To
STANLEY CURSITER AND ERIC LINKLATER
Fellow-Orkneymen

Edwin Muir (1887–1959) was born and raised in the Orkney Islands until his family moved to Glasgow in 1901. He found employment there as a clerk and educated himself during these years, moving to London and marrying Willa Anderson in 1919. Muir gradually established himself as a literary critic and novelist and, with Willa, as a translator—most notably of the works of Kafka. His novels are *The Marionette* (1927), *The Three Brothers* (1931), and *Poor Tom* (1932) which was closely based on his own grim years in Glasgow and Greenock.

The Muirs travelled abroad in the years before World War II, and Edwin began to take an outsider's look at his native land in *Scottish Journey* (1935), and in a telling critique of Scottish culture, *Scott and Scotland* (1936), which led to a breach with his friend Hugh MacDiarmid. Muir was in his late 40s before he started to write the poetry for which he is best known today. His verse is marked by a fascination with time and timeless symbols—haunted no doubt by what he came to see as an idyllic childhood in Orkney. His early collections *First Poems* (1925) and *Chorus of the Newly Dead* (1926) were followed by *Variations on a Time Theme* (1934), *Journeys and Places* (1937), *The Narrow Place* (1943), *The Voyage* (1946), *The Labyrinth* (1949), *One Foot in Eden* (1956), and *Collected Poems 1921–1958* (1960).

Muir worked for the British Council in Prague and Rome after the war, before becoming, in 1950, the warden at Newbattle Abbey, a residential adult education college outside Edinburgh. He was a visiting Professor at Harvard from 1955 to 1956 before retiring to a village outside Cambridge.

EDWIN MUIR
an autobiography

Introduced by Professor Peter Butter

CANONGATE
CLASSICS
50

First published in Great Britain in 1954 by The Hogarth Press. First published as a Canongate Classic in 1993 by Canongate Press plc, 14 Frederick Street, Edinburgh EH2 2HB. Copyright © Edwin Muir. Introduction © Peter Butter 1993. Memoir © George Mackay Brown 1993.

British Library Cataloguing-in-Publication Data
A catalogue record for this book is available on request from the British Library

ISBN 0 86241 423 7

The publishers gratefully acknowledge general subsidy from the Scottish Arts Council towards the Canongate Classics series and a specific grant towards the publication of this title.

Set in 10pt Plantin by The Electronic Book Factory Ltd, Fife, Scotland. Printed and bound in Great Britain by BPCC Paperbacks Ltd

Contents

	Edwin Muir: A Personal Memoir	vii
	Introduction	xi
	Preface	xix
1	Wyre	1
2	Garth	57
3	Glasgow	81
4	Fairport	122
5	London	148
6	Prague	176
7	Interval	189
8	Dresden and Hellerau	192
9	Italy and Austria	204
10	England and France	221
11	Scotland	238
12	Prague Again	247
13	Rome	270
	Appendix I	278
	Appendix II	282
	Index	295

Edwin Muir: A Personal Memoir

I had to go and have tea with Edwin and Willa Muir at Stromness Hotel, Orkney, one summer afternoon in 1951.

I was so nervous I drank a couple of pints of beer in the bar below. It was a rather awesome prospect, to be meeting for the first time the author of *The Story and the Fable* and *The Labyrinth*.

All I remember of the meal was that Willa told stories and laughed a great deal. Edwin sat among swirls of cigarette smoke, silent and smiling.

They had given a lift in their car to two travelling booth boxers, from Kirkwall to Stromness. The pugilists thanked Edwin for the lift. 'And thanks to your mother,' said one (meaning Willa). Willa laughed delightedly about that.

At the end of the tea and cakes, Edwin said he'd liked a story of mine in *The New Shetlander*. On the strength of that, he'd take me as a student when the new session began in October 1951.

*   *   *

A nervous train journey it was from Aberdeen to Edinburgh, for someone new to railways. A simple islander might overshoot the mark, or get off too soon. But there at Waverley Edwin was waiting to drive me to Newbattle, safely. (Edwin and cars didn't get on; the cars may have resented his two marvellous poems about horses.)

Again, I can't remember what we spoke about.

*   *   *

Newbattle 1951–52 was the happiest time of my life. The snow lay thick that winter and the heating failed in the great Abbey for a week or so, and we had to cut down trees on the far bank of the Esk so we could huddle round the fire in

vii

the Abbey crypt (the students' common room). No wonder I got a bad cold at the end of the Spring term.

*   *   *

The students came from Scotland, England, India, Yugoslavia, Africa. There were not as many students as there ought to have been; education authorities were reluctant to give grants for non-vocational courses. *Sero Sed Serio* was the motto carved on the Abbey stones ('Late but in Earnest'). We could study English Literature, Philosophy, Economics, History: whatever we chose.

We happy few got on very well, on the whole.

*   *   *

Because Edwin was a famous writer, most students attended his lectures. The Elizabethan Dramatists was his subject that year. Edwin would come drifting in to the lecture room, sit down, and begin to speak about Marlowe, Chapman, Shakespeare, in a kind of mild Orcadian lilt. There seemed to be no attempt at eloquence at all; so some students were a bit disappointed. The lecturer appeared to be in a kind of gentle trance. One could sense depths under the tranquil surface. Sometimes he would open a text and take off his glasses and read a passage. The substance of some of those lectures appeared in his excellent book *Essays on Literature and Society* . . . Then the voice trailed off, and the lecture was over.

Another lecture he gave every Friday on Language. This was mostly about where to put commas and semicolons in sentences. Edwin advocated a simple plain prose style . . . I found those language lectures a bit boring, and maybe didn't attend them all. I thought I knew all that elementary stuff anyway.

Once a month we were expected to hand in an essay. Then one by one we were summoned to discuss the essay in Edwin's study that overlooked the formal Italian garden and a great beech tree (it was blown down in a January gale that year) and the murky South Esk river. There was no set subject for an essay; an essay could be a poem, a story, a fragment of an autobiography—anything.

A mild ritual took place, once you had knocked and been invited in. Edwin sat at his desk among hanks of cigarette smoke; there lay your essay on the desk . . . Some time passed before discussion of the essay. There were frequent pauses while Edwin looked through the window. He never said anything to hurt anyone's feelings (though many of the essays must have been dreadful) . . . 'How are you getting on?' he would say. Then, 'I hope you're quite happy here . . .' The masterpiece of an essay lay on the desk, but at last, after all the kind enquiries and the silences, the manuscript had to be talked about. He sifted through the pages. 'Oh, it's interesting,' he might say at last. (One of the students, Tom Wilson from Larbert, said you could always tell by the *way* Edwin said 'It's interesting', whether it was pure trash or had some really good things in it . . .) Another smoke swirl—another tranquil silence and gentle valediction—then you gathered up your manuscript and came away.

*   *   *

So, he was not a spectacular performer. But there was a wonderful atmosphere at Newbattle all that year. I'm sure it had much to do with that Prospero weaving spells there in the heart of the ancient Abbey. In the crypt we sat till midnight talking about everything under the sun, mainly politics and literature. There was a quickening of poetry in some of us. Even one student of politics took to writing verse. We read and recited to each other; never before or since have I enjoyed poetry so much. It is well enough since printing began, to read poetry alone out of a book. But when two or three poetry-lovers come together, everything is enriched beyond measure. (The audience at the Globe Theatre, the townsfolk of Kelso or Perth when a wandering balladman began to chant in the market-place—both poet and audience illiterate—experienced the full glory of verse). Edwin *seemed* to do nothing about it, but I think his mere presence at Newbattle opened those horizons.

*   *   *

Looking back on that time from a distance of forty years, I often think how tired he must have been—how he must have longed for a few hours to do the work he was here on earth to do. Often that year he was unwell. But the corporate aspect had to be seen to. Edwin appeared at the mid-morning tea breaks, smoking and sipping tea that had only a few grains of sugar in the cup; and again for the life of me I can't remember any words of his on those many mornings. Sometimes he might say to a student, 'I don't think I've seen an essay from you for a good long while now, Bob . . .' That same Bob Fletcher won a scholarship to King's College, Cambridge, with an essay on Milton that he wrote at Newbattle. Bob had been a tube worker in Airdrie. There were frequent get-togethers of a few students in the Muirs' sitting room of an evening: wine and cakes. Willa dominated on those occasions, smoking cigarettes in a long holder, with vivid pastiches and caricatures and clerihews, and peals of laughter . . . Again, Edwin sat in a corner sipping wine and weaving cigarette smoke, and saying little.

On a fine afternoon Edwin and Willa would walk round the garden, very slowly because Willa had arthritis and went on a stick, and Edwin seemed to glide rather than walk through the grass.

In the end the poet, weary of administration and bureaucracy, was glad to be summoned from Newbattle to give the Charles Eliot Norton lectures (*The Estate of Poetry*) at Harvard.

He left behind him a little group of young men and women whose lives have been perpetually enriched by his presence among them.

George Mackay Brown

Introduction

In 1938, aged fifty, Edwin Muir began to take 'notes for something like a description of myself, done in general outline, not in detail, not as a story, but as an attempt to find out what a human being is in this extraordinary age which depersonalises everything . . . It may be that I have found at last a form which suits me'.[1] These last words refer back to his three novels, and acknowledge that fiction had not been the right form for him. Actually, those early novels had become increasingly autobiographical and (except in the first and best, *The Marionette*), the autobiographical elements had burst out of the fictional structure imposed on them, revealing its weakness. Now the memories are to be allowed to speak for themselves. 'I would like to avoid all make-believe; the arranged patterns of modern novels give me such a stale, second-hand, false and tired feeling'. But Muir still wants form, not an indiscriminate gush. 'I have no wish to confess either, for the sake of confession: I am too old for that: I want some knowledge'.[2] Form will be given by making the description of himself 'an attempt to find out what a human being is'. So the first version of the autobiography, published in 1940, was called *The Story and the Fable*—the story of one man enacting the fable of Man. 'The Eternal Man is what has possessed me during most of the time that I have been writing my autobiography, and has possessed me in most of my poetry'.[3] Perhaps too much so in the poetry written up to then. *The Story and the Fable* better combines vivid detail with the search for meaning. To do this convincingly is the main task of this kind of autobiographer. If he puts in only those items of his story which most clearly reveal the underlying fable he may seem to be making an 'arranged pattern'; if he pours in everything he can remember much of it will be trivial and meaningless.

For this reason, even after starting *The Story and the Fable*, Muir still hankered after the autobiographical novel, in which a writer can bring out the correspondences between an individual life and a larger pattern freely. 'As it is, I have to stick to the facts', and try to fit the larger images in where they will fit in. The facts—about a man's appearance, social position, routine life, etc,—he rather curiously calls 'a dry legend'. When such things are known in a merely external way they give no knowledge of what a man is. The 'legend', even if made up of true facts, is 'deceptive', whereas the 'fable' is the inner truth. The key is imagination, which can transform what might be 'dry legend'; and which can operate on actual facts as well as on fictions. The bone-yard at 'Fairport' was a fact, and expands in the imagination into an emblem.

> My childhood all a myth
> Enacted in a distant isle.

Readers of George Marshall's *In a Distant Isle* may be tempted to say that Muir's account of his childhood is indeed a myth—in a sense not intended by him. Marshall shows that far from life in Orkney having remained, as Muir says, 'almost unchanged for two hundred years' there had been great and continuing changes in the fifty years up to the boy's 'seven years Eden' on Wyre: changes in agriculture, methods of land tenure, education, etc. Much was going on that the child did not know or was not much impressed by. But that does not mean that Muir's recreation of his childhood is a falsification. Marshall himself recognises that 'the vision presented in the autobiography seems utterly convincing in literary, if not in historical terms'.[4] He rightly wants us to see that this autobiography, like all the best ones, is a work of art, an act of imagination, a recreation of the past not just a feat of memory. But in stressing its truth in literary terms one does not want to lose a sense of its integrity, its truth in the obvious sense. Sometimes there are errors of fact—of dating, order of events, etc; sometimes of judgement, due to lack of historical knowledge. But in creating an image of Eden Muir's imagination was using elements in the landscape and life of Wyre that were really there, and striking deeper into life than a historian's more comprehensive account could do. And the same is true of the contrary image based on the Glasgow years. Much of the strength of these early chapters is in the detail, the intensity with which ordinary, even ugly and frightening, things are seen. Eden is not escape, but acceptance, a vision of an inclusive order. The chief distorting factor in most autobiographies is vanity. Muir is not at all concerned to excuse or justify himself, to complain or fight old battles, only to see and understand.

He writes of a 'seven years Eden'. Eden and the Fall, Innocence and Experience were both known in Orkney before he left at fourteen for Glasgow. The account of the Glasgow years could no doubt be faulted by a historian; but again it strikes deeper into the life of an individual and into universal experience—of alienation, inner division and division from people and things. There are horrific visions of men as animals, but also visions of transfiguration. Muir's great toughness is shown—in his survival, his winning through to limited successes even though divided from his deeper self. *The Story and the Fable* takes us to the point when at thirty-five his imagination woke and he began to write poetry. This is the turning point in his life. 'When my past life came alive in me after lying so long, a dead weight, my actual life came alive too as that new life passed into it; for it was new, though old; indeed, I felt that only now was I truly living it since only now did I see it as it was, so that at last it could become experience'.[5] This reliving of the past was expressed in poems and novels, but not fully until *The Story and the Fable*, the writing of which was therefore itself an important stage in his development, releasing him from obsession with time and the past and leading to the more wide-ranging, less introspective poetry of his later years.

The fable is found in the story, and more directly in moments of special vision and in dreams. No autobiography 'can confine itself to conscious life'; our dreams are part of reality, through which we can reach knowledge of ourselves, and hence of other people, beyond what the conscious self can attain. The most distinctive feature of this autobiography is the number and quality of the dreams.

Most of them are quite different from our usual confused and trivial dreams; and the most interesting are more than the working out of personal psychological problems. As Thetis Blacker says of the dreams she records in *A Pilgrimage of Dreams*, 'They possess a clarity, a coherence, a vividness, a translucence and a significance never found in the ordinary dreams of every night'. They 'seem to have come to me from some place deeper than my ordinary ego, or my analysable subconscious self.'[6] This is true also of Muir. His long waking dream in London 'came' to him, he believed: 'it was not "I" who dreamt it, but something else which the psychologists call the racial unconscious, and for which there are other names'. Such dreams and visions come at least from a deeper level of the self than we are normally aware of, and so seem to come from outside. Whence do they get into that deeper self? From the collective unconscious? From God? From some more sinister source? We can only conjecture, on the basis of the wisdom or otherwise conveyed. Some of Muir's dreams—such as that of the dreamer murdering a man in a moonlit street —can be related to his life at the time, and given a simple psychological interpretation. But the most interesting—such as the dream of the praying animals, of the dreamer bringing a statue of a girl to life, and the waking trance—have the quality of poetry, being endlessly suggestive, beyond explanation.

The Story and the Fable came out in May 1940, an unpropitious time; and it was not until 1953 that a new edition with additions to bring it up to date was called for. Muir was no longer moved by an inner compulsion to relive his past; so the new chapters have not quite the intensity of the old. In a notebook he listed incidents and people that might go in; and concluded 'All this fairly external'. He cast round for a central theme, and settled on the 'terrible impersonality', that 'is the mark of the last twenty or thirty years'—something observed rather than a part of his inner life.

There is not so much 'fable' in the new chapters, and even the 'story' is in important ways less complete. Willa noted in her journal in August 1953 that he was having difficulty in writing about their early time in Italy because he was leaving out so much. The chief thing he was leaving out was his infatuation with a German student they had known at Hellerau, Gerda Krapp. It was only a brief interruption of a long and loving marriage, but it caused much emotional turmoil at the time. Another important relationship only slightly touched on is that with his son. Partly due to the accident suffered in London Gavin never fully realised his potential as a musician, became nervous and withdrawn, and at times at odds with his parents. Willa wrote in her Newbattle journal of his defensiveness: 'and yet there is *inside* him a fountain of affection, a childlike naiveté, a warmth and simplicity, that would make him very lovable and charming were he to let it flow out spontaneously'. Perhaps there was a failure of flow on both sides. In any case Muir's strong feelings about his son did not flow into the autobiography. There is not even very much about Willa.

This protection of his own and others' privacy is admirable; but it does result in our meeting in the new chapters more the observer of the life around him, less the suffering and enjoying individual. Though his life between 1921 and 1945 was unspectacular, it touched many movements characteristic of the time. Earlier he had plunged in; now he looked with understanding scepticism, standing apart from fashion on his own ground of faith in the imagination—the answer to the growing depersonalisation. By imagination he saw in small incidents much that was happening under the surface. So his story of a quiet life grows not so much now into the fable of eternal man as into the story of mid-twentieth century man. In his journey out to Prague after the war and his life there he came closer than before to great events. His account is lighted by the poet's eye for telling detail. He notes the expressionless eyes of a Russian soldier at the frontier 'giving out the interior light of glowing, highly polished stones', and the menacing, unhappy eyes of young Gestapo men in a photograph; and by imagination he tries to penetrate behind the eyes to the spiritual state. The exploration of these images takes place mainly in poems—'The Interrogation', 'The Helmet' and 'The Usurpers'. The deeper currents of his being were now flowing into poetry—poetry which more than before arose from the immediate and the particular—leaving the prose a bit drier. By now he was not much interested in prose, however well he wrote it. He was still vulnerable, still a dreamer and visionary; and occasionally the movements of his deeper self are felt pulsing even in prose. This is so in the account of his unhappiness in St Andrews followed by a sense of resurrection, given by the sight of childrens' play and by his experience of the Lord's Prayer. It is significant that this, the most introspective passage in the new chapters, is based on earlier writing, as are the retrospective last three pages of 'Dresden and Hellerau'. But at least one new section adds to the fable as well as to the story—that on his depression on returning from Prague followed by recovered happiness in Rome. He had written in preliminary notes:—'I can write of Rome with a full heart . . . Laura . . . The sense of Incarnation.' 'The sense of Incarnation' completes his journey back to the innocent vision of childhood, and is a journey on to larger vision. The full humanity of Italian friends, the beauty and vitality of swifts swooping over his flat, 'the ages assembled in a tumultuous order' in works of art, the images which 'are the outward sign that the Word had been made flesh' form a whole, a whole greater than anything experienced in childhood. In *The Story and the Fable* he interrogated the past, and felt the relived past flowing into and illuminating the present; now he moves on to a new vision which illuminates and enlarges the past. In a later notebook he wrote of his father and mother:- 'Realising long after their deaths their virtue and goodness. How could they have been what they were but for Incarnation. The incarnation of a soul in a body.'

Peter Butter

NOTES

1 *Selected Letters of Edwin Muir*, P.H. Butter, ed. (1974), p. 100.
2 *Ibid.*, p. 101.
3 Edwin Muir, *The Story and the Fable* (1940), p. 261.
4 'Muir's Orkney: The Place and the Idea', *Edwin Muir: Centenary Assessments*, C. MacLachlan and D.S. Robb, eds. (1990), p. 24.
5 *The Story and the Fable*, p. 235.
6 Thetis Blacker, *A Pilgrimage of Dreams* (1973), p. xv.

Preface

The first part of this account of some things in my life appeared in 1940 as 'The Story and the Fable'. Some slight alterations have had to be made in it so as to fit it into the longer story.

The late Hugh Kingsmill kindly gave me permission many years ago to quote from a letter to him by John Holms which appears in the first section. I owe gratitude to my wife for numerous invaluable suggestions and criticisms. And my warm thanks are due to Miss Flora Jack for the sometimes difficult work of deciphering and typing the whole of the last section.

CHAPTER ONE

Wyre

I was born on the 15th of May, 1887, in a farm called the Folly, in the parish of Deerness in Orkney. My father left it when I was two, so that I have no early memories of it, and as the house has since been pulled down and the farm joined to another farm, all that I know of it are the foundations, which I was shown a few years ago: a long, narrow house looking down towards the sea and the isle of Copinsay over a sloping field.

My father came from the island of Sanday, which is filled with Muirs and Sinclairs, families who came over from Caithness after the Stewarts at the beginning of the sixteenth century. I can follow my own branch no further back than my father's father, who had a farm in Sanday called Colligarth. My mother's name was Elizabeth Cormack, and my knowledge of her family again goes back only to her father, Edwin Cormack, after whom I was named. There is in Deerness a ruined chapel which was built in the eighth or ninth century by an Irish priest called Cormack the Sailor, who was later canonized; it is only a few miles from Haco, the farm where my mother was born. Whether the names are connected over that great stretch of time in that small corner no one can say; but it is conceivable, for in Orkney families have lived in the same place for many hundreds of years, and I like to think that some people in the parish, myself among them, may have a saint among their ancestors, since some of the Irish priests were not celibate.

My mother lived much more in the past than my father, so that when I was a child Deerness became a lively place to me, while Sanday remained blank except for its witches, since the tales my father told me were mainly about the supernatural. One of my mother's stories has stuck in my memory. The family had moved from Haco to Skaill, a farm on the edge of a sandy bay, beside the parish church and the churchyard. She was eighteen at the time. The rest of the family had gone up to the Free Kirk, two miles away, for an evening prayer meeting, a great revival having swept the islands. It was a wild night of wind and sleet, and she was sitting in the kitchen reading, when the door opened and ten tall men, dripping with water, came in and sat round the fire. They spoke to her, but she could not tell what they were saying. She sat on in a corner, dumb with terror, until the family came back two hours later. The men were Danes, and their ship had split on a rock at the end of the bay.

Both her memory and my father's were filled with wrecks, for the Orkney coast is dangerous, and at that time there were few lighthouses. When the wrecks were washed ashore the people in the parish gathered and took their pick. Stories were told of men luring ships on to the rocks by leading a pony along a steep road with a green light tied to one side and a red light to the other. It was said, too, that ministers sometimes prayed for a wreck in bad times. A strange tale often told in our family is indirectly connected with all this. One bright moonlight night my father and my cousin Sutherland were standing at the end of the house at the Folly after feeding the cattle, when they saw a great three-masted vessel making straight for the shore. They watched in amazement for a few minutes—there was only a field between them and it—until it melted into a black mist on the water. I was enchanted by this story when I heard it, but as I grew older I naturally began to doubt it. Then when I was seventeen or eighteen I was speaking to a farmer who had lived on the neighbouring farm of the Barns, and he told me the very same story. He had been at the end of his house that night, and he too had seen the three-master standing in for the shore and then disappearing. At the time he was amazed at its behaviour, like my father and my cousin Sutherland, for in the bright moonlight the cliffs must have been clearly visible from the ship; but they all accepted it, I think, as a magical occurrence.

My father's stories were drawn mostly from an earlier age, and I think must have been handed on to him by his own father. They went back to the Napoleonic wars, the

press-gang, and keelhauling, which still left a memory of
terror in Orkney. But in his own time he had known several
witches, who had 'taken the profit of the corn,' turned the
milk sour, and wrecked ships by raising storms. Many of
these stories I have heard since in other versions, and these
obviously come from the store of legends that gathered when
witch-burning was common in Scotland. In one a Sanday
farmer, coming back for his dinner, saw the local witch's
black cat slinking out of his house. He rushed in, snatched
up his gun, and let fly at it. The cat was leaping over a stone
dyke when he fired; it stumbled and gave a great screech,
then ran away, dragging one hind-leg after it. Next day the
witch sent for the doctor to set her leg. My father told this
story so well that I could see the farmer with the smoking
gun in his hands, and the black cat stumbling over the grey
stone wall and running away with a twisted, crablike glide.
When my father told his witch stories we sat up very late;
we were afraid to go to bed.

The devil himself, as Auld Nick, sometimes came into
these tales, and generally in the same way. A farmer would
be in the barn threshing his corn with a flail, when he would
notice another flail keeping time with him, and looking up
would see an enormous, naked, coal-black man with a fine
upcurling tail standing opposite him. He fainted at this
point, and when he awoke all the corn in the barn would
be neatly threshed. But these visits were always followed by
bad luck.

My father had also a great number of stories about the
Book of Black Arts. This book could be bought only for
a silver coin, and sold only for a smaller silver one. It
ended in the possession of a foolish servant-girl who paid a
threepenny-piece for it. It was very valuable, for it gave you
all sorts of worldly power; but it had the drawback that if
you could not sell it to some one before you died you would
be damned. The servant-girl of my father's story tried every
means to get rid of it. She tore it to pieces, buried it, tied a
stone to it and flung it into the sea, burned it; but after all
this it was still at the bottom of her chest when she went to
look there. What happened in the end I can't remember; I
fancy the poor girl went off her head. I always thought of

the book as a great, black, hasped, leather-bound volume somewhat like a family Bible.

My father also knew the horseman's word—that is, the word which will make a horse do anything you desire if you whisper it into its ear. Some time ago I asked Eric Linklater, who knows Orkney now better than I do, if he had ever heard of the horseman's word up there. He said no, but he told me that when he was a student at Aberdeen University young ploughmen in Buchan were willing to pay anything from ten shillings to a pound out of their small wages to be told the horseman's word. From what my father said I imagine that the word was a shocking one.

The Orkney I was born into was a place where there was no great distinction between the ordinary and the fabulous; the lives of living men turned into legend. A man I knew once sailed out in a boat to look for a mermaid, and claimed afterwards that he had talked with her. Fantastic feats of strength were commonly reported. Fairies, or 'fairicks,' as they were called, were encountered dancing on the sands on moonlight nights. From people's talk they were small, graceful creatures about the size of leprechauns, but pretty, not grotesque. There was no harm in them. All these things have vanished from Orkney in the last fifty years under the pressure of compulsory education.

My father left the Folly for a farm called the Bu in the island of Wyre. There were seven other farms on the island, with names which went back to the viking times: Russness, Onziebist, Helzigartha, Caivit, Testaquoy, Habreck, the Haa. The Bu was the biggest farm in the island, and close beside a little green knoll called the Castle. In the eleventh century this had been the stronghold of a viking freebooter called Kolbein Hruga, or Cubby Roo, but we did not know this at the time, nor did any of our neighbours: all that remained was the name and the knoll and a little cairn of big stones. Between the house and the knoll there was a damp green meadow which waved with wild cotton in summer. Then came the dry, smooth slope of the Castle, and on the top the round cairn of square grey stones, as high as a man's shoulder and easy for us to climb. My younger sister and I would sit there for hours in the summer evenings, looking across the sound at the dark, hilly island of Rousay, which also had its castle, a brand-new one like a polished black-and-white dice, where a retired general lived: our landlord. He was a stylish, very little man with a dapper walk, and the story went that because of his size he had been the first to pass through the breach in the wall of Lucknow when that town was relieved during the Indian Mutiny. He came over to Wyre every spring to shoot the wild birds. I remember one soft spring day when the light seemed to be opening up the world after the dark winter; I must have been five at the time, for it was before I went to school. I was standing at the end of the house; I think I had just recovered from some illness, and everything looked clean and new. The General was walking through the field below our house in his little brown jacket with the brown leather tabs on the shoulders, his neat little knickerbockers and elegant little brown boots; a feather curled on his hat, and his little pointed beard seemed to curl too. Now and then he raised his silver gun, the white smoke curled upward, birds fell, suddenly heavy after seeming so light; our cattle, who were grazing in the field, rushed away in alarm at the noise, then stopped and looked round in wonder at the strange little man. It was a mere picture; I did not feel angry with the General or sorry for the birds; I was entranced with the bright gun, the white smoke, and particularly with the soft brown tabs of leather on the shoulders of his jacket. My mother was standing at the end of the house with me; the General came over and spoke to her, then, calling me to him, gave me a sixpence. My father appeared from somewhere, but replied very distantly to the General's affable words. He was a bad landlord, and in a few years drove my father out of the farm by his exactions.

Between our house and the school there was a small, roofless chapel which had once been the chapel of the Castle. In summer it was a jungle of nettles and rank weeds, which on hot days gave out a burning smell that scorched my nostrils. At the school, which stood on a slight rising, a new group of more distant islands appeared, some of them brown, some green with light sandy patches. Not a tree anywhere. There were only two things that rose from these low, rounded islands: a high, top-heavy castle in Shapinsay, standing by itself with the insane look of tall, narrow houses in flat, wide landscapes, and in Egilsay a black chapel with a round, pointed tower, where St Magnus had been murdered in the twelfth century. It was the most beautiful thing within sight, and it rose every day against the sky until it seemed to become a sign in the fable of our lives.

Besides my father and mother and my three brothers and two sisters there were two other members of our household: my aunt Maggie and my cousin Sutherland. Maggie was an elder, unmarried sister of my father. She had a perfectly grey face, the colour of peat ash, a well-shaped nose a size too large for it, a mouth like a handsome young man's, and clear, almost colourless eyes. She always wore a napkin round her head, tied so as to form a little penthouse over her brow, so that looked at from the side she seemed to have two noses of the same shape and size, one above the other. She was a small woman, but had a long, loping stride which made her look as if she were always running. Like most old people in Orkney at that time, she was bothered with all sorts of ailments—rheumatics in the joints, wind, pains at the pit of the stomach; and she always kept in her own room what she called a 'phial,' her fond diminutive for 'bottle,' though whether it contained medicine or alcohol we were never sure. She used snuff, and drank a great quantity of baking-soda with water. I think she must have been a bitter, disappointed woman, for she was always talking of the lovers she had rejected as a young girl. But to us she was merely odd, and we teased her a great deal, especially after we caught her one night trying to get rid of a wart on her finger by pointing a straw first at it and then at the moon, and muttering something to herself.

My cousin Sutherland was the most original character in the house. I remember him as a little man in a blue jersey and trousers with a dashing fall. His body swung forward from his hips, as if he were always on the point of offering something with his hands. His head was like a battering-ram, and dusty brown hair like an animal's fell stood stiffly up from it. His sparkling grey eyes were nautical, his bulbous nose ecclesiastical, his bushy brown moustache military. Before he made a joke he would pass the back of his hand under his moustache with a casual succulent sweep which left his arm negligently hanging in the air, as if he had forgotten it for the moment but would presently remember it again. All his movements melted into each other with the continuity of a tree. His skin was reptilian; his head sloped, like a tortoise's, into his neck, his shoulders into his trunk. He was very strong and crafty, and in wrestling could bring down men much younger and heavier than himself. His ordinary stance then was a lazy crouch; he would roll waggishly on his feet, as if he were keeping his balance in a slight swell; he was very light-footed. His appearance never changed while I knew him; he looked thirty-five all the time.

Sutherland had more natural slyness of a harmless kind than any man I have ever known. Since he was lecherous as well he was a great danger to the young women of Wyre, Rousay, and Egilsay; for on calm summer nights he would sail to these other islands with a boatload of young men and try his fortune with the strange women. I fancy he never attempted to display himself to them in a romantic light, for when he wanted a favour he always referred to himself as 'Old Sutherland' in an objective yet cajoling way. His language was very free, and his advances shockingly direct, but always with a show of reason. He never tried to show the women why they should yield to him, but concentrated on the much more subtle question 'Why not?' a question very difficult to answer. He was the father of a number of illegitimate children, and I remember my father once saying in a vexed voice, 'Why, the man canna look at a woman, it seems, withoot putting her in the family way!' I was too young at the time to understand these words.

Whenever Sutherland got drunk he began to invent language. I can't remember now many of his feats in this way, but he liked words with a dashing Spanish sound, like 'yicka-hooka' and 'navahonta.' He was so pleased with the word 'tramcollicken,' which he invented himself, that he gave it a specific meaning which I had better not mention; but the word became so popular that it spread all over Wyre. From somewhere or other he had picked up 'graminivorous,' which struck him by its comic sound, and for a long time his usual greeting was, 'Weel, boy, how's thee graminivorous tramcollicken?' Macedonia, Arabia, Valparaiso, and Balaclava became parts of his ordinary vocabulary, giving him a sense of style and grandeur. He was a great singer at concerts, or *soirées*, as he always called them, and gave dashing renderings of 'Poor blind Joe' and 'When Jack comes home again.' On Sunday afternoons he sat on the kitchen bed snuffling the Psalms with his face sanctimoniously lengthened. But in the evening he set out for some neighbouring farm to see what he could get out of the women.

My first definite memories are connected with the Bu; but there is one composite one which may conceivably go back to the house where I was born, it brings such a sense of timelessness with it. I was lying in some room watching a beam of slanting light in which dusty, bright motes slowly danced and turned, while a low murmuring went on somewhere, possibly the humming of flies. My mother was in the room, but where I do not know; I was merely conscious of her as a vague, environing presence. This picture is clear and yet indefinite, attached to one summer day at the Bu, and at the same time to so many others that it may go back to the day when I first watched a beam of light as I lay in my cradle. The quiet murmuring, the slow, unending dance of the motes, the sense of deep and solid peace, have come back to me since only in dreams. This memory has a different quality from any other memory in my life. It was as if, while I lay watching that beam of light, time had not yet begun.

My first definite memory is of being baptized. Why I was not baptized in Deerness, where there were two churches, I have never been able to find out; but the ceremony was postponed for some reason until I was three years old. I was dressed for the occasion in a scarlet suit with petticoats instead of breeches, for boys were not given boys' clothes then until they were five. The suit was made of some fine but slightly rough material like serge; the sun must have been shining that day, for the cloth seemed to glow from within with its own light; it was fastened with large glittering golden buttons. I think it must have been the first time that I saw the colour of gold and of scarlet, for it is this suit that makes me remember that day, and it still burns in my memory more brightly than anything I have ever seen since. In the afternoon my father and mother led me by the hand to the school, where Mr Pirie, the minister of Rousay, had come to baptize me. Some people had gathered. I was lifted up by my father, face upward; I saw Mr Pirie's kind face with its thin beard inclined diagonally over me (for he had a glass eye and looked at everything from the side), then I felt the cold water on my face and began to cry. As if the baptismal water had been a deluge, all the rest of that day is damp and drowned, the burning scarlet and the gold sunk in darkness.

Most of my childhood is drowned as deep as the rest of that baptismal day; I have no recollection of the routine of my first seven years, though it was there, giving me my first realization of order in the world. A fragment of that age swam up recently after being lost for more than sixty years. It was another suit of clothes, and it returned by a curious road. I was down in Edinburgh a few years ago with some time on my hands. I went into a tea-room, and after having my tea looked round to see what the hour was, but there was no sign of a clock. As the waitress was giving me the bill I asked her the time; she glanced at a wrist-watch she was wearing, and told me with a condescending air that it was a quarter to six. As I still had some time left I went to the Café Royal for a drink. Where I sat I was directly facing the clock set in the wall above the buffet, a round, plain clock with a face like that of an old-fashioned watch very much enlarged. My mind returned to the waitress; I remembered an evening in Prague when my wrist-watch had been stolen from me in a tramcar without my noticing it. My thoughts wandered on, and I found myself thinking that I was too old now for a wrist-watch; for some reason this seemed a perfectly sensible notion. But in that case —I was still paying very little attention to my thoughts—what sort of watch should I wear, for it was inconvenient to be without a watch? Then I saw dangling in the air a big, heavy watch such as the ploughmen used to wear when I was a boy.

This troubled me, for what pocket could I keep it in? The watch settled the matter by dropping into my breast pocket, where it attached itself by a black, twisted cord to the top buttonhole of my coat, under the lapel. But this is a very juvenile arrangement, I told myself, wakening into another layer of daydream, though not into complete awakeness. Then, as if all these windings had been deliberately leading up to it, all at once I saw a boy's blue sailor suit with a yellow twisted hempen cord loosely knotted round the collar, and at the end of it a canary-yellow wooden whistle. The sailor suit startled me so much that I did not know what to do with it. Next moment I realized that I had worn it once; I could remember distinctly the feel and the smell of the smooth wooden whistle; it had a faint, fragrant smell. But I could not say when I had worn that suit, and the fact that after being buried for all these years it should come back now by such a tortuous and yet purposive road struck me as very strange. Yet it seemed still stranger that it could have disappeared at all, for the yellow whistle must have been one of the things which I loved most as a child, since even in memory I could feel the delight it had given me. Could some disaster have befallen the yellow whistle, so that I put it so completely out of my mind that it had never returned since? If that could happen once it might have happened hundreds of times.

I can still see the scarlet dress and the sailor suit; I can see the rough grey stones spotted with lichen on the top of the Castle, and a bedraggled gooseberry bush in a corner of the garden whose branches I lovingly fingered for hours; but I cannot bring back the feelings which I had for them, the sense of being magically close to them, as if they were magnets drawing me with a palpable power. Reasonable explanations can be found for these feelings: the fact that every object is new to a child, that he sees it without understanding it, or understands it with a different understanding from that of experience— different, for there may be fear in it, but there cannot be calculation or worry; or even the fact that he is closer to things, since his eyes are only two or three feet from the ground, not five or six. Grass, stones, and insects are twice as near to him as they will be after he has grown up, and when I try to re-create my early childhood it seems to me that it was focused on such things as these, and that I lived my life in a small, separate underworld, while the grown-ups walked on their long legs several feet above my head on a stage where every relation was different. I was dizzily lifted into that world, as into another dimension, when my father took me on his shoulders, so that I could see the roof of the byre from above or touch the lintel of the house door with my hand. But for most of the time I lived with whatever I found on the surface of the earth: the different kinds of grass, the daisies, buttercups, dandelions, bog cotton (we did not have many flowers), the stones and bits of glass and china, and the scurrying insects which made my stomach heave as I stared at them, unable to take my eyes away. These insects were all characters to me, interesting but squalid, with thoughts that could never be penetrated, inconceivable aims, perverse activities. I knew their names, which so exactly fitted them as characters: the Jenny Hunderlegs, the gavelock, the forkytail, the slater—the underworld of my little underworld, obsessing me, but for ever beyond my reach. Some were not so horrible, such as the spider, impersonal compared with the others, whose progress was a terrifying dart or a grave, judge-like, swaying walk. Unlike the others, he was at home in the sun, and so did not need to scuttle; I thought of him as bearded and magistral. I could never bear to touch any of these creatures, though I watched them so closely that I seemed to be taking part in their life, which was like little fragments of night darting about in the sun; they often came into my dreams later, wakening me in terror. How many hours I must have spent staring with fixed loathing at these creatures! Yet I did not want to know anything about them; I merely wanted them away. Their presence troubled me as the mind is troubled in adolescence by the realization of physical lust. The gavelocks and forkytails were my first intimation of evil, and associations of evil still cling round them for me, as, I fancy, for most people: popular imagery shows it. We cannot tell how much our minds are influenced for life by the fact that we see the world first at a range of two or three feet.

The insects, of course, were only a small part of that three-foot world; I think I must have passed through a phase of possession by them, comparatively short. The grass was a reliable pleasure; the flowers were less dependable, and after I picked a dandelion one day and found it writhing with little angry, many-legged insects, the faces of the flowers took on a faithless look, until my mother taught me which could be relied upon. The crevices in stone walls were filled with secrets; a slab of hard cement on the wall of the house had a special meaning. Mud after new rain was delicious, and I was charmed by everything that flew, from the humble bee to the Willie Longlegs. At that stage the novelty of seeing a creature flying outweighed everything else.

My height from the ground determined my response to other things too. When my father and Sutherland brought in the horses from the fields I stood trembling among their legs, seeing only their great, bearded feet and the momentary flash of their crescent-shaped shoes flung up lazily as they passed. When my father stopped with the bridle in his hands to speak to me I stood looking up at the stationary hulks and the tossing heads, which in the winter dusk were lost in the sky. I felt beaten down by an enormous weight and a real terror; yet I did not hate the horses as I hated the insects; my fear turned into something else, for it was infused by a longing to go up to them and touch them and simultaneously checked by the knowledge that their hoofs were dangerous: a combination of emotions which added up to worship in the Old Testament sense. Everything about them, the steam rising from their soft, leathery nostrils, the sweat staining their hides, their ponderous, irresistible motion, the distant rolling of their eyes, which was like the revolution of rock-crystal suns, the waterfall sweep of their manes, the ruthless flick of their cropped tails, the plunge of their iron-shod hoofs striking fire from the flagstones, filled me with a stationary terror and delight for which I could get no relief. One day two of our horses began to fight in the field below the house, rearing at each other like steeds on a shield and flinging out with their hind-legs, until Sutherland rushed out to separate them. A son of our neighbour at the Haa had a crescent mark on his forehead where a horse had kicked him; I stared at it in entrancement, as if it were a sign in the sky. And in a copy of *Gulliver's Travels* which my eldest brother had won as a school prize there was a picture of a great horse sitting on a throne judging a crowd of naked men with hairy, hangdog faces. The horse was sitting on its hindquarters, which had a somewhat mean and inadequate appearance; its front hoofs were upraised and its neck arched as if to strike; and though the picture was strange and frightening, I took it to be the record of some actual occurrence. All this added to my terror of horses, so that I loved and dreaded them as an explorer loves and dreads a strange country which he has not yet entered.

I had no fear of the cows, and wandered confidently among their legs. There seemed to be no danger *in* cows, as there was in horses, nothing to fear except their size and weight; I could not imagine a cow sitting in judgment on a throne. I did not fear the big black, curly-browed bull either as I feared the horses; I merely felt wary of him, knowing that he was dangerous in a comprehensible way, and that my father and Sutherland approached him with caution. One evening early in summer he followed an old woman from a neighbouring farm as she was walking to the Bu. I was standing with my two sisters at the end of the house, and as the old woman drew near, walking quite slowly, we saw the black bull rollicking behind her, flinging up his heels raffishly and shaking his head, nonplussed because she never altered her pace. She was deaf and did not hear him. He pulled up before he reached her, and my sister called the dog Prince and drove him off. To the three of us there was something extravagantly funny in the sight of the old woman walking quietly along and the bull prancing behind her; but my father was alarmed, and on Sutherland's advice decided that the bull would have to wear a ring in his nose. The bull was dragged by a strong rope into the shed where the farm implements were kept. All the young men of Wyre gathered; it was a long, clear summer evening, and every sound could be heard for miles. The bull was fastened by stout ropes with his body inside the shed and his head and neck sticking through a window. The young men hung on to a cord fastened behind his ears to hold his head down, and Sutherland came round the corner of the byre with a red-hot iron in his hand. At that point my father drove me into the house, and Sutherland playfully threatened to scorch the roof of my mouth with the iron, saying that it would make me sing better; that frightened me, and I ran. I listened inside the kitchen door to the shouting of the men and the bellowing of the bull, which seemed to fill the island. When it stopped I went out again. The bull's head was still sticking through the window; there was a look of deep surprise on his face, and drops that looked like tears were rolling from his eyes; he kept tossing his head as if to shake off the neat, shining ring sticking in his nose. The ring, like everything new, delighted me. The men stood discussing the job in thoughtful voices. A chain was fixed to the ring, and after that the bull had to drag it after him wherever he went.

That summer my father took me one evening to the Haa with him. The farmer of the Haa had bought a cow and had just let it into the field where his other cows were grazing. He and his sons were standing at the gate of the field to watch how the herd would welcome the new cow. For a while the cows paid no attention; then they all began to look in the same direction and drew together as if for protection or consultation, staring at the strange cow, which had retreated into a corner of the field. Suddenly they charged in a pack, yet as if they were frightened, not angry. The farmer and his sons rushed into the field, calling on their dog, and managed to head off the herd. The new cow, trembling, was led back to the byre. My father and the farmer philosophically discussed the incident as two anthropologists might discuss the customs of strange tribes. It seemed that this treatment of new members of the herd was quite common. It frightened me, yet it did not shake my belief in the harmlessness of our own cows, but merely made me despise them a little for being subject to foolish impulses, for as they charged across the field they looked more foolish than dangerous.

The distance of my eyes from the ground influenced my image of my father and mother too. I have a vivid impression of my father's cream-coloured moleskin breeches, which resisted elastically when I flung myself against them, and of my mother's skirt, which yielded, softly enveloping me. But I cannot bring back my mental impression of them, for it is overlaid by later memories in which I saw them as a man and a woman, like, or almost like, other men and women. I am certain that I did not see them like this at first; I never thought that they were like other men and women; to me they were fixed allegorical figures in a timeless landscape. Their allegorical changelessness made them more, not less, solid, as if they were condensed into something more real than humanity; as if the image 'mother' meant more than 'woman,' and the image 'father' more than 'man.' It was the same with my brothers and sisters, my cousin Sutherland, and my aunt Maggie. We begin life not by knowing men and women, but a father and a mother, brothers and sisters. Men and women, and mankind in general, are secondary images, for we know them first as strangers; but our father and mother were never strangers to us, nor our brothers and sisters if we were the last born, as I was. When I was a child I must have felt that they had always been there, and I with them, since I could not account for myself; and now I can see them only as a stationary pattern, changing, yet always the same, not as a number of separate people all following the laws of their different natures. Where all was stationary my mother came first; she certainly had always been with me in a region which could never be known again. My father came next, more recognizably in my own time, yet rising out of changelessness like a rock out of the sea. My brothers and sisters were new creatures like myself, not in time (for time still sat on the wrist of each day with its wings folded), but in a vast, boundless calm. I could not have put all this into words then, but this is what I felt and what we all feel before we become conscious that time moves and that all things change. That world was a perfectly solid world, for the days did not undermine it but merely rounded it, or rather repeated it, as if there were only one day endlessly rising and setting. Our first childhood is the only time in our lives when we exist within immortality, and perhaps all our ideas of immortality are influenced by it. I do not mean that the belief in immortality is a mere rationalization of childish impressions; I have quite other reasons for holding it. But we think and feel and believe immortally in our first few years, simply because time does not exist for us. We pay no attention to time until he tugs us by the sleeve or claps his policeman's hand on our shoulder; it is in our nature to ignore him, but he will not be ignored.

I can see my father quite clearly still with my later sight, though he has been dead for fifty years. He was a little, slight man with the soft brown beard of one who had never used a razor. His head was inclined sideways like the heads of statues of medieval saints; this had a natural cause, a contracted neck muscle; yet it seemed merely the outward mark of his character, which was gentle and meditative. His face was narrowish, with a long, delicate nose and large, fastidious lips almost hidden by his beard. He was slightly deaf and very embarrassed by it, and this may have been the reason why he was so fond of talking to himself. He would hold long conversations in the fields when no one was near; dialogues or monologues, I do not know which; but one could tell by the posture of his body and an occasional pensive wave of the hand that he was occupied. He was a religious man, but not strict or ostentatiously pious; he attended church irregularly but reverently; he often omitted grace before meals for long stretches; then he would remember and begin again. Every Sunday night he gathered us together to read a chapter of the Bible and kneel down in prayer. These Sunday nights are among my happiest memories; there was a feeling of complete security and union among us as we sat reading about David or Elijah. My father's prayer, delivered in a sort of mild chant while we knelt on the floor, generally ran on the same lines; at one point there always came the words, for which I waited, 'an house not made with hands, eternal in the heavens.' As a young man he had been saved, but he was not confident of his salvation, and I once heard him saying to my mother that he wished he was as certain of going to heaven as Jock M., a strict elder. I think there was a touch of irony in his words.

My father never beat us, and whether he was unlike his neighbours in that I cannot say. A distant relation of

ours, Willie D., a brave and pious man, beat his family
mercilessly. My father regretted his harshness, and often
told of a day when he had been walking home from church
with Willie and another man, talking of their children, when
the other man turned to Willie and said, 'Never lift your
hand to a bairn in anger. Wait, and you may change your
mind.' My father admired these words, and often repeated
them. Yet Willie went on thrashing his family; why I do
not know; perhaps in a sort of panic, terrified what might
happen to them if the evil were not driven out of them.

He came to see us once in Wyre. As I had heard so much
about him I kept staring at him in guilty curiosity. He was
not a big man, as I had expected, being scarcely taller than
my father, but deep-chested and powerful and deliberate in
his movements. He had a gentle, handsome, sad face and a
grave voice, and perhaps because I knew he was so harsh
to his family and yet so gentle to me I worshipped him. He
must have been very attractive to women, for children are
often drawn to men by the same qualities as women are. A
few years later he lost his life setting out to sea in a storm
which no other man would face.

The worst punishment we knew was an occasional clip
across the ears from my father's soft cap with the ear-flaps,
which he always wore, outside and inside; and this never
happened unless we were making an unbearable noise.
Afterwards he would sit back looking ashamed. Like most
gentle people he was long-suffering, but when his anger was
roused it frightened us. It was roused against me only once,
and that was after we left Wyre. I had been sliding on the
mill-dam all one Sunday morning against his orders, and
when I came back at dinner-time he threatened to thrash
me with a rope-end if I did it again. I felt outraged; such
a thing had never been heard of in our house before. But I
knew that he was terrified that the ice might break and leave
me to drown, for the mill-dam was deep. It may have been
some such terrifying vision of the future that made Willie D.
thrash his children, that and the common belief that evil can
be beaten out of children— violently driven out with blows.

My mother had more practical sense than my father, but
was just as gentle. I cannot remember ever hearing them

exchanging a discourteous word or raising their voices to each other. Their form of address was 'boy' and 'lass,' as it is still in Orkney among men and women, no matter of what age. My mother had a greater regard for appearances than my father, and a deeper family sense; her children were always in the right to her. She was inclined to worry, and wanted us to 'get on.' She too had passed through a religious experience as a young woman, and had a deep respect for religion, but not the spontaneous piety of my father. Yet it was she who taught me the story of Jesus out of a child's book whose name I cannot remember. It must have been written in a vein of mawkish sentiment, for it gave me the impression that Jesus was always slightly ill, a pale invalid with the special gentleness of people who cannot live as others do. My mother often lamented, as she read from this book, that she no longer had another one called *The Peep o' Day*, and for a long time I carried about an imaginary picture of it; I could see the frontispiece showing a bearded Jesus in a wide cloak, bearing a lamb in His arms. But it lay in the past, in a place I could never reach.

My mother liked the hymns in the Moody and Sankey hymn-book, and on Sunday evenings we would sing these catchy, self-satisfied tunes together: 'Hold the fort, for I am coming,' 'Dare to be a Daniel,' 'Bringing in the sheaves.' I always disliked them, but this only made me sing them more loudly, as if that would rid me of my dislike. Revivalist Christianity was saturated at that time with ideas of self-help, and my mother's wish that we might 'get on' may have gone back to her conversion. A paper called *The Christian Herald*, which we got weekly, helped to encourage this. It contained every week a sermon by the Reverend Charles Haddon Spurgeon, and another by the Reverend Doctor Talmage, as well as a page of prophecies by the Reverend Doctor Baxter, in which the date of the Millennium was calculated by comparing texts from Scripture. These speculations on the Millennium sank deep into my mind, as I was to discover many years later. There were stories too, showing the virtues of thrift and the dangers of drinking. *From Log Cabin to White House*, a Smilesian biography of President Garfield, had somehow got into our small library. I read it, as I read everything else. We had, of course, *The Pilgrim's Progress*, a book which thoroughly terrified me; and as a young man my father had taken out Goldsmith's *Natural History* in monthly parts with coloured plates, as well as a book called *The Scots Worthies*, a collection of biographies of reformers and Covenanters, abundantly illustrated with woodcuts. It was badly written, biased, and untruthful, but it contained some exciting stories of heroism and endurance. At one time it was to be found in every farmhouse in Scotland.

My mother was fond of singing, and she did not confine herself to hymns, though she drew a strict distinction between sacred and 'carnal' songs. I sang all her songs, carnal and sacred, after her. I can recollect singing at a concert in the Wyre school when I was four and not yet in trousers; it was an old Scots ballad about James V and his habit of going among his people disguised as a gaberlunzie man, or beggar; but I can remember only the end of the tune now and the last four lines of the text:

> Then doon he loot his duddy cloots,
>   An' doon he loot them fa',
> An' he glittered in go-o-old
>   Far abune them a'.

This gave me a great sense of glory. Another old ballad of my mother began:

> Of all the ancient Scottish knights
>   Of great and warlike name
> The bravest was Sir James the Rose,
>   That knight o' mickle fame.

I have never come across it since. There were also popular songs of a hundred or half a hundred years befcre, ballads of the Peninsular and the Crimean Wars, one of them telling how 'we stormed the heights of Alma.' There were eighteenth-century broadsheet ballads too, sung in the monotonous rhythm which the ploughmen love, containing many verses such as

> He was a very gallant lad,
>   But I'm sorry for to say

> That for some bad crime or other
> He was sent to Botany Bay.

My brother Johnnie, who had an irreverent mind, brought back one day a hymn which he had heard the Salvation Army singing in Kirkwall:

> My old companions, fare ye we-ell;
> I will not go-o with you to He-e-ell;
> I mean for ever with Christ to dwe-ell.
> Will you go-o, will you go?

He never sang it when my father or mother was there, but the rest of us were delighted by it. My mother had also a lovely old Cockney song; how it reached her I do not know:

> But, oh, she was as beautiful as a butterfly
>   And as proud as a queen,
> Was pretty little Polly Perkins
>   Of Paddington Green.

There was a great difference between the earlier and the later songs. The ballads about James V and Sir James the Rose had probably been handed down orally for hundreds of years; they were consequently sure of themselves and were sung with your full voice, as if you had always been entitled to sing them; but the later ones were chanted in a sort of literary way, in honour of the print in which they had originally come, every syllable of the English text carefully pronounced, as if it were an exercise. These old songs, rooted for so long in the life of the people, are now almost dead.

We had two fiddles in the house and a melodeon. My two eldest brothers played the fiddle, and we were all expert on the melodeon. John Ritch, our neighbour at the Haa, was a great fiddler in the traditional country style, and he had a trick of making the bow *dirl* on the strings which delighted us, especially in slow, ceremonious airs such as *The Hen's March to the Midden*. Then one year we were all caught with a passion for draughts, and played one another endlessly through the long winter evenings, always wary when we met Sutherland, for he had a trick of unobtrusively replacing his men on the board in impregnable positions after they had been captured. If we pointed this out to him he would either deny it loudly or else show amazement at seeing them there. When I think of our winters at the Bu they turn into one long winter evening round the stove—it was a black iron stove with scrollwork on the sides, standing well out into the kitchen—playing draughts, or listening to the fiddle or the melodeon, or sitting still while my father told of his witches and fairicks. The winter gathered us into one room as it gathered the cattle into the stable and the byre; the sky came closer; the lamps were lit at three or four in the afternoon, and then the great evening lay before us like a world: an evening filled with talk, stories, games, music, and lamplight.

The passing from this solid winter world into spring was wild, and it took place on the day when the cattle were unchained from their stalls in the six months' darkness of the byre, and my father or Sutherland flung open the byre door and leaped aside. The cattle shot through the opening, blind after half a year's night, maddened by the spring air and the sunshine, and did not stop until they were brought up by the stone dyke at the other end of the field. If anyone had come in their way they would have trampled over him without seeing him. Our dog Prince, who kept a strict watch over them during the summer, shrank before the sight. That was how spring began.

There were other things connected with it, such as the lambing; I think our lambs must have been born late in the season. I have a picture of my mother taking me by the hand one green spring day and leading me to the yard at the back of the house to see two new-born lambs. Some bloody, wet, rag-like stuff was lying on the grass, and a little distance away the two lambs were sprawling with their spindly legs doubled up. Everything looked soft and new—the sky, the sea, the grass, the two lambs, which seemed to have been cast up without warning on the turf; their eyes still had a bruised look, and their hoofs were freshly lacquered. They paid no attention to me when I went up to pat them, but kept turning their heads with sudden gentle movements which belonged to some other place.

Another stage in the spring was the sowing. About that

time of the year the world opened, the sky grew higher, the sea deeper, as the summer colours, blue and green and purple, woke in it. The black fields glistened, and a row of meal-coloured sacks, bursting full like the haunches of plough-horses, ran down each one; two neat little lugs, like pricked ears, stuck up from each sack. They were opened; my father filled from the first of them a canvas tray strapped round his middle, and strode along the field casting the dusty grain on either side with regular sweeps, his hands opening and shutting. When the grain was finished he stopped at another sack and went on again. I would sit watching him, my eyes caught now and then by some ship passing so slowly against the black hills that it seemed to be stationary, though when my attention returned to it again I saw with wonder that it had moved. The sun shone, the black field glittered, my father strode on, his arms slowly swinging, the fan-shaped cast of grain gleamed as it fell and fell again; the row of meal-coloured sacks stood like squat monuments on the field. My father took a special delight in the sowing, and we all felt the first day was a special day. But spring was only a few vivid happenings, not a state, and before I knew it the motionless blue summer was there, in which nothing happened.

There are zones of childhood through which we pass, and we live in several of them before we reach our school age, at which a part of our childhood stops for good. I can distinguish several different kinds of memory during my first seven years. There is first my memory of lying watching the beam of light, which I associate with no period and when I still seemed to be in the cradle. After that come my memories of the baptism and the singing at the concert; these belong to my petticoat stage, when I was conscious of myself as a small child moving safely among enormous presences. Next—as if my mother's fitting me out with trousers had really changed me—I remember myself as a boy, aware that I was different from little girls; no longer in the world where there is no marriage or giving in marriage.

This stage seems to have coincided with an onset of pugnacity, for my first memory of it is a fight with another boy over a knife. The memory is dim, and the figures in it huge and shadowy, making me think of the figures in the Scottish ballads, the Douglases and Percys. It must have been in autumn, for a sad light hangs over it. The other boy, whose name was Freddie, was standing with me at a place where two narrow roads crossed, and a little distance away two older girls with cloths over their heads were watching. Dusk was falling; the wet clouds hung just over our heads, shutting us in and making a small circular stage for the combat. I remember my anger rising and lifting my hand to strike. I knocked Freddie down and snatched the knife from him. He did not get up again, and that frightened me. I went over and shook him by the shoulder, and saw that he was crying as he lay with his face in the damp grass. A doctor had been to the house a little while before to attend to my mother, and I decided to be a doctor, went over to Freddie again, pretended to feel his pulse, and declared that he had recovered. How it ended and what became of the knife I do not remember.

This memory belongs to a different world from my other memories, perhaps because my pugnacious phase lasted only a short time, for after an attack of influenza I became timid and frightened. Other things as well may have helped to bring this about: I can give no clear explanation of it. In an island everything is near, for compressed within it are all the things which are spread out over a nation or a continent, and there is no way of getting away from them. A neighbouring farmer who had often brought me sweets in his snuff-lined pockets had died in great pain a little time before, and I had heard all about his death: I can still feel the terror of it. I have often fancied, too, that in a child's mind there is at moments a divination of a hidden tragedy taking place around him, that tragedy being the life which he will not live for some years still, though it is there, invisible to him, already. And a child has also a picture of human existence peculiar to himself, which he probably never remembers after he has lost it: the original vision of the world. I think of this picture or vision as that of a state in which the earth, the houses on the earth, and the life of every human being are related to the sky overarching them; as if the sky fitted the earth and the earth the sky. Certain dreams convince me that a child has this vision, in which there is a completer harmony of all things with each other than he will ever know again. There comes a moment (the moment at which childhood passes into boyhood or girlhood) when this image is broken and contradiction enters life. It is a phase of emotional and mental strain, and it brings with it a sense of guilt. All these things, the death of a man I knew, the sense of an unseen tragedy being played out around me, the destruction of my first image of the world, the attack of influenza, may have together brought about the change. In any case I became timid and frightened. Of the influenza all I remember is the sweetish taste of the medicine; it seemed to taste of the metal teaspoon which I took it out of, and like the spoon was a light golden colour.

My phase of acute childish guilt—how long it lasted I do not know; it may have been months or merely weeks—was associated with a sack of sheep-dip which my father had brought from Kirkwall. As the dip was poisonous the sack was left in the middle of a field some distance from the house; my father gave us strict orders not to go near it and on no account to touch it. I took care to keep away from it; yet after the sheep had been dipped and the sack destroyed I could not feel certain that I had not touched it, and as I took my father's words literally, and thought that even to touch the sack might bring death, I went about in terror. For my hands might have touched the sack. How could I know, now that the sack was gone and I had no control over the boy who might have touched it or might not have touched it, being quite unable to stay his hand in that other time and that other place? My fear was beyond any argument, so I washed my hands many times a day, until they had a wasted, transparent look, and pored upon them afterwards in a sort of agony, as if I were trying to read something from them. My fear went about with me, never leaving me: I would turn corners to get away from it, or shut myself in a little closet with one window, where there seemed to be no room except for myself; but the closet was big enough to hold my fear too. Sometimes I would run for a long way to escape from it, until I could run no farther, and if I fell and

cut my knee I felt that the blood trickling down must take
me back to the ordinary world where other children too cut
their knees and bled. My mother often looked anxiously at
me, as if she thought I had gone away from her and she could
not follow me; I often surprised that look in her face. And
I had actually gone away into a world where every object
was touched with fear, yet a world of the same size as the
ordinary world and corresponding to it in every detail: a sort
of parallel world divided by an endless, unbreakable sheet
of glass from the actual world. For though my world was
exactly the same in appearance as that world, I knew that
I could not break through my fear to it, that I was invisibly
cut off, and this terrified and bewildered me. The sense that
I was in a blind place was always with me; yet that place was
only a clear cloud or bubble surrounding me, from which I
could escape at any moment by doing something; but what
that was I did not know. My sister, playing in the sun a
few feet away, was in that other world; my brothers cut and
gathered the hay in it, the ships passed, the days followed
one another in it. I could not reach it by getting close to
it, though I often tried; for when my mother took me in
her arms and laid my head on her shoulder she, so close
to me, was in that world, and yet I was outside. How long
this lasted I cannot tell, but at last the actual world appeared
again in twisted gleams, as through running glass, and the
fear and the frenzied longing to cleanse myself went away.

I cannot account for this passion of fear and guilt; perhaps
at the root of it was the obsession which all young children
have with sex, their brooding curiosity, natural in itself, but
coloured with guilt by the thoughts of their elders. Children
live in two worlds: in their own and that of grown-up people.
What they do in their own world seems natural to them;
but in the grown-up world it may be an incomprehensible
yet deadly sin. A child has to believe things before he can
prove them, often before he can understand them; it is
his way of learning about the world, and the only way.
Accordingly he can believe that he is sinning without
feeling that he is sinning; but the sin, accepted at first
on trust and made plausible by make-believe, may later
take on an overwhelming imaginative reality, and guilt may

fall upon him from an empty sky. The worst thing about my fears was that I could not tell my father and mother about them, since I did not understand them; and the knowledge that there were things in which their help, no matter how willing, could be of no use to me bewildered me most of all. When that film dissolved, the world my eyes saw was a different world from my first childish one, which never returned again. This fit of guilt and terror came when I was seven, and in summer, for it is associated with bright, glassy, windless weather. I know I was seven, for we had just moved from the Bu to the neighbouring farm of Helzigartha, or Helye, where we stayed only for a year.

A farm is such a carnival of birth and death, there is no wonder that it should frighten a child. With my first sight of the two lambs that foreign, dirty-red, rag-like stuff is associated like a stain, and I still cannot see them without seeing it. Perhaps if it had not been for the attack of influenza I might have thought less of it, might have tucked it into that non-committal pocket of the mind where, when our bodies are sound and our senses working normally, we put away what startles or disgusts us. I must have been convalescent at the time, with the pitiless hypersensitiveness of convalescence. Yet these first fears, coming from things so bound up with life, were probably good, and a child could not grow up in a better place than a farm; for at the heart of human civilization is the byre, the barn, and the midden. When my father led out the bull to serve a cow brought by one of our neighbours it was a ritual act of the tradition in which we have lived for thousands of years, possessing the obviousness of a long dream from which there is no awaking. When a neighbour came to stick the pig it was a ceremony as objective as the rising and setting of the sun; and though the thought never entered his mind that without that act civilization, with its fabric of customs and ideas and faiths, could not exist—the church, the school, the council chamber, the drawing-room, the library, the city—he did it as a thing that had always been done, and done in a certain way. There was a necessity in the copulation and the killing which took away the sin, or at least, by the ritual act, transformed it into a sad, sanctioned duty.

My mother always kept us in the house when cows were brought to the bull; we would listen to the shouts of the men in the yard with very little idea of what was happening, for the shouts were like the shouts of warriors or of men playing some heroic game. My mother tried to keep me in too when the pig was killed—I must have been about seven the first time—but I slipped out when her back was turned, ran over to the byre, and from a window there stared into the yard. The farmer who acted as pig-killer for the island was a strong, sandy-haired man with a great round lump on the side of his neck, from which a sheaf of lighter bristles, somewhat like a pig's, stuck out. He always brought his gully with him, a large, broad-bladed knife with a sharp point and a wooden handle. When I reached the window the pig had a great gash in its throat, and blood was frothing from it into a basin which Sutherland was holding in his hands as he knelt on one knee on the ground. My father and the farmer were clinging to the pig to keep it still; but suddenly it broke loose, knocking Sutherland down; the basin toppled over; the blood poured over the ground, and Sutherland rose cursing, wiping his red hands on his trousers. It was a bright, windy day, and little flurries and ripples ran over the pool of blood. The pig seemed to be changed. It flew on, quite strange to me, as if seeking something, with an evil, purposive look, as if it were a partner in the crime, an associate of the pig-killer. As it ran it kept up a saw-like screaming which seemed to come from the slit in its throat. It stopped now and then to consider what it should do next; for it was not acting at random, but with a purpose which I could not fathom, and which therefore frightened me. Once it stopped to sniff at a docken in a corner of the yard, and then it looked like itself again and I was not afraid of it. But at once it made another stumbling charge, and what glared out of its eyes was mortal cruelty, the cruelty of the act itself, the killing. Then it began to make little top-heavy lurches; every moment it seemed about to fall forward on its snout. I ran into the house and hid my face, crying, in my mother's skirt. She scolded me and comforted me.

Later, in memory, it seemed to me that I had pitied the

pig; but I know that I did not; my terror was too great, and what I felt for it was hatred, for the pig seemed formidable and evil, except for the moment when it stopped to sniff at the docken. I did not go out again, and when, much later, the pig-killer came into the kitchen, his arms red with blood up to the elbows, to wash in a basin of hot water. I crawled under the table. He tried to coax me out, but I would not come. Later I went out to the barn, where the pig, neatly slit open, was hanging from the rafters by two cords passed through the sinews of its hind-legs. A warm, sweet smell filled the place, making me feel giddy; in a tub the entrails were floating in water; the pig swayed; the rafters creaked softly, as they did when we swung from them; the inside of the pig was pink and clean, with little frills and scallops of fat like convoluted shells running down either side. There was no one there but myself and the dead pig. I stared at it as at some infamous mystery and went away.

When I returned to the house Sutherland was sitting on a stool blowing up the bladder through a straw. It hung limp and purse-like for a moment; then it gradually filled; thin red veins stood out, stretching, on the stretched surface, which changed, growing thinner and thinner, like a gross bubble. He blew and blew, then tied a piece of string round the neck of the bladder and flung it to me. I dropped it, for it felt wet and slippery and had a strong smell. In a few days it grew stiff and dry, and I used it now and then as a football.

My memory of Sutherland killing a sheep in the barn is dim and ignominious, perhaps because Sutherland was an amateur and approached the business in a jaunty, conspiratorial vein. I have an impression of darkness and silence, as if the barn door had been closed to shut out the light and hide the deed; and I can see no one there but Sutherland and myself, which is so improbable that it must be due to a trick of memory. I can see the ewe lying on a bench on its side, meek and stupid, and Sutherland standing with a penknife in his hand, an infamously small penknife it seems to me now, though that must be another trick of memory. The whole scene is shameful, and gives me a feeling of cowardly stealth; I can remember nothing more about it.

Fortunately the barn was associated with happier memories, for about the same time Hughie o' Habreck, who was a skilled joiner as well as a farmer, came to build a yawl for my father. He was thickset and very strong, with a deep, rumbling voice and mutton-chop whiskers: a slow, consequential man who whenever he spoke seemed to be delivering a verdict, so that people were always asking his advice. He would stand over the growing boat and deliberate for a long time on what he should do next, at last saying in a judicial voice, as if he had just convinced himself, 'We'll do this now,' or 'We'll do that now.' He was never in a hurry; he sawed and planed and chiselled in a particular way of his own, absorbed in the thought of the boat, as if there were nothing but it and himself in the world, and his relation to it had a complete, objective intimacy. I cannot remember much about the actual building of the boat, except for the bending of the boards in steam, the slow growth of the sides as one smooth ply of wood was set on another, the sides bulging in a more swelling curve from bow to stern as the days passed in delicious slowness, the curly shavings, the scent of wood and resin, and a pot of bubbling tar into which you could thrust your hand without being burned if you dipped your hand in water first. The boat was eventually finished, and my brothers often went out in it in the evenings to fish, taking me with them.

I must have been seven when the great storm came. I can still remember distinctly the first day, which was dull and windless, the sky filled with clouds which hung without movement, like the full, suspended sails of a great fleet, yet seemed to expand and to be forced lower and lower as the darkness fell, until they were just over my head. I was coming back from school when, as I passed the little pond below the house, I became aware of the intense stillness: I can see myself for that moment; before and after there is a blank. When I went into the kitchen my mother said that she did not like the look of the weather, which surprised me, for I had loved the dull, sad stillness, the dense air which made each motionless blade of grass sweat one clear drop, the dreary immobility of the pond. A little while afterwards we heard an iron pail flying with a great clatter along the

length of the house. My father and Sutherland ran out to see
that all the doors and windows of the steading were fast shut.
I wanted to go with them to see the storm, but my mother
forbade me, saying that the wind would blow me away: I
took it for a fictitious warning, for I did not know then that
wind could do such things. The storm itself made very little
impression on me, for I was in the house, and looking out
of the windows I could not see that there was anything to
see except the dull sky with its low-flying clouds, and the
flattened look of everything, and the desertion of the fields.
On the second day Sutherland reported that a boat anchored
in the sound had dragged its anchor for several miles. This
seemed to impress him and my father a great deal, and I
tried to be impressed too. But what really excited me was
the knowledge that this was a storm, and not merely a wind;
for I thought of a storm as something different from a wind.
The storm must have lasted for several days; when the wind
fell news came across from Rousay that a boat returning
from the mainland with two men and two women had been
lost on the first day. The sea was still high, but my father
and Sutherland set out in our boat, along with the other
boats of Wyre and Rousay, to look for the drowned party.
In the evening Sutherland talked of what the sea did to the
dead, swelling their bodies and sending them to the surface
on the third day. Other cases of drowning came up; at that
time, when most farmers had a share in a boat and went out
in the fishing season, death at sea was common in Orkney.
The bodies were eventually found.

It was about the time when my first world was crumbling
and I was frightened and ill that I was sent to school. This
was not until I was seven, on account of bad health. I had
come very little in contact with other boys, but had struck
up a great friendship with a little girl at a neighbouring
farm who was a year younger than myself. What we did
and what games we played I cannot remember now; but
we were together every day throughout the summer, and
often played for hours in the roofless chapel, where the
weeds were as tall as ourselves. It was not one of those
precocious imitative love affairs which seem to waken in
children of that age if their parents so much as suggest

it. We were very friendly; we hardly ever quarrelled, for
there was no rivalry between us. Our friendship was more
intimate than a friendship between two boys of the same age
would have been; it was more quiet and settled too; very like
the friendship of an old married couple. Sometimes it was
interrupted by bouts of showing off; but these never lasted
long, for we found they spoiled everything. What we could
have done during all these long summer days, how we could
have filled in the time with enjoyment, effortlessly, as in a
dream, I cannot imagine. My brothers and sisters were all
at the school, so that we were left quite to ourselves day
after day.

Out of this friendship I was flung into the school, a small
school with only fifteen or sixteen pupils, but all of them
strange. The teacher—I had often sat on her knee when
she came to see us at the Bu—was kind to me, but I
soon realized that she was different in the classroom, and
it took me a long time to understand why. I was a backward
child, good at nothing but singing; and the examiner who
visited the school at the end of my first summer term was
so disappointed with my answers that he said in a more
formidable voice than I had ever heard in my life before,
'This must be a particularly stupid boy.' He was a tall,
big-faced man in a brown tweed suit smelling of peat, and
his large hands were terribly scrubbed and clean.

I disliked school from the start. The classroom which had
to serve us all, with its smell of ink, chalk, slate pencils,
corduroy, and varnish, made me feel as if my head were
stuffed with hot cotton-wool, and I realized quite clearly
that I was caught and there was no escape. A map of
the world covered one of the walls, a small, drab world,
smaller even than the classroom; the light brown benches
with the inkpots let into them seemed too hard and new;
the windows showed nothing but the high clouds floating
past. Time moved by minute degrees there; I would sit for
a long time invisibly pushing the hands of the clock on with
my will, and waken to realize that they had scarcely moved.
I was afraid of the other boys at first, who seemed to have
grown up in a different world from mine. Gradually I made
friends with the younger ones on an uneasy footing which

might crumble at any moment without my knowing why. Some of my dread and dislike of school was certainly due to bad health.

I had to leave for Edinburgh by the morning train a few years ago—I was living at St Andrews at the time—and as I walked to the station I passed the children going to school. It was a dismal morning draped with discoloured rags of clouds like a great washing; a few drops of rain splashed down at meaningless intervals; sodden leaves were plastered to the pavements and low walls. I watched the children, their satchels on their backs, walking through the school gate and trudging towards a door in the high wall; there was little sound anywhere, for it was an unfrequented street; everything had an air of secrecy. I can give no idea of the dreariness of the scene; the earth bleared and wet; the dejected children. I seemed to see an enormous school, higher even than this one, and millions of children all over the world creeping towards it and disappearing into it. The picture rose of itself, and it brought back a still Sunday evening in Wyre, when my mother and I had gone for a walk. The walk took us past the school, which, being shut, had a clean, forsaken look. My heart beat faster as we drew near, and I looked with dread at the ragged grass of the playground, not pounded now by the boots of the other boys, but lying peaceful and lost. I lingered to glance at the classroom windows, and my head grew hot and tight, as if I had been shut in a clothes cupboard. That was the feeling which my first year at school gave me, a feeling of being shut in some narrow, clean, wooden place: it must be known to every one who has attended a school, and the volume of misery it has caused will not bear thinking of. One day it made me so sick that Miss Angus took me outside and told me to sit down in a grassy field. It was a warm summer day. She came out later and told me to go home.

The day I remember best was the day when Freddie Sinclair chased me home: it was after we had gone to Helye, and his road lay in the same direction as mine. He was the boy I had fought over the knife, and this day he wanted to fight me again, but I was afraid. The road from the school to Helye lay on the crown of the island, and as I ran on, hollow with fear, there seemed to be nothing on either side of me but the sky. What I was so afraid of I did not know; it was not Freddie, but something else; yet I could no more have turned and faced him than I could have stopped the sun revolving. As I ran I was conscious only of a few huge things, monstrously simplified and enlarged: Wyre, which I felt under my feet, the other islands lying round, the sun in the sky, and the sky itself, which was quite empty. For almost thirty years afterwards I was so ashamed of that moment of panic that I did not dare to speak of it to anyone, and drove it out of my mind. I was seven at the time, and in the middle of my guilty fears. On that summer afternoon they took the shape of Freddie Sinclair, and turned him into a terrifying figure of vengeance. I felt that all the people of Wyre, as they worked in their fields, had stopped and were watching me, and this tempered my fear with some human shame. I hoped that none of my family had noticed me, but when they came in from the fields at tea-time Sutherland said, 'Weel, boy, I see thu can run!' I had got over my panic by then, and pretended that Freddie and I had been merely having a race. Sutherland laughed. 'Ay, a fine race, man, a fine race!' He called me 'man' when he wanted to be sarcastic.

I got rid of that terror almost thirty years later in a poem describing Achilles chasing Hector round Troy, in which I pictured Hector returning after his death to run the deadly race over again. In the poem I imagined Hector as noticing with intense, dreamlike precision certain little things, not the huge simplified things which my conscious memory tells me I noticed in my own flight. The story is put in Hector's mouth:

> The grasses puff a little dust
> Where my footsteps fall,
> I cast a shadow as I pass
> The little wayside wall.
>
> The strip of grass on either hand
> Sparkles in the light,

> I only see that little space
> To the left and to the right,
>
> And in that space our shadows run,
> His shadow there and mine,
> The little knolls, the tossing weeds,
> The grasses frail and fine.

That is how the image came to me, quite spontaneously: I wrote the poem down, almost complete, at one sitting. But I have wondered since whether that intense concentration on little things, seen for a moment as the fugitive fled past them, may not be a deeper memory of that day preserved in a part of my mind which I cannot tap for ordinary purposes. In any case the poem cleared my conscience. I saw that my shame was a fantastically elongated shadow of a childish moment, imperfectly remembered; an untapped part of my mind supplied what my conscious recollection left out, and I could at last see the incident whole by seeing it as happening, on a great and tragic scale, to some one else. After I had written the poem the flight itself was changed, and with that my feelings towards it. A psychologist would say that this was because I had suppressed my knowledge of my cowardice, and that it could trouble me only so long as I suppressed it. That may be so, but what it was that made me stop suppressing it is another question. I think there must be a mind within our minds which cannot rest until it has worked out, even against our conscious will, the unresolved questions of our past; it brings up these questions when our will is least watchful, in sleep or in moments of intense contemplation. My feeling about the Achilles and Hector poem is not of a suppression suddenly removed, but rather of something which had worked itself out. Such events happen again and again in everyone's life; they may happen in dreams; they always happen unexpectedly, surprising us if we are conscious of them at the time. It is an experience as definite as conviction of sin; it is like a warning from a part of us which we have ignored, and at the same time like an answer to a question which we had not asked, or an unsolicited act of help where no help was known to be. These solutions of the past projected into the present, deliberately announced as if they were a sibylline declaration that life has a meaning, impress me more deeply than any other kind of experience with the conviction that life does have a meaning quite apart from the thousand meanings which the conscious mind attributes to it: an unexpected and yet incontestable meaning which runs in the teeth of ordinary experience, perfectly coherent, yet depending on a different system of connected relations from that by which we consciously live.

The winter before we left the Bu a curious thing happened. One of the farmers in Wyre, an old friend of my father's, had left, and a new tenant had come in his place. The new farmer was a big, fat, sandy-haired man with a face the colour of porridge and eyes with almost white lashes. He was coarse and overbearing, and the other farmers, being quiet, peaceable men, did not like him. He had a jeering, over-familiar way with him, and was fond of strolling across to his neighbours' fields and criticizing them while they worked, all under a cloak of jocularity. One winter evening a few months after he had come to the island the new farmer burst in upon us in great agitation. He had been coming from the shop, which was at the other end of Wyre. As he returned along the shore he decided to have a look at his boat and see that it was safe; it was a wild night and very dark. When he reached his boat he heard voices at the other side of it and stopped to listen. The voices belonged to two young lads, and the older one was trying to persuade the younger to take out the plug, so that when the farmer went out the boat would fill and drown him. The farmer jumped up with a shout and made for them, and the two boys ran off. He chased them half across the island, stumbling over dykes and falling into burns. When he reached the Bu he was in a dreadful state. My father was deeply shocked, for the boys were sons of close neighbours of ours. The farmer kept saying, 'I'll have the law o' him! I'll have the law o' him!' This raised him in my eyes, for to have the law of anyone was something we only read about in *The Orcadian* or *The People's Journal*. He praised the younger lad as an honest boy who would do nobody any harm, but when he came to the older one he kept saying, 'He's wicked! He's wicked!' in an incredulous voice, as if wickedness were a thing he did not expect to find in an island like Wyre. My father tried to pacify him and make him believe that the older boy had not meant it. But after the farmer left he said, 'That Willie A. is a bad, sly boy.' 'Sly' was the worst word he could find for anyone. The scandal blew over somehow, and the farmer was treated more kindly by his neighbours afterwards.

During our last year at the Bu there was a wedding at one of the farms, and we were all invited to it. We went in the afternoon and returned early next morning. I remember the dancing in the lighted barn, and a crowd of young women who were unaccountably kind to me, pressing cakes upon me and filling my pockets with sweets until they stuck out at both sides. My strangest memory of the wedding is a vivid, dreamlike glimpse of a young farm-servant, whom we called Goliath of Gath, as he gazed at one of the girls. He was strong, proud of his strength, stupid, and always at a loss for a word. He had an ox-like head set on a strong neck. Large drops of sweat were rolling down his face, and his eyes seemed to be melting in a soft, invisible flame. I had never seen a look like that in a man's face before, and if I had known anything about adult passions I would have seen him as a shaven ox slowly basting in the fires of love. As it is, he is like a part of a mythological picture to me now, and a line which was left in my mind by a dream one morning some years ago probably came from that glimpse of his face more than forty years before. The line was:

> Jove with the ponderous glory of the bull,

which is quite unlike any poetry that I write. I have always thought of Jove's brow as broad and a little stupid and yet glorious like that of a bull. I do not like the line; it is an echo, perhaps even a line unconsciously cribbed from some Elizabethan poet, though I do not know its source.

The dream itself was a curious one. I was in a town in Spain or Portugal (I have never been to Spain or Portugal). I was wandering about the streets in bright sunshine in a stiff, creased tweed suit, feeling annoyed that I was wearing a waistcoat; yet the heat was not so great as I had expected, though it made my face feel stiff and salt and sore. I had a

soft felt hat pulled down over my brow. I could see myself
objectively, without illusion, so that the figure did not seem
to be really like me; more like an old friend.

As I walked along I was struck by a bas-relief on the gable
of an old house. It represented an enormous muscular figure
which I took to be Hercules; the body and limbs swelled out
heavily yet resiliently from the wall like a great cluster of
grapes, though it had the look too of an opulent heraldic
inn-sign; there was a great deal of dark blue and purple
surrounding the main figure, suggesting the wine-cup and
the vine-press. It was like an ancient and rich relic which
had survived the long, watery wash of Time from an age
when animal and man and god lived densely together in the
same world: the timeless, crowded age of organic heraldry.
Somewhere in this picture, transfigured, was that young
farm-servant in Wyre whose face, caught in a moment of
animal glory, had been such a revelation. Yet I had not
known at the time what the revelation was; I had merely
seen the glow, the transformation, without understanding,
in a sort of wonder. 'The ponderous glory of the bull'
suggested Spain; the rich colours, which might have been
either wine or blood, were colours of sacrifice and rejoicing;
the Hercules himself was probably an idealization of the
farm-servant, whom now, after forty years, I was offering
up to some unknown ancestral god in my mind.

I have always been fascinated by a part of us about which
we know far less than our remote ancestors did: the part
which divined those immediate though concealed relations
that made them endow their heroes with the qualities of the
animals whose virtues they incarnated, calling a man a bull
for strength, a lion for courage, or a fox for cunning. That
age is fabulous to us, populated by heraldic men and legendary beasts. We see a reflection of it in the Indian reliefs
where saints and crowned emperors wander among tigers,
elephants, and monkeys, and in the winged bulls of the
Assyrians with their human heads: angel, beast, and man
in one. The age which felt this connexion between men and
animals was so much longer than the brief historical period
known to us that we cannot conceive it; but our unconscious
life goes back into it. In that age everything was legendary,

and the creatures went about like characters in a parable of beasts. Some of them were sacred and some monstrous, some quaint and ugly as house gods; they were worshipped and sacrificed; they were hunted; and the hunt, like the worship and the sacrifice, was a ritual act. They were protagonists in the first sylvan war, half human and half pelted and feathered, from which rose the hearth, the community, and the arts. Man felt guilty towards them, for he took their lives day after day, in obedience to a custom so long established that no one could say when it began. Though he killed them, they were sacred to him, because without destroying them he could not live; and so when they lay in heaps, in hecatombs, they were a vast sacrifice offered by the animal kingdom, and they gave their lives in hundreds of thousands, guiltlessly, by a decree of destiny. Man tamed some of them and yoked them to the plough and the mill; he fattened them so that he might eat their flesh; he drank their milk, used their fleeces and their hides to clothe him, their horns as ornaments or goblets, and lived with them under the same roof. This went on for ages beside which the age we know is hardly more than a day. As their life had to be taken and the guilt for it accepted, the way of taking it was important, and the ritual arose, in which were united the ideas of necessity and guilt, turning the killing into a mystery.

My passion for animals comes partly from being brought up so close to them, in a place where people lived as they had lived for two hundred years; partly from I do not know where. Two hundred years ago the majority of people lived close to the animals by whose labour or flesh they existed. The fact that we live on these animals remains; but the personal relation is gone, and with it the very ideas of necessity and guilt. The animals we eat are killed by thousands in slaughter-houses which we never see. A rationalist would smile at the thought that there is any guilt at all: there is only necessity, he would say, a necessity which is laid upon all carnivores, not on man only. But our dreams and ancestral memories speak a different language. As it is, the vegetarians are more honest than the rest of us, though their alternative is probably a false one, for they merely avoid the guilt instead of accepting it.

I do not know whether many people have dreams of animals; perhaps these dreams die out in families which have lived for two or three generations in a big city; I have no means of knowing. But it is certain that people who have been brought up in close contact with animals, including the vast majority of the generations from whom we spring, have dreamed and dream of animals, and my own experience shows that these dreams are often tinged with a guilt of which consciously we are unaware. As I feel that these dreams go back to my world as a child, the best place to speak of them is here. If I were recreating my life in an autobiographical novel I could bring out these correspondences freely and show how our first intuition of the world expands into vaster and vaster images, creating a myth which we act almost without knowing it, while our outward life goes on in its ordinary routine of eating, drinking, sleeping, working, and making money in order to beget sons and daughters who will do the same. I could follow these images freely if I were writing an autobiographical novel. As it is, I have to stick to the facts and try to fit them in where they will fit in.

It is clear that no autobiography can begin with a man's birth, that we extend far beyond any boundary line which we can set for ourselves in the past or the future, and that the life of every man is an endlessly repeated performance of the life of man. It is clear for the same reason that no autobiography can confine itself to conscious life, and that sleep, in which we pass a third of our existence, is a mode of experience, and our dreams a part of reality. In themselves our conscious lives may not be particularly interesting. But what we are not and can never be, our fable, seems to me inconceivably interesting. I should like to write that fable, but I cannot even live it; and all I could do if I related the outward course of my life would be to show how I have deviated from it; though even that is impossible, since I do not know the fable or anybody who knows it. One or two stages in it I can recognize: the age of innocence and the Fall and all the dramatic consequences which issue from the Fall. But these lie behind experience, not on its surface; they are not historical events; they are stages in the fable.

The problem that confronts an autobiographer even more urgently than other men is, How can he know himself? I am writing about myself in this book, yet I do not know what I am. I know my name, the date and place of my birth, the appearance of the places I have lived in, the people I have met, the things I have done. I know something of the society which dictates many of my actions, thoughts, and feelings. I know a little about history, and can explain to myself in a rough-and-ready fashion how that society came into being. But I know all this in an external and deceptive way, as if it were a dry legend which I had made up in collusion with mankind. This legend is founded on a sort of agreement such as children presuppose in their games of make-believe: an agreement by which years and days are given certain numbers to distinguish them, and peoples and countries and other things certain names: all this is necessary, of course, for the business of living. But it is a deception as well: if I knew all these figures and names I should still not know myself, far less all the other people in the world, or the small number whom I call friends. This external approach, no matter how perfect, will never teach me much either about them or about myself.

Take the appearance of a man, which is supposed to tell so much about him. He can never see that appearance: he can never see himself. If he looks at his face in a mirror, which faithfully reflects not only him, but the anxiety or hope with which he stares into it, he does not feel that this is himself. The face he sees has a certain convincing quality, it is true, like all faces; there is experience, thought, evasion, resolution, success, failure, suffering, and a certain comfort in it; there is in it everything that one can ask from a face. It imposes without effort—there can be no doubt of that—on every one else. He knows that it was made by him and time in a curious, often reluctant collaboration, and time is so much the stronger partner that at certain moments there seems to be nothing there but time. For though he incised every line himself—with no idea that these lines would remain—time fixed each of them by a principle of selection which had no regard whatever for him. If he looks honestly at the result it is time that convinces him, time that tells him, 'You must accept this, for I have preserved it.' Yet what time preserves is not what he would have liked to preserve. So that there are moments when he is so oppressed by this face which he carries about wherever he goes that he would like to take it down and put it up again differently; but only death can do that. There is no getting away from this result of time's collaboration. This face constructed to look like a face has an absolute plausibility. Yet if the man sees that face in a photograph it looks like the face of a stranger.

Or take a man's actions. We may know that he works in an office or in a coal-mine, that he has made a great deal of money by speculating on the Stock Exchange, that he once reached the South Pole, that he governed a province in India, that he won a race, that he threw up his post to nurse lepers or save the souls of heathens. These things tell us something about him; working in an office, winning money on the Stock Exchange, reaching the South Pole, and converting heathens leave their mark on a man, and *condition* him. A clerk is not like a coal-miner, or a stockbroker like an explorer. It is the same with countless other things. A man who lives in Kensington is different from a man who lives in Wapping. The differences are important, and they are caused by various distortions. It distorts a man to work in a coal-mine or an office; it distorts him in a different way to make a fortune on the Stock Exchange, though in a commercial society the distortion may be less apparent. It need not distort a man so much to be an explorer or a missionary. The miner cannot live a civilized life, and society sins against him; the stockbroker will not live a civilized life, and sins against society. Or at any rate the sin is there, though it is difficult to establish where its roots lie. These things are of enormous importance, and we shall never settle them until the miner and the stockbroker live a civilized life.

But they are not of much help to us when we set out to discover what we are, and there is a necessity in us, however blind and ineffectual, to discover what we are. Religion once supplied that knowledge, but our life is no longer ruled by religion. Yet we can know what we are only if we accept some of the hypotheses of religion. Human beings are understandable only as immortal spirits; they become natural then, as natural as young horses; they are absolutely unnatural if we try to think of them as a mere part of the natural world. They are immortal spirits distorted and corrupted in countless ways by the world into which they are born; bearing countless shapes, beautiful, quaint, grotesque; living countless lives, trivial, sensational, dull; serving behind counters, going to greyhound races, playing billiards, preaching to savages in Africa, collecting stamps, stalking deer in the Highlands, adding up figures in an office for fifty years, ruining one another in business, inventing explosives which will destroy other men and women on a large scale, praying for the cessation of war, weeping over their sins, or trying to discover what sin really is: doing everything that is conceivable for human beings to do, and doing it in a different way at every stage of history. I do not have the power to prove that man is immortal and that the soul exists; but I know that there must be such a proof, and that compared with it every other demonstration is idle. It is true that human life without immortality would be inconceivable to me, though that is not the ground for my belief. It would be inconceivable because if man is an animal by direct descent I can see human life only as a nightmare populated by animals wearing top-hats and kid gloves, painting their lips and touching up their cheeks and talking in heated rooms, rubbing their muzzles together in the moment of lust, going through innumerable clever tricks, learning to make and listen to music, to gaze sentimentally at sunsets, to count, to acquire a sense of humour, to give their lives for some cause, or to pray.

This picture has always been in my mind since one summer evening in Glasgow in 1919. I did not believe in the immortality of the soul at that time; I was deep in the study of Nietzsche, and had cast off with a great sense of liberation all belief in any other life than the life we live here and now, as an imputation on the purity of immediate experience, which I had intellectually convinced myself was guiltless and beyond good and evil. I was returning in a tramcar from my work; the tramcar was full and very hot; the sun burned through the glass on backs of necks, shoulders, faces, trousers, skirts, hands, all stacked there impartially. Opposite me was sitting a man with a face like a pig's, and as I looked at him in the oppressive heat the words came into my mind, 'That is an animal.' I looked round me at the other people in the tramcar; I was conscious that something had fallen from them and from me; and with a sense of desolation I saw that they were all animals, some of them good, some evil, some charming, some sad, some happy, some sick, some well. The tramcar stopped and went on again, carrying its menagerie; my mind saw countless other tramcars where animals sat or got on or off with mechanical dexterity, as if they had been trained in a circus; and I realized that in all Glasgow, in all Scotland, in all the world, there was nothing but millions of such creatures living an animal life and moving towards an animal death as towards a great slaughter-house. I stared at the faces, trying to make them human again and to dispel the hallucination, but I could not. This experience was so terrifying that I dismissed it, deliberately forgot it by that perverse power which the mind has of obliterating itself. I felt as if I had lived for a few moments in Swift's world, for Swift's vision of humanity was the animal vision. I could not have endured it for more than a few minutes. I did not associate it at the time with Nietzsche. But I realized that I could not bear mankind as a swarming race of thinking animals, and that if there was not somewhere, it did not matter where—in a suburb of Glasgow or of Hong Kong or of Honolulu—a single living soul, life was a curious, irrelevant desolation. I pushed away this realization for a time, but it returned again later, like the memory of my cowardice as a boy.

The animal world is a great impersonal order, without pathos in its suffering. Man is bound to it by necessity and guilt, and by the closer bond of life, for he breathes the same breath. But when man is swallowed up in nature nature is corrupted and man is corrupted. The sense of corruption in *King Lear* comes from the fact that Goneril, Regan and Cornwall are merely animals furnished with human faculties as with weapons which they can take up or lay down at will, faculties which they have stolen, not inherited. Words are their teeth and claws, and thought the technique of the deadly spring. They are so *unnatural* in belonging completely to nature that Gloucester can explain them only by 'these late eclipses in the sun and moon.' In *King Lear* nature is monstrous because man has been swallowed up in it:

> A serving-man, proud in heart and mind; that curled my hair; wore gloves in my cap; served the lust of my mistress' heart and did the act of darkness with her; swore as many oaths as I spake words and broke them in the sweet face of heaven: one that slept in the contriving of lust and waked to do it: wine loved I deeply, dice dearly, and in woman out-paramoured the Turk: false of heart, light of ear, bloody of hand; hog in sloth, fox in stealth, wolf in greediness, dog in madness, lion in prey.

That is a picture of an animal with human faculties, made corrupt and legendary by the proudly curled hair. The conflict in Lear is a conflict between the sacred tradition of human society, which is old, and nature, which is always new, for it has no background. As I sat in that tramcar in Glasgow I was in an unhistorical world; I was outside time without being in eternity; in the small, sensual, momentary world of a beast.

But I believe that man has a soul and that it is immortal, not merely because on any other supposition human life would be inconceivable and monstrous; for I know that there are many people who believe that man is merely a thinking animal and yet do not consider him monstrous, and that there are a few people who, believing this, consider him monstrous, but do not find him inconceivable: who accept the nightmare and acknowledge nothing beyond it, as Swift did. But I think there are not many people who have the strength to do this; the great majority of those who see man as a thinking animal cannot do so without idealizing him, without seeing him ascending to some transcendent height in some future: they are sentimentalists with a passionate faith in self-help. My belief in immortality, so far as I can divine its origin, and that is not far, seems to be connected with the same impulse which urges me to know myself. I can never know myself; but the closer I come to knowledge of myself the more certain I must feel that I am immortal, and, conversely, the more certain I am of my immortality the more intimately I must come to know myself. For I shall attend and listen to a class of experiences which the disbeliever in immortality ignores or dismisses as irrelevant to temporal life. The experiences I mean are of little practical use and have no particular economic or political interest. They come when I am least aware of myself as a personality moulded by my will and time: in moments of contemplation when I am unconscious of my body, or indeed that I have a body with separate members; in moments of grief or prostration; in happy hours with friends; and, because self-forgetfulness is most complete then, in dreams and day-dreams and in that floating, half-discarnate state which precedes and follows sleep. In these hours there seems to me to be knowledge of my real self and simultaneously knowledge of immortality. Sleep tells us things both about ourselves and the world which we could not discover otherwise. Our dreams are part of experience; earlier ages acknowledged this. If I describe a great number of dreams in this book I do so intentionally, for I should like to save from the miscellaneous dross of experience a few glints of immortality.

I have had many dreams about animals, domestic, wild, and legendary, but I shall describe only one at this point, as it seems to me to throw into an imaginative shape two of the things I have been writing about: our relation to the animal world, a relation involving a predestined guilt, and our immortality. All guilt seeks expiation and the end of guilt, and our blood-guiltness towards the animals tries to find release in visions of a day when man and the beasts will live in friendship and the lion will lie down with the lamb. My dream was connected with this vision. I dreamed that I was lying asleep, when a light in my room wakened me. A man was standing by my bedside. He was wearing a long robe, which fell about him in motionless folds, while he stood like a column. The light that filled the room came from his hair, which rose straight up from his head, burning, like a motionless brazier. He raised his hand, and without touching me, merely by making that sign, lifted me to my feet in one movement, so that I stood before him. He turned and went out through the door, and I followed him. We were in the gallery of a cloister; the moon was shining, and the shadows of the arches made black ribs on the flagstones. We went through a street, at the end of which there was a field, and while we walked on the moonlight changed to the white light of early morning. As we passed the last houses I saw a dark, shabby man with a dagger in his hand; he was wearing rags bound round his feet, so that he walked quite soundlessly; there was a stain as of blood on one of his sleeves; I took him to be a robber or a murderer and was afraid. But as he came nearer I saw that his eyes, which were fixed immovably on the figure beside me, were filled with a profound, violent adoration such as I had never seen in human eyes before. Then, behind him, I caught sight of a confused crowd of other men and women in curious or ragged clothes, and all had their eyes fixed with the same look on the man walking beside me. I saw their faces only for a moment. Presently we came to the field, which as we drew near changed into a great plain dotted with little conical hills a little higher than a man's head. All over the plain animals were standing or sitting on their haunches on these little hills; lions, tigers, bulls, deer, elephants, were there; serpents too wreathed their lengths on the knolls; and each was separate and alone, and each slowly lifted its head upward as if in prayer. This upward-lifting motion had a strange solemnity and deliberation; I watched head after head upraised as if proclaiming some truth just realized, and yet as if moved by an irresistible power beyond them. The elephant wreathed its trunk upward, and there was something pathetic and absurd in that indirect act of adoration. But the other animals raised their heads with the inevitability of the sun's rising, as if they knew, like the sun, that a new day was about to begin, and were giving the signal for its coming. Then I saw a little dog busily running about with his nose tied to the ground, as if he did not know that the animals had been redeemed. He was a friendly little dog, officiously going about his business, and it seemed to me that he too had a place in this day, and that his oblivious

concern with the earth was also a sort of worship. How the
dream ended I do not remember: I have now only a memory
of the great animals with all their heads raised to heaven.

I had this dream a long time after I left Orkney; I was
living in London and being psychoanalysed. I had so many
dreams about this time that I could hardly keep count of
them. In a great number of them I encountered dragons
and mythological monsters, the explanation of the analyst
being that I had for many years suppressed the animal
in myself, so that it could come up now only in these
wild and terrifying shapes. He was right up to a point in
assuming this, for I had grown up a Puritan, and though
I had liberated my mind, my senses were still bound. But
he was right only up to a point, for the strange thing about
these monsters was that they did not terrify me; instead I felt
in a curious way at home with them. I can remember only
one of them that frightened me: a great roaring sea-beast
which I was trying to fight with an oar as I stood in a boat. I
have had many dreams of fear, but except for this one hardly
any of them have been connected with animals. It seems
to me that most of the dreams I had about this time were
ancestral dreams or Millennial dreams like the one I have
just described. Our minds are possessed by three mysteries:
where we came from, where we are going, and, since we
are not alone, but members of a countless family, how we
should live with one another. These questions are aspects of
one question, and none of them can be separated from the
others and dealt with alone. In my dream about the animals
all three questions are involved; for the dream touches the
relation between man and the animals and points to his
origin, while in the image of the animal kingdom glorified
and reconciled with mankind it points simultaneously to
man's end, and with that to the way in which he should
live in a society, for that question is inseparable from the
question of his end.

There were Millennial airs in that dream, or in the
analyst's words, themes from the racial unconscious. But
there was also in it something of my first few years; the
hills were the little green hills of childhood; the figure
who appeared by my bedside was a childish image of

Christ; and the event itself, the Millennium, had often been discussed by my father and mother at the Bu after a reading of the Reverend Doctor Baxter, while I listened and almost without knowing it fashioned my own delightful pictures, long since forgotten. There was a great deal of Biblical discussion in our house, and the brazier of burning hair may be a far-off reminiscence of a long debate between me and my Aunt Maggie, who was a tough casuist, on the translation of Elijah to heaven. That summer D., the husband of a relative of my mother who lived in Edinburgh, had come to Orkney for his holidays, and stayed for a while at the Bu. He was a commercial traveller, a good violinist, and a man of some intelligence, with an inflamed, pimply face and what seemed to us curious views on religion: he was a Christadelphian. He had a close but pedantic knowledge of the Bible, and in spite of his enlightened views—for he did not believe in a hell—he was as literal in his interpretation of texts as any Plymouth Brother. He had discovered that Elijah did not go to heaven in a chariot of fire, as people generally thought, and in support of this he adduced Second Kings chapter ii, verse 11:

> And it came to pass, as they still went on, and talked, that, behold, there appeared a chariot of fire, and horses of fire, and parted them both asunder; and Elijah went up by a whirlwind into heaven.

D. read from this that Elijah did not go up to heaven in the chariot, but in a whirlwind; but Aunt Maggie would not have it; she had been taught that Elijah went up in a chariot, and she refused to give up the chariot. For some reason I was attracted by the fancy of the whirlwind. The debate between Aunt Maggie and me went on long after D. had gone, leaving a pile of tracts behind him which my father put in the fire one day. There was a great deal of discussion among us about King David too, and how, considering all the sins he had committed, he could be a man after God's heart. My father had a soft side for David, and nodded his head in a sort of Plutarchian wonder over his character; but my mother could never quite reconcile herself to him.

There was no church in Wyre, so that on Sunday the

Wyre people had to set out in their boats for Rousay across the narrow sound. Half a dozen boats would sometimes leave together on a calm summer morning, but there were many days when the weather was too rough for anyone to risk the journey. I can remember these expeditions, and Mr Pirie standing in the pulpit nodding his head, which was inclined diagonally as he followed the lines of his written sermon with his one good eye; I can see his thin hair brushed across the crown of his head to hide a small coin-like bald patch in the middle, and his straggling beard, and his brown, seamed face. He was greatly loved, though every one disapproved of his reading his sermons: people still had a strong belief in spontaneous inspiration.

We always returned from church to a good dinner of soup with a chicken, or, as we called it, more honestly, a hen, cooked in it, followed by 'spotted dog.' Now that my sailor suit has come back again I find it is associated with these Sunday dinners and the shining spoons and knives and forks laid out on the white tablecloth. During the week we did not bother much about knives and forks and tablecloths. A big plate of herring or other fish was set in the middle of the table, along with a dish of potatoes, and we simply stretched out our hands. The traditional Orkney invitation to a visitor was, 'Put in the hand,' though when a visitor appeared knives and forks were usually laid out. We hardly ever ate meat or fowl more than once a week. It was the same at all the other farms, and nobody seemed to be the worse for it. Our supper was porridge. The porridge-pot was set down in the middle of the floor, and we all sat round it with great bowls of milk and ladled the porridge into the milk.

Our diet was a curious one by town standards. We went without many necessaries, or what are considered necessaries—beef, for instance—and had a great number of luxuries which we did not know to be luxuries, such as plovers' eggs, trout, crab, and lobster: I ate so much crab and lobster as a boy that I have never been able to enjoy them since. Our staples were home-made oat bannocks and barley bannocks, butter, eggs, and home-made cheese, which we had in abundance; white bread, bought at the Wyre shop, was looked upon as a luxury. In the kitchen there was a big girnel with a sliding top; inside it was divided in two, one compartment being filled with oatmeal and the other with barley-meal. The meal had to be pressed firmly down, otherwise it would not keep. The girnel, when the top was slid aside, gave out a thick, sleepy smell which seemed to go to my head and make me drowsy. It was connected with a nightmare which I often had, in which my body seemed to swell to a great size and then slowly dwindle again, while the drowsy smell of meal filled my nostrils. It is from smell that we get our most intense realization of the solidity of things. The smell of the meal pressed tightly down in the girnel made me realize its *mass*, though I could see only its surface, which was smooth and looked quite shallow. My nightmares probably came from an apprehension of the mere bulk of life, the feeling that the world is so tightly crammed with solid, bulging objects that there is not enough room for all of them: a nightmare feeling powerfully conveyed in the stories of Franz Kafka.

Our life at the Bu was virtually self-supporting. The pig, after being slaughtered each year, was cut up and salted, and the pork stored away in a barrel. I helped with the salting when I was quite small, and got a sense of pleased importance from rubbing the raw slices of meat on coarse salt strewn on a wooden board: these neat cubes did not seem to have any connexion with the butchered pig. We had fish almost as often as we wanted it, and crabs when Sutherland went to lift his creels; and Aunt Maggie was often down on the beach gathering whelks. The oat bannocks and barley bannocks, the milk, butter, cheese, and eggs, were our own produce. We sent part of the wool after the sheep-shearing down to a Border town, and it came back as blankets and cloth. We bought at the shop such things as white bread, sugar, tea, treacle, currants and raisins, and paraffin oil for the lamps.

Old Fred of the shop was a very genteel man with an accent which he had picked up in his young days while serving in a grocery store in Edinburgh. He was the only man on the island who shaved and put on a collar every day, and this set him apart from other men as a sort of priest smelling perpetually of the clean odours of tea, tobacco, and paraffin oil. He emphasized the difference by wearing a straw hat, summer and winter, both outside and inside the shop. Having seen the world, he looked down on us for our insularity, and showed that he thought his Edinburgh manners, suitable for a fine Princes Street shop, were cast away on us islanders. He was a thin, sensitive little man, terribly proper: a gentle bachelor with pernickety ways. He is long since dead.

The Lammas Market was the great yearly event. It was held in Kirkwall, but though my father and my older brothers and sisters usually went to it, I was never taken, for the journey was considered too long and tiring. On the first Monday of the market the *Fawn*, which plied between Rousay and Kirkwall, stopped a little distance out from Wyre—for there was no pier—and some one rowed out the people who wanted to go to the market. I cannot recollect my family ever setting out, but I remember clearly my brothers and sisters returning from it one year. I had bronchitis and was not allowed outside; but when they came in sight my mother let me go to the end of the house and watch them coming. I can see them still passing the corner of the ruined chapel; they were all in their best clothes; it was a still, warm summer evening. They brought presents for me, pink sweets I had never seen before, ribbed like snowdrifts, rough chunks of yellow rock, and new, dark brown, smooth sweets which I did not much care for: chocolates. I had expected a jumping-jack as well, for my mother had often described one to me which had once been in the house; but no jumping-jacks could be had at the market; they were out of fashion, and I had to put up instead with a large wooden egg, out of which a snake shot, rustling, when you opened it. I never had many toys, and never got much genuine satisfaction from them: the enjoyment was conscious make-believe with an undercurrent of disappointment: I always expected every toy to do more than it could do.

We had very few visitors in Wyre, for the island was difficult to reach except in perfectly calm weather. Mr Pirie sometimes came across from Rousay to call on his parishioners or to hold a prayer meeting in the school. An auctioneer from Kirkwall, a jolly young man in a blue serge suit, came one wet, cold afternoon—he had some business at another farm—and gave me a sandwich, the first I had ever seen: he seemed to have a great number of them in his pockets. And a queer man in a soft, grey suit with a very high, stiff collar knocked at our door one summer evening. He spoke in a shrill voice with a thin, whining accent; he was extravagantly polite and amiable; but his face was dead white and jumped about so much as he chattered and giggled that I hid behind my father and peeped out at him from there. We did not know what to make of him, but after he had left Sutherland said that he was 'moonstruck' —the adjective still used at that time in Orkney to describe lunatics. Rich young men who were not in their right minds were often sent to farms in remote islands then; a good number of them reached Orkney, and the Orkney people had a name for them, calling them 'feeders', since they ate without doing any work. The poor man who had called on us and tried to amuse us was a 'feeder' kept by a Rousay farmer who, wanting to give him a change, had rowed him across to Wyre to wander about there, and presently rowed him back again.

Our greatest friends in Wyre were the Ritches of the Haa, a handsome family with a sense of fun, and gentle manners. John Ritch, the father, was my father's closest friend; they had been next-door neighbours in Deerness, and in Wyre they got farms next to each other again. John Ritch was a skilled tailor and a fine fiddler as well as a farmer. He was one of the most handsome men I have ever seen, tall and straight, with a fine solid brow and nose and a square trimmed beard; he was more particular about his appearance than most farmers, and had a dignified jocosity which quite beguiled us. There was a sort of feud between him and Sutherland, who had no dignity, and whenever John Ritch came to our house Sutherland would tell one thundering lie after another, hoping to annoy him. But John Ritch, without losing his temper, would say gravely, 'Thu kens in the conscience, Sutherland, that thu's telling a lee.' And Sutherland would answer brazenly, 'And *I* ken in *me* conscience that I'm *no* telling a lee.' This dialogue would go on for a long time, while the rest of us looked on as at a play.

The language we spoke was a mixture of Norse, Scots, and Irish. The second person singular was in full working order, and we used it as it is used in French and German, addressing our friends as 'thu' and 'thee' and strangers and official personages as 'you'; we had a sure sense of the distinction and were never at a loss. The men spoke for the most part in a slow, deliberate voice, but some of the women could rattle on at a great rate in the soft sing-song lilt of the islands, which has remained unchanged for over a thousand years. For the Orkney people, or the Norse part of them, came more than that length of time ago from two little valleys in the south of Norway, and the inflection of their voices is still the same as that of the present inhabitants of these valleys, having remained unchanged while the whole fabric of speech was transformed. It is a soft and musical inflection, slightly melancholy, but companionable, the voice of people who are accustomed to hours of talking in the long winter evenings and do not feel they need to hurry: a splendid voice for telling stories in. It still keeps some of the quality of a chant, and I feel that in its early stages a language is always changed, since it is new enough still to be cherished as an almost miraculous thing. The strangeness fades, and language becomes workable and commonplace.

The idiom of the Orkney language has some fine old inversions and a few archaic words like 'moonstruck' and 'phial' and 'sib.' 'Tells thu me yon?' ('Tell you me that?') is the habitual order. 'That wad I no' is an emphatic 'I wouldn't think of such a thing.' The syntactical feeling is much stronger than in ordinary urban or educated speech, and has more resemblance to that of the seventeenth century. These traditional inversions, which give such an exact value to the order of words in a sentence, have been ironed out by the Educational System, and very few of them remain now. Most of the local poets who appear in Orkney write in an English laboriously learned from the grammar books; but I except from this generalization two very fine poets, Robert Rendall and George Brown. The islands produce a terrible number of professors. But simple, uneducated people here and there still speak a beautiful language and know where to set a word in a sentence.

I cannot say how much my idea of a good life was influenced by my early upbringing, but it seems to me that the life of the little island of Wyre was a good one, and that its sins were mere sins of the flesh, which are excusable, and not sins of the spirit. The farmers did not know ambition and the petty torments of ambition; they did not realize what competition was, though they lived at the end of Queen Victoria's reign; they helped one another with their work when help was required, following the old usage; they had a culture made up of legend, folk-song, and the poetry and prose of the Bible; they had customs which sanctioned their instinctive feelings for the earth; their life was an order, and a good order. So that when my father and mother left Orkney for Glasgow when I was fourteen, we were plunged out of order into chaos. We did not know it at the time, and I did not realize it for many years after I had left Glasgow. My father and mother and two of my brothers died in Glasgow within two years of one another. Four members of our family died there within two years. That is a measure of the violence of the change.

I have only a vague memory of our year at Helye, at the end of which we left Wyre for a farm on the mainland near Kirkwall. My attack of terrified guilt came on me during that year; but except for it all I can remember is that I never liked Helye as well as the Bu, which was a kindly house.

For many years after leaving Wyre I never dreamed about it once; it was as if that part of my life had been forgotten. My first dream of it came twenty-five years later, when I was being psychoanalysed in London. I dreamed that I was standing at the bow of a boat; it was early morning, and the sky and the sea were milk-white. The ship went on with a rustling motion, and cut more deeply into the ever-deepening round of the horizon. A spire rose above the rim of the sea, and at once, as the ship rushed smoothly on, I could see the little streets, the prickly weeds growing out of the walls, the tangle dripping from the pier. The houses opened out, melted and ran together; in a moment I would be there; but then I saw that this was not the town I knew, and that the people walking about the streets were strangers. Then, the ship clean gone, I was wandering along the top of a high, craggy coast. Far beneath me the sea snarled in the caves, which like marine monsters gnashed at it and spat it out again; opposite, across the boiling strait, so near that I felt I could touch it, was Rousay with its towering black mountain. I had never thought that the coast of Wyre, was so wild and rocky, and even as this thought formed in my mind the isle grew tamer, grew quite flat, and I was walking along a brown path level with the sea, picking great, light, violet-hued, crown-shaped flowers which withered at once in my hands. I came to a little chapel or shrine on the shore. On one wall a brown clay image was hanging: a weatherbeaten image of an old woman naked to the waist, with sun-burned, wrinkled dugs. I went up to the image, and as if I were fulfilling some ritual pressed one of the nipples with my finger. A trembling flowed over the figure, and, like a wave running across another in counter-motion, the texture changed; the clay quivered and rippled with life, all the marks of age vanishing in that transparent flood; the breasts shone smooth and round, and rose and fell with living breath. At the same time in the centre of my breast I felt a hot, tingling fire, and I knew that a yellow sun was blazing there, and with its beams, which filled my body with light and soft power, was raising the image from the dead. The figure came down from the wall, a dark brown girl, and stood beside me. That is all I remember about the dream, which ended before I reached the Bu, though I felt a great longing to return there. It was as if the dream, having set out to take me back to that house which I loved so much, were offering me something else instead, reanimating another image of whose existence I did not know.

I had a dream later of the Bu itself, though again everything was strangely transfigured and transposed. I was walking up a little winding road; I had been away for a long time, and now, an old man, I had returned. Great trees stood round the house, their foliage darker and thicker than any I had ever seen, the leaves hanging like dark green tongues one over the other in a motionless security which no wind could reach. The walls appeared behind them, thick walls so rounded and softened by time that no jutting angle or corner remained: in the middle was a great wooden gate like the gate of an old castle. Above the house rose a low grey sky, a particular sky arched over it alone: there was nothing but the great walls, the dark trees, and the low, round sky. I stood and looked at the house, filled with quiet expectation, but I did not go in.

Another dream also points back to Wyre, but even less directly than these two: I set it down to show how early impressions may grow and take on the form of myth. One day when I was about five or six my Aunt Maggie pointed at a gleaming grey bird standing on the farther edge of the pond below the house, and cried, 'Look, there's a heron!' As she pointed the heron rose in the air and effortlessly flew away on its wide-spread wings. I was filled with fear and wonder at the slow winging of the great bird, and its very name, the 'heron,' seemed to have a strange significance. In the dream I was walking with some people in the country, when I saw a shining grey bird in a field. I turned and said in an awed voice, 'It's a heron.' We went towards it, but as we came nearer it spread its tail like a peacock, so that we could see nothing else. As the tail grew I saw that it was not round, but square, an impenetrable grey hedge of feathers; and at once I knew that its body was not a bird's body now, but an animal's, and that behind that gleaming hedge it was walking away from us on four feet padded like a leopard's or a tiger's. Then, confronting it in the field, there appeared an ancient, dirty, earth-coloured animal with a head like that of an old sheep or a mangy dog. Its eyes were soft and brown; it was alone against the splendid-tailed beast; yet it stood its ground and prepared to fight the danger coming towards it, whether that was death or merely humiliation and pain. From their look I could see that the two animals knew each other, that they had fought a countless number of times and after this battle would fight again, that each meeting would be the first meeting, and that the dark, patient animal would always be defeated, and the bright, fierce animal would always win. I did not see the fight, but I knew it would be ruthless and shameful, with a meaning of some kind perhaps, but no comfort.

CHAPTER TWO

Garth

My father was driven out of the Bu, which was a good farm, and then out of Helye, which was a bad one, by the exactions of his landlord. During a prospecting visit to the mainland he decided to rent a farm of about a hundred acres called Garth, four miles out from Kirkwall. We moved into it when I was eight. From the start everything went wrong. The land was poor and had constantly to be drained; the dwelling-house was damp; in the rooms where we slept worms writhed up between the stone flags in wet weather. My mother was always ill; my brothers and sisters, one after another, left to take up jobs in Kirkwall or Glasgow or Edinburgh; the family slowly broke up; horses and cows died; my father grew more and more discouraged, strained his heart, and was unable to carry on his work. We all hated the dreary place, which gave a spiteful return for the hard work flung into it. We were five years at Garth. At the end of them the only members of our family left at home were my father and mother, my sister Clara and myself, my Aunt Maggie and Sutherland.

My memories of these five years are vague and clouded, because I was unhappy and felt my father's and mother's unhappiness; to exchange a good farm for a bad one is a calamity. I had lost my first clear vision of the world, and reached the stage when a child tries desperately to see things as his elders see them, and hopes to grow up by pretending to be grown up. At the Bu I had lived my life separately and in peace, but now I felt that need to become at once like grown-up people which tortures growing boys: it was as if time had suddenly spoken aloud within me. Under that compulsion I could not see things with my own eyes; instead I tried to see them as I thought my father and my mother and Sutherland saw them. I eagerly falsified them, knowing that the falsification was expected by every one: my parents, my teachers, visitors to the house, even other boys, who were enthusiastically doing the very thing that I was doing. Perhaps this is the only way in which children can learn to live in the adult world, which to every one but the man of faith or imagination is a dry legend consisting of names and figures. I did not come to see things with my own eyes again until my growing up was finished and I no longer needed to pretend that I was grown up, or to feel elated or astonished by the fact. It is in these years between eleven and eighteen that we construct little by little, with the approval of all the world, the mask which we shall wear with such ease when we reach manhood, feeling then that we were born with it, though it is merely a face which was made to look like a face by our own clumsy hands at an age when we did not know what we were doing: a crude imitation of our romantic conception of some grown-up figure such as never existed except in our imagination. We really grow up by pretending to grow up.

From Garth we could not see any of the hills or islands that we had known in Wyre. The house looked down from the bare hillside on Inganess Bay, a large, semi-circular bight, beyond which the open Atlantic quivered, an always straight line. At one end of that line the rump of the island of Shapinsay stuck out like the tail of a peaceful sea-monster; at the other, past the flat lands of Tankerness, the Mull Head, a black, blunt hammer-shape, jutted into the sea. At the foot of our land, a little distance from the shore, ran the main road to Deerness, my mother's parish, which now seemed to come much nearer; then the road took a sharp turn to the right and disappeared over the crown of a hill. Ships from Leith to Kirkwall passed in the open stretch of water beyond Inganess Bay; trawlers appeared in all weathers, ploughing the dark sea white; gigs, brakes, bicycles, and vans went along the Deerness Road. I had never seen these vehicles before, as there were no roads and therefore no use for them in Wyre. In Shapinsay there was a battery used by the local volunteers, and on clear summer evenings we would watch the white, cotton-wool smoke puffed in the air, and listen for the boom of the guns, which came quite a long time afterwards.

A burn ran past the house from the two mill-dams above it, whose water turned the threshing mill. On the green bank overlooking the burn there was a little over-hanging shelf of turf, covered in May with primroses, where I used to play. Below the shelf lay a pool where a frog—there seemed to be only one—swam about year after year: it was the first frog I had seen, for there were none in Wyre. In Garth too I saw my first rats and mice, and beside the Wideford Burn, which I crossed every day on my way to and from school, my first hawthorn and wild roses. The country was bare, except for a clump of wizened trees along the Deerness Road, and a black thicket beside a big house on the edge of Inganess Bay. All round were farms with Norse names, many of which I have forgotten: Quoydandy, Wideford, Grimsquoy, Grimster. The landscape was rough and desolate, the landscape of a second-rate saga; it did not have the beautiful soft colours of Wyre and the islands round: the red island of Eday, the dark green island of Egilsay with its tower, the blue-black hills of Rousay. Even the sea seemed a duller blue.

Garth—the local pronunciation, and probably the original one, was Gert—stood on the side of a hill, with all its fields but one below it, towards the sea. Behind that one field stretched bog and heather, and in winter the water in the watery ground seeped down and turned the farmyard into a wilderness of black mire. The mill-dams overflowed; the burn came down, swollen and brown, while we navigated it in a tub—a precarious game, for the stream with mechanical accuracy kept the tub spinning like a teetotum. Water rushed, trickled, and seeped everywhere; the mire sucked at our boots; the stone flags of the house sweated a thin layer of moisture. But in summer it was a pleasant enough place.

One morning shortly after we went to Garth my father took me by the hand and set off for Kirkwall, three miles away. We crossed the Wideford Burn, walked through the fine big steading and past the handsome dwelling-house, then took the main road, climbed the hill beside Quoydandy, and saw Kirkwall lying below us, with the great red church of St Magnus standing up in the middle of it.

We came to Dundas Crescent with its handsome houses and gardens in which the rich shopkeepers lived, passed the clean, businesslike school where the children were already shouting in the playground, their shouts uniting every now and then to make a single high note, and then separating like a flock of birds flung into confusion. My father turned in at the gate of a high, solid-looking house before which there was a big tree, knocked at the door, and when the maid opened asked for Mr McEwan. In a little while the maid returned and led us into a room filled with books where a short, round, brown-eyed man with a bald head and a brown, pointed beard was sitting. Mr McEwan got up and shook hands with my father, who told him he had come to enter me in the Kirkwall Burgh School. They talked for a little while; then Mr McEwan, without rising from his chair, stretched out his hand and took me by the arm and pulled me close to him, so that I could feel the smell of his clothes, a clean, dry, brushed smell. From that short distance he looked straight into my face, as if he were interested only in it and not in me at all, and had pulled my arm (as he might have pulled a lever) simply to bring my face close to him. He looked at it for some time, then smiled, released my arm, giving it a slight pinch at the same time, told me he hoped I should like the school, and in a little while, for it was now almost nine, set out with my father and myself for the school, where I said goodbye to my father, who looked back at me sadly but encouragingly. After the bell rang Mr McEwan led me through the bustle of the passages to one of the infant classrooms, introduced me to the teacher and the other children, and saw me installed at my desk. I never reached his own class—he took only advanced pupils—but he had the reputation of being a brilliant teacher, and though that first close scrutiny rather daunted me, he was always perfectly kind.

The Kirkwall Burgh School was a big school with a large staff and several hundred scholars. I did not hate it as I had hated the school in Wyre; I no longer tried to push on the hands of the clock with my will; the feeling of imprisonment faded, since part of my mind agreed now with the school: I had begun to grow up. Yet there were months on end when

I dreaded, morning after morning, as separate things, for each seemed fatal, the setting out from Garth, the slinging of the school-bag over my shoulder, the first few steps, and the steady trudge along the road; yet at each of these stages there was still a vestige of hope left; but when I reached the top of the hill and saw Kirkwall lying directly before me my last hope vanished, and I went down the slope as if my arms were bound and a warder were walking behind me. The sound of the school bell ringing as I loitered down Dundas Crescent seemed to be telling me for the last time to fly; but instead I ran as fast as I could towards it, knowing that there was only that one road, which grew harder the nearer I approached its end. I have never managed to see St Magnus' Cathedral with an untroubled eye since then; a film of fear clings to it simply because it is associated with those mornings when I looked down on Kirkwall, where, hidden behind houses, stood the school.

Yet there were times when I enjoyed going to school; it all depended on who was teaching me. I passed under a whole regiment of teachers there, male and female: teachers who shouted at me, who hit me over the head with the pointer, who strapped me (for the tawse was used vigorously), who took an interest in me, who sneered at me (and they were the worst); teachers whose personal habits I came to know as I grew older; who drank, or were infatuated with the pretty girls in their class, or had a curious walk or some curious habit. We studied them with the inquisitiveness of visitors to a zoo; for to us they were really animals behind bars. There were teachers who terrified us, and whose eyes, fixed on us, could assume the hypnotic glare of an animal-tamer. I knew the appearance of all the straps in all the classrooms: there were thick, voluptuous ones, and thin, mean, venomous ones; laid down on the desk after execution, they folded up with ruthless grace like sleepy cats. In some of them the tails had been burned over a fire to make them sting more sharply. Certain boys were punished day after day as part of the routine: a brutal ceremony which we watched in a silent fascination and dread which might easily have implanted in us a taste for sadism and insidiously corrupted us. The punishment varied from three strokes on the hand to twelve.

There were teachers who did not use the strap more than three or four times in a year, and others who flogged on monotonously day after day, as if they were pounding some recalcitrant substance, not the hands of living boys. I avoided the strap as well as I could; in some classes I could completely forget it, and then I liked school, for the teachers were invariably good at their work. One teacher, Miss Annan, did not use the strap at all. She had a cheerful, impudent, devoted class who only needed her presence to become inspired. She taught us English, and but for her we might never have realized what the subject meant beyond the drudgery of parsing and analysis. She opened our eyes; we felt we were a sort of aristocracy, for what we did for her we did freely. She must have been a remarkable woman; she seemed to have endless charm, vitality, and patience. She filled us with confidence and a kind of goodness which was quite unlike the goodness asked from us by the other teachers. Yet she never put us on our honour; she simply took us as we were and by some power changed us.

After the first shock of being flung among some hundreds of boys I found that they were not so terrifying as they seemed, and that I could make friends and avoid making enemies: a sure sign that I was growing up. On the other hand, I had lost my first delight in things; life had a purpose and had grown drier; mere learning gave me a bookish enjoyment. I got praise from my teachers; this gave me a sense of responsibility, and I might have become a model pupil if it had not been for bad health, the weather, and the long distance I had to go to school, which often kept me at home. Sometimes my father needed me to herd the cows. In the dead of winter I had to be let off at one o'clock, so as to get home before dark. When the peat-cutting came in the spring I begged hard to stay at home, for the long, sunny days up in the hills enchanted me. With all this I was more often absent than present, and one day when I had returned after a long break Dr George Reid greeted me with the resigned words, 'Well, Edwin, your visits are like angels' visits, few and far between.' My 'subjects' got hopelessly behind, and I did not really begin to catch them up until, when I was thirteen, my father gave up the farm

and we came to live in Kirkwall. The result was that I had
only one good year of school, for at the end of it we went
to Glasgow and my schooling stopped.

During the years at Garth, as I say, I was growing up,
and so my memories are vague and untrue, for I was only a
shifting mirror, or hardly even that, since I did not reflect
things as they were, but as I wished them to be in many
years' time. My games became rehearsals for the serious
business of life. I sailed a toy boat in the mill-dam, and
raced the boats of the boys in the neighbourhood. We had
toy ploughing matches, delving little drills in the turf with
a spade and then judging the result. We made expeditions
to Inganess Bay to gather whelks and mussels, and fished
for trout in Wideford Burn with a line and a pin. I got far
more satisfaction out of these games than out of the toys
I had barrenly brooded over in Wyre, for they pointed
to the state which I longed to reach, in which I divined
an unknown glory. The work I did on the farm merely
wearied me; to herd the cows and keep them out of the
corn was a boring, necessary task to one who lived in
that dream, and the toy regattas and ploughing matches,
the bent pin which never caught a fish, were like magical
spells which, if I persisted with them, would bring manhood
within my reach.

But why, about the age of nine, I began to bolt printed
matter as if it were some precious nourishing substance I
cannot imagine; for there was nothing in the house which
was worth reading, apart from the Bible, *The Pilgrim's
Progress*, *Gulliver's Travels*, and a book by R. M. Ballantyne
about Hudson Bay. The previous tenant of the farm had
left in a loft over the kitchen a great jumble of weekly
papers and old books. There were numbers of a paper
called, I think, *The Christian World*, dating from several
years back. They contained nothing but accounts of meetings and conferences, announcements of appointments to
ministries, and obituary notices; yet I read them from
beginning to end. There was also a thick volume bound
in calf and containing a verbatim report of a controversy between a Protestant divine and a Roman Catholic
priest some time about the middle of last century, with

a long argument on transubstantiation and many references to the Douai Bible which greatly puzzled me, for I did not know what the Douai Bible was. There was a novel all about young women, which I think now must have been *Sense and Sensibility*: I could make nothing of it, but this did not keep me from reading it. And the monthly parts of *The Scots Worthies* which my father had carried with him from Sanday, and which were now in hopeless confusion, I went over carefully, arranging and repairing them until the book assumed consecutive form. My father was so touched by this act of piety— for he regarded the book as almost a sacred one—that he had it handsomely bound in leather for me: a big tome of a thousand pages. All this passed through my mind; it was poor stuff without a vestige of nourishment, and it did not leave a trace behind. I read as if I were under some compulsion, as if my mind were crying for food and if there was none to be had must eat bran instead. I read all my new school-books as soon as I got them; I read *The People's Journal*, *The People's Friend*, and *The Christian Herald*. I read a complete series of sentimental love tales very popular at that time, called *Sunday Stories*. I read novels illustrating the dangers of intemperance and the virtues of thrift. I read a new periodical called *The Penny Magazine* which my brother Willie got: it was modelled on *Tit-bits*, and contained all sorts of useless information. But I had no children's books and no fairy-tales: my father's witch stories made up for that.

Out of all that reading only one memory survives now. The story itself I have forgotten, but the scene was laid in Italy, and there was a chapter in which a beggar arrived at a cottage carrying a heavy sack, which he left in a corner while he went, as he said, to the barn to get some sleep. The woman of the house, who lived by herself, happened to touch the sack, felt it moving, and knew at once that there was a man in it who had come to murder her. The image of the murderer in the sack, a murderer carried on a man's back and dumped down to do his work, oppressed my mind and entered my dreams, where I was pursued

over fields and ditches by a maniacal sack tumbling head
over heels, rolling, leaping, climbing, sliding, a deaf and
dumb and bound and yet deadly shape. When I read
Treasure Island a few years later the horrible figure of
the blind seaman Pew brought back again the terrors of
that dream.

There was another impression, almost as horrible, but
this time it was caused by an illustration, not a story.
Sutherland sometimes had sent to him by a cousin in
Leith a weekly paper called, I think, *The Police News*,
a record of brutal crimes. He left it lying in the kitchen
one day, and with my usual hypnotized interest I went
across to take it up. On the cover was the picture of a
powerful man standing in his shirt-sleeves with an axe
raised above his head. His moustache was curled at the
ends; there was a neat parting in the middle of his hair;
he stood there as straight as a soldier, with the expression
which one sees in old-fashioned photographs. On a bed
in front of him a woman wearing a shawl was sprawling with her head cloven in two. My father snatched
up the paper as I put out my hand for it, crammed it
into his pocket, and said sternly, 'That's no for thee!'
Sutherland came in shortly afterwards, and my father
shouted, 'Here, Sutherland, keep this rubbish o' thine tae
theesel.' Sutherland looked sheepishly at him and then at
the paper, and went out carrying the paper in his hand
to read it elsewhere. But that picture did not have nearly
such a deep effect on my mind as the murderer in the sack,
who, being hidden and shapeless, was capable of assuming
innumerable shapes which kept recurring in my dreams for
years afterwards.

A child's imagination is unbelievably vivid, and I do
not know whether it was a benefit or a calamity when
my brother Willie, out of pure kindness, began taking
Chums for me. *Chums* was at that time the chief rival of
The Boy's Own Paper, which I did not see until years later,
when it bored me with its stories of public-school life, filled
with incomprehensible snobbery. The line of *Chums* was
adventure stories in savage lands. There was always a hero
with a pointed beard, sailors with soft bushy beards and

honest faces, and a boy called Frank. This small company passed through sunless canyons, forded alligator-infested rivers, cut their way through dense jungles, and fought savage tribes set on by bad, white, clean-shaven men, meanwhile foiling the attacks of lions, tigers, bears, and serpents. Returned to England with their riches, they dropped through trap-doors in rotting wharves and languished in dripping dungeons, until the sailors, having broken out, returned like a benevolent music-hall chorus to rescue the others, with a vast tattoo of sturdy fists on villainous faces. The excitement of following these adventures was more a pain than a pleasure, and everything was so real to me that when I was herding the cows on the side of the hill I would often glance over my shoulder in case a tiger might be creeping up behind me. I knew with one part of my mind that there were no tigers in Orkney, but I could not resist that nervous backward jerk of the head.

I battened on this rubbish, some of it dull, some too exciting, until when I was eleven a school history-book containing biographies of Sir Thomas More, Sir Philip Sidney, and Sir John Eliot showed me that reading could be something quite different. My reading-books up to then must have been poor, for I can remember nothing of them except a description of Damascus, with a sentence to the effect that at night the streets were 'as silent as the dead.' I had had, of course, to learn *Casabianca* and *Lord Ullin's Daughter* and *Excelsior* and the other vapid poems which are supposed to please children, but like every one else I was bored by them. Then, when I was twelve, we had a really good poetry-book which contained extracts from *The Excursion*, part of *Childe Harold's Pilgrimage*, *The Eve of Saint Agnes*, *Adonais*, *The Pied Piper of Hamelin*, and Matthew Arnold's *Tristram and Iseult*. We were given *Childe Harold's Pilgrimage* and *The Pied Piper* to learn by heart in consecutive years. I never liked *The Pied Piper*, which, being written consciously as a child's poem, made me feel conscious, and most of *Childe Harold's Pilgrimage* seemed unreal to me, so that when I stood up to recite,

> There was a sound of revelry by night,
> And Belgium's capital had gather'd then
> Her Beauty and her Chivalry, and bright
> The lamps shone o'er fair women and brave
>   men,

I had the uncomfortable feeling that I should be more deeply moved than I was. A collection of Scottish ballads would have appealed far more directly to children of my age, and I am astonished that these beautiful poems are not used more in Scottish schools. The poems in the book which I liked best were *The Eve of Saint Agnes* and *Tristram and Iseult*, and certain lines which moved me then still move me more deeply than I can account for:

> Northward he turneth through a little door,
> And scarce three steps, ere Music's golden tongue
> Flatter'd to tears this aged man and poor.

I do not know why, out of a poem containing more beautiful lines, these should have moved me most at twelve. The line from Arnold's poem

> Christ! what a night! how the sleet whips the pane!

probably struck me so much because it gave such an intense picture of a wild Northern night, with the lighted room and the darkness and fury outside, and showed me that poetry could be made out of things I myself knew. *Adonais* seemed to be filled with a nobility which I did not understand, and I could make nothing of the extracts from *The Excursion*, though, since the book was a good one, they were probably well chosen.

By this time I had made up my mind that I would be an author when I grew up, but as my father and mother regarded 'profane' literature as sinful, had a great horror of 'novells,' as they called them, and thought poetry a vanity, I did not feel easy in my mind about my intention, and by a piece of childish casuistry decided that the book I should write would be a life of Christ, for in that way I could satisfy without offence the claims both of religion and literature. I had seen a life of Christ by Dean Farrar mentioned with commendation in *The Christian World*, and this gave me the idea. But this stage lasted only a short time, for one day in Kirkwall my brother Johnnie, who had gone to work in a shop there, gave me three pennies to spend, and I went at once to a bookseller's which sold 'The Penny Poets' and bought *As You Like It*, *The Earthly Paradise*, and a selection of Matthew Arnold's poems. Johnnie, meeting me later, was angry and a little hurt that I had spent the money in such a way, for he had wanted me to enjoy myself. I could not make out how I had offended him, but I felt guilty as I stood holding the three yellow-covered books in my hand.

I did not get much out of the selection of Arnold's poems, for there was nothing, except *The Forsaken Merman*, that was in the least like *Tristram and Iseult*, and the rich feeling of the countryside of Southern England in *The Scholar Gypsy* and *Thyrsis* woke no response in me, since all I knew was our bare Northern landscape. My enjoyment of poetry was pure hit and miss, for I knew nothing of the world I was adventuring into. *As You Like It* delighted me, but it was *The Earthly Paradise* that I read over and over again. The little book did not, of course, contain all of Morris's huge poem; but it told the stories in simple language, with occasional extracts from the poetry: the story of Atalanta and the apples, of Perseus and Andromeda, of Ogier the Dane and all the Northern heroes and heroines; and it seemed to me that I was watching the appearance of a new race in my familiar countryside: a race of goddesses, beautiful women, and great warriors, all under the low Northern sky, for even the Greek stories unfolded for me in a landscape very like Orkney.

From that point I followed up with a sort of devotion every reference I found in my school-books or in the weekly papers to great writers. I worshipped their names before I knew anything of their work. Spenser, Shakespeare, Milton, Dryden, Swift, Goldsmith, Wordsworth, Coleridge, Tennyson, Swinburne, Macaulay, Carlyle, Ruskin—these names thrilled me. And when I discovered a new one such as Christopher Marlowe or George Crabbe it was like an addition to a secret treasure; for no one knew of my passion, and there was none to whom I could speak of it. One day I

saw a life of Carlyle in a bookshop window in Kirkwall and
begged a shilling from my mother to buy it; but I found
that it was a shilling and threepence, and I had to return
dejectedly with a book on Wallace and Bruce instead. It
was not a good book, and all I remember of it is a few lines
quoted from Burns:

> At Wallace' name, what Scottish blood
> But boils up in a spring-time flood!
> Oft have our fearless fathers strode
> > By Wallace' side,
> Still pressing onward, red-wat-shod,
> > Or glorious died!

These lines had a rich, dark, wintry magic then which has
faded now, and 'red-wat-shod' is the only phrase that brings
back my original excitement.

My acquaintance with literature increased in a haphazard
way, by chance discovery, while I was at Garth. I never
had a course of English literature, or any guidance either
in my reading or my method of reading; and this was an
enormous drawback. When we went to live in Kirkwall my
opportunities for reading greatly increased, for there was a
lending library; but the use I made of it was unwise, and I
read a great number of books which I was quite incapable of
understanding. Various histories of English literature were
my most sensible choice; but critical studies of Hume and
Sterne were far beyond my reach, and my father, on seeing
me with the book on Hume, was greatly upset and made
me take it straight back again, for to him Hume was 'the
Atheist,' a dreadful term in our house. I wasted a great deal
of time in wrong reading from eleven to fourteen, always
hoping for the enjoyment which rarely came, but going
on with surprising persistence. A sense of overpowering
gloom is connected in my mind with Hugo's *Notre Dame
de Paris*, which I read in English, and an impression of livid
brightness with *The Scarlet Letter*; but that is all. Of Carlyle's
French Revolution all that remains is a sentence like a radiant
hillside caught through a rift in a black cloud: the passage
where he describes the high-shouldered ladies dancing with
the gentlemen of the French Court on a bright summer

evening, while outside the yellow cornfields stretched from end to end of France.

Curiously enough the story I remember best is a grotesque and rather silly one which appeared in an annual almanac issued by *The Orkney Herald*. It was an account of the origin of the Orkney and Shetland Islands. A great dragon, it related, lived somewhere in the North in the old days, and fed on the sons and daughters of the people. At last a king's son arose who could not bear to see the land laid waste, and made up his mind to put an end to the monster. He set out alone in a little boat, and sailed up under darkness to the dragon as it lay sweltering on the waves. The dragon was asleep, and as the Prince came alongside it happened to yawn. The Prince, seeing his opportunity, sailed into its mouth, and began rowing down its throat and into its capacious passages. After a few hours, striking a light, he saw that he had reached its liver, and, kindling some tow, set fire to it, and began to row back again. At first the heat merely tickled the monster and made it shudder with pleasure. When the Prince reached its throat he could see the glow of the conflagration far behind him. At last he found himself breached against the great teeth, and at this point the monster gave a great reeking belch which shot him half a mile out to sea. He hoisted his sail, and, taking to his oars as well, made all haste to get away. Presently a great storm arose, and looking back he saw the dragon lashing the water on the horizon, its head and neck rising and twisting and falling behind the rim of the sea. In its death-agony the beast shed all its teeth, which became the Orkney and Shetland Islands, then wrapped its body round the earth like a great belt, and this, subsiding, turned into the Atlantic Ocean. Who the author of this story was I do not know. It may be an old story, or the recent invention of some enterprising Orkney man; I have never come across it again. It may partly account for the fact that I have had so many dreams about dragons. At the time it merely amused me.

During these years I began to grow aware of the people round me as individuals. At the Bu my family had been a stationary, indivisible pattern; now my brothers and sisters hardened into separate shapes, and without my knowing it division entered the world. The breaking up of our family, the departure of one member after another, strengthened this feeling greatly, for with my eldest brother Jimmie working in Kirkwall I could now think of him as separate from us, yet when he came out to see us at Garth he was obviously a member of the family still. This paradox of unity and separateness troubled my mind a great deal, for Jimmie in Kirkwall lived a life of his own, quite unlike our life; yet when he came to see us he was still the brother I had known and worshipped as a child. Soon after our shift to Garth he went still farther away, to Glasgow, and after that we saw him only once a year, during his summer holidays. Then Willie, my second oldest brother, grew discontented in turn, and my father, knowing he was unhappy, allowed him to enter a lawyer's office in Kirkwall. The process continued; it was as if a fermentation had set up in our family which no power could stop. My third brother, Johnnie, and my sister Elizabeth had a harder struggle to get away, for they were urgently needed on the farm; but my father had to give in, though he could not understand. Elizabeth went to Edinburgh, and Johnnie to Kirkwall. At its heart the family held together; there was no inward break, no enmity: it was as if something quite impersonal were scattering us to all the quarters of the compass. If Garth had been a better farm, or if it had been twenty instead of three miles from a town, all this might not have happened, and some of us might have had a happier life; for to be a farmer in Orkney now is a pleasant lot: Orkney is probably the most prosperous, well-run, and happy community in Britain. But Garth was a thankless farm, Kirkwall was near, Edinburgh and Glasgow, from Kirkwall, seemed merely the next stepping-stone, and no power on earth could have kept us from taking that road. When my father had to give up farming he too, after a year's hesitation, and against Jimmie's strong advice, decided to go to Glasgow and take the rest of us with him: a terrible mistake.

Jimmie was the one of us, I think, who most resembled my father; he had the same sensitive, gentle nature, and the same sense of fun. Willie, now long since dead, was a strange, sardonic, very intelligent boy, who might have made his name if he had lived. He was quite unlike the rest of us both in appearance and disposition, being tall, awkward, long-faced, and subject to deep fits of despondency. The things we did casually he did deliberately and well. He was not satisfied to play the fiddle in the country style, but set himself to master the theory of music, and though the local fiddlers complained that he did not have the natural touch, he played far better than any of them and knew it, his knowledge being sufficient for him. He was much the strongest of us, and could lift two 56-pound weights from the ground above his head in one movement. He was silent and impatient of pretence or display. He had a far clearer picture of the world—a somewhat Swiftian picture—than the rest of us, and knew what he wanted to do and how to set about it. When he died he was studying for his law course while working in an office in Edinburgh. I did not have much to do with him as a child, but we became close friends in Glasgow, when I was beginning to discover the intellectual world for myself.

Johnnie was quick-tongued and adventurous, and had the eyes and chin of a sailor. He was careless and merry, made friends easily, and was always ready for a wild prank; but the work on the farm chafed him, so that he had recurrent bursts of discontent. He wanted to go to sea, and once made a strong bid to join the Army; that really alarmed and displeased my father. It would probably have been better for Johnnie if he had gone to sea, for he was stifled in the shop in Kirkwall. He was attracted to men who had travelled about the world, and his quick and witty tongue amused them and kept us laughing for evenings on end. He died in great agony in Glasgow about two years after Willie.

My sister Elizabeth, who came next to Johnnie, had an eager mind and a spirit equal to anything. Even as a girl she scorned stupidity and easy sentiments and shouldered responsibilities far beyond her years. My younger sister, Clara, was my great companion as a child, for we were nearest in age; she was kind, patient, and unexacting, and grew up into an easy, comfortable woman. Both are now dead.

I became conscious in Garth of my brothers and sisters as separate characters. We were a family, but we were individuals too, moving each in a different direction, and straining the fabric of the family. As if it were the physical manifestation of this inward tension, we fell ill one after another, my mother several times; Clara and I went down with typhoid, and had to be taken away to the fever hospital in Kirkwall; even Sutherland, who had never felt a pain in his life, got toothache, and sat groaning in bed in great alarm, for he thought his last day had come—pain was so strange to him. Only those of us who left kept their health.

All this time much of my life too was passed outside the family, for I struck up many friendships with the boys at the Kirkwall school. These friendships were mostly make-believe, like everything else at that time; they did not last long, but, being make-believe, they could be replaced with almost cynical ease. The clash of the countryside too now came to my ears; I listened, where I would not have listened before, to gossip of girls being put in the family way and of farmers seducing their maid-servants, and if I met one of those farmers I would look at him curiously, expecting to see in his face some exposure of his inclinations. All this gossip, which in another community would have been scandalous, was merely amusing and good-natured in ours, for illegitimacy was indulgently regarded in Orkney, and in any case the father of the child almost always married the girl. My mother often talked of a woman in Deerness who had had seven illegitimate children, yet had always refused marriage, and though she regarded this, naturally, with disapproval, she never mentioned this lady without saying, 'She was a fine lass.' I listened, then, to the country gossip, but my listening too was make-believe, and generation might have taken place by an exchange of thoughts for all I knew. Yet I felt, listening to the gossip, that I was in the grown-up world.

At Garth for the first time beggars came about the house. There was one in particular, an old man called John Simpson, half lay-preacher and half vagrant, who came often and ate enormously each time: these beggars were always taken in and given food. John Simpson had a black beard and a resonant voice; he wore a frock-coat very much soiled by food, and a battered black hat, but no collar: he always carried a Bible with him, and at the least encouragement would flop down on his knees in the kitchen and burst into prolonged prayer, pulling us down with him—a habit which embarrassed us, for we knew that he was not right in the mind. My father once, out of kindness, offered him work on the farm as a potato-picker, but John Simpson groaned so loudly over his job, saying that he felt very ill—actually he was a big, strong man—that my father told him he could stop. He went away in a few days, after eating his fill. I saw him once or twice afterwards in Kirkwall, pursued by a crowd of jeering boys, and I felt sorry and ashamed for him. He preached whenever the children would let him, but his words were quite without sense.

I had often heard my mother talking about another beggar who had come regularly to the Folly in the old days, bringing his own tea and food to be cooked over the fire, and sleeping in the barn. His name was Fred Spence, and he was a man of education and breeding who had lost his money and his wits, but still kept his fine manners. He sometimes told a story of how he had strangled his wife, concluding in a well-bred, finicking voice, 'Her neck was very tough.' I met him one summer day as I was returning from school. He was a good-looking man with a high forehead and a pointed beard; very elegant and very dirty, like a grimy version of Cunninghame Graham. With great condescension he asked me my name, which I gave him somewhat fearfully, for I recognized him at once from my mother's description. His extreme courtesy, being half mad, was frightening; but I stood my ground, for I was curious. Fred was wearing a swallow-tail coat and a soft black hat on his matted grey hair, which fell down over his shoulders. As if he were some noble patron he inquired into my progress at school, saying at intervals, 'Latin! Latin is very important!' And then, with a royal absent-mindedness, he abruptly dismissed me, asking me, however, to remember him to my father and mother. He was a harmless madman, but as I stood listening to him on the deserted road I could not help thinking of his wife, whose neck had been so tough. I never saw him again.

When I was thirteen my father gave up the farm, sold off

his stock and farm implements, and went to live in a small house in Kirkwall. My Aunt Maggie went to stay with a sister. A relative of Sutherland in America had died and left him some money, and he sailed to join his cousins in Leith, where we lost sight of him for a while. Only my father and mother, my sister Clara and myself, remained.

Except for my reading, which went on still more eagerly, my year in Kirkwall was drab and sordid. I had reached the stage when boys stick together to hide the shame of their inexperience, and turn without knowing it against their parents and the laws of the house. My rough friendships were an indirect challenge to my father and mother, a hidden gesture of rebellion. I played a great deal of football; it was as if my body demanded explosive action. The place where we played was called the Craftie; it was a little field of grass, worn bare in patches, close by the slaughter-house. To us in our raw and unhappy state the slaughter-house had an abominable attraction, and the strong stench and sordid colours of blood and intestines seemed to follow us in our play. Our language and manners grew rough; even our friendship had an acrid flavour. There were savage fights in the Craftie, and the boys, crying with rage, would have killed each other if they could; yet behind their fury there was a sort of sad shame and frustration.

I do not know why boys of this age, the age of awakening puberty, should turn against everything that was pleasant in their lives before and rend it in a fit of crude cynicism. Perhaps it comes from their first distorted knowledge of the actual world, which is not the world of childhood, and a divination that all their childish games in which they played at being grown-up were of no use, something sterner being needed. Or it may be merely that I was unlucky in my friends, for I had far less worldly knowledge at the time than town boys of my age, and I was always perfectly prepared to be friendly with anyone who was friendly with me. I remember one fine summer day spent with another boy in wandering along the Wideford Burn, picking flowers and looking at birds' nests, without a single rough word. Why did I not have more days like that one in which I was perfectly happy, instead of all those days in the Craftie, when I was really miserable, though I did not know it? The Craftie seemed to hypnotize us; we kicked the football in hatred; there was a deep enmity in the bond between us.

All this was in the year before we left for Glasgow. That winter a revivalist preacher, a thin, tense young man called Macpherson, came to Kirkwall and began to make converts. While we were at Garth the famous John McNeill, a large-scale evangelist, had made a short visit to Orkney, and had preached in the church we attended in Kirkwall. I can remember him dimly; a big, stout, genial man with a black beard, who greatly embarrassed the congregation by keeping them laughing during the whole service, for he was a great wit. He did not make many converts; our people refused to be chaffed into salvation. Later two other revivalists appeared together: one of them, thin, small, and tense, preached hell fire, and the other, tall, stout, and expansive, radiated the love of God. We all went in to hear them one Sunday evening; many people at the end of the service rose from their seats when the preachers summoned them to Christ: I looked on with excitement, but did not understand the glad perturbation of the people round me. As we left the church the two preachers, standing at the door, shook hands with the congregation. It was the big, benevolent preacher who was at our side of the door, and as he took my hand in his large, comforting one he looked down at me and said to my father, 'Will not this little fellow come to Christ?' My father, to shield me, murmured something to the effect that perhaps I was too young and tender yet. 'What! Too young and tender to come to gentle Jesus!' the preacher said in a shocked voice. My father was much impressed by this answer, and often repeated it afterwards; but I felt that the preacher was not really so shocked as he appeared to be.

This must have happened when I was ten or eleven; I was now fourteen, and, except when I was reading, very unhappy. I paid no attention to the visit of Mr Macpherson; the boys I went about with jeered at his converts whenever they met them; some of their acquaintances had already been saved. Then my sister Clara was converted, and my mother in her delight drew closer to her. I felt alone in the house; but I was reading *Les Misérables*, and consoled myself with the thought that I too was capable of loving noble things. Yet gradually, by a power independent of myself, I felt impelled towards the only act which would make me one with my family again; for my father and mother and sister were saved, and I was outside, separated from them by an invisible wall. A tremor of the fear which had cut me off in a world of my own at Helye returned, and I began to listen to Mr Macpherson's outdoor services at the head of the pier, standing well back in the crowd so as not to be seen by my friends. Then one dark cold night—how it happened I do not know—I found myself in the crowd which marched after the preacher, all the length of Kirkwall, to the mission hall. As we passed through the narrow streets groups standing there turned round and stared at us: the unredeemed, whom I still feared so much that I slipped for safety deeper into the heart of the crowd. The people round me marched on side by side, ignoring one another in a sort of embarrassment at still being lost sinners, their eyes fixed straight before them. At last we reached the hall; after the darkness outside the whitewashed walls and the yellow benches were so bright that they dazzled me; the worshippers entered, ordinary men and women and children now, smiling at one another as if in secret understanding; the doors were shut; the service began. I remember nothing of it; I probably did not listen, for I was filled with an impatience which did not have anything to do with the words the preacher was saying; all round me people were bursting into sobs and loud cries, as if they too felt the same agonized anticipation and could wait no longer for redemption; and when Mr Macpherson stopped at last and asked those who had accepted Christ to rise in their places the whole audience rose, lifting me with them, and I found myself on my feet with a wild sense of relief. But the great majority of the audience had accepted Christ already, and the difficult moment came now, for when we had all sat down again the new converts, a mere handful, were asked to walk up to the platform and kneel down at the penitent form, a long wooden bench set there in full view. I hesitated; I was appalled by this naked exposure before people whom I did not know; but when a small group—men, women, boys, and girls—had risen, I rose too and followed them and knelt down. The preacher went along the bench where we were kneeling and asked each of us in turn, 'Do you accept Jesus Christ as your personal Saviour?' and when my turn came and I replied, 'I do,' I felt that these words, which were the seal of my salvation, yet were uttered deliberately, not torn from me, must bring with them an overwhelming assurance; and I was deeply disappointed when they did not, for they seemed merely to be two words. The preacher asked me to offer up a prayer, but I could not think of one, and felt that it would be presumptuous of me, so newly converted, to address God out of my own invention. Beside me was kneeling a red-haired, spectacled young man who served in a shop. He had been the most conspicuous groaner during the service, exclaiming so emphatically that people had looked round at him with surprise and respect; he now burst into a loud and rapid prayer, as if he were already resolved to make a record in the world of the saved. My exaltation did not keep me from feeling slightly annoyed with him for his forwardness; but I suppressed the feeling, telling myself that I must love him. When I got up at last, dazzled, an involuntary smile of joy on my face, and returned to my seat with the others, all the faces of the congregation melted into one great maternal face filled with welcome and wonder, and I felt I was walking straight into a gigantic pair of loving arms.

I went home and told my mother, and returned with a sense of absolute security to *Les Misérables*, which now seemed a new and holy book, with meanings which I had never guessed at before. But a doubtful look came into my mother's face when she saw me returning so eagerly to a profane story; she stood and thought for a moment, then smiled whimsically, glancing at the book and then at me. I felt she doubted that my conversion was real, and was deeply offended.

What was the nature of my experience that night? For some time afterwards I certainly felt a change within myself; coarse thoughts and words to which I had become hardened during the last year became unendurable to me; I was perpetually happy, and found it easy to reply gently to insults and sneers. The slightest suggestion of evil pierced me to the heart; yet I remained unaffected in some part of myself, as if I were invulnerable. At the same time I found myself often reflecting with relief that I should be leaving Kirkwall in a fortnight, so that I should not have to testify for long before those who had known me: in Glasgow, I told myself, I should associate with the saved from the start; they would be all round me. At times I actually felt ashamed of my new state, belittling it to my friends instead of proclaiming it loudly like the ardent, red-haired shop assistant. I made friends with the Kirkwall boys of my own age who had been saved, and avoided my old companions. Among the saved were some of the roughest boys at the school; they were now incapable of speaking a rude word, and their faces shone with grace. A sort of purification had taken place in us, and it washed away the poisonous stuff which had gathered in me during that year; but it was more a natural than a spiritual cleansing, and more a communal than a personal experience, for it is certain that if the whole audience had not risen that night I should not have risen. To pretend that it was a genuine religious conversion would be ridiculous; I did not know what I was doing; I had no clear knowledge of sin or of the need for salvation; at most I wished to be rescued from the companions among whom I had fallen and to be with the good, with my father and my mother and my sister. Yet the change itself was so undeniable that it astonished me. I was not trying to be changed; I was changed quite beyond my expectation; but the change did not last long.

Though they were glad at the conversion of my sister and myself, my father and mother had doubts of the virtue of these revivals which periodically swept over the country. Much later I remember some one telling me that each revival was followed by a great increase in the number of illegitimate children. In one of them which took place when my mother was a young girl people fell down in fits in the church and rolled on the floor. How these orgiastic movements were set going I do not know; their effect while they lasted was probably good in some ways; they made people forget their narrow concerns and open their hearts to one another. But the wave passed, and people returned to their private concerns again and became more sparing of love. These revivals were communal orgies such as were probably known long before Christianity came to these islands, and they cleansed people's hearts for the time being; but they had very little to do with religion, and, like most orgies, they often left behind them a feeling of shame.

Later on, in Glasgow, I was flung among the violently converted just as I had wished to be, and though I experienced a second dubious conversion before I was finished with that kind of religion, I came to know so much about the way in which revivals are organized that I was soon disillusioned with them. I was in Glasgow during the famous Torry and Alexander campaign, and a pious second cousin kept begging me so often to go with him that at last I went. The meetings were held in an enormous hall. Alexander, a willowy, sleek, slightly bald young man, kept the audience cheerful with catchy hymns:

> We're marching to Zion,
> Beautiful, beautiful Zion,
> We're marching onward to Zion,
> That beautiful city of God.

After he had prepared the way Dr Torry, a burly, grey-haired clubman, got up and fired off a number of wisecracks on salvation, which he made out to be a good business proposition. The time came to summon the saved to rise in their places; everybody round me rose, and to my great astonishment I found myself getting up too, although I had had no intention of doing so: it is very hard to remain sitting when everybody else has risen. I did not go up to the penitent form, of course, but my rising greatly pleased my second cousin, who probably fancied he had won a soul.

A friend of mine who attended a Baptist church in Glasgow which I also attended for a while disillusioned me finally with revivals. He had himself taken part in one, and one night after a meeting, the minister having asked him how many had been saved, he said somewhat shortly, 'Five.' 'What, a mere wretched five!' the minister replied, whereupon my friend retorted, 'I think you should remember, Mr X, that they're precious in God's sight!' He came away in a rage, and after that refused to have anything more to do with revivals.

CHAPTER THREE

Glasgow

Our setting out for Glasgow was delayed for a while. My father decided to trim his beard in honour of the occasion, and he trimmed it so radically that he caught a bad cold. We sailed from Stromness in the middle of winter, on a dark, windy day. Jimmie and Johnnie were on the pier at Leith to meet us; we arrived in darkness, and the bluish lights of the great electric globes angrily glared down on the wharf. A dirty train was standing in the station; I had seen trains only in school-book illustrations, and had thought of them as shining and new. My brothers in their city clothes seemed strangely efficient and at home in this unknown world.

We stayed in Edinburgh that first night, and I must have lodged with my brother Willie. I remember walking with him next morning down a clean, stony street with innumerable gates leading down to basements where maids were polishing steps. We came to a green hill on which a number of monuments stood about, and then, after an interval, we were in a dark picture-gallery. Near the door there was a statue of a naked woman, and two ragged, dirty boys were standing before it nudging each other and tittering as they stared at a black thumb-mark on one breast of the statue. I had never seen boys like them before. We walked through the gallery looking at the dark and bright pictures. After that I remember nothing until we were in Glasgow.

Jimmie had taken a flat for us in Crosshill, a respectable suburb near the Queen's Park. For some reason we did not stay long in our first house, but soon moved to a second one, and then to a third. For a few months I wandered about, quite friendless, trying to get used to Glasgow. My father was interested in everything, and got into long, informative conversations with strangers; but after a lifetime in Orkney he found it hard to accustom himself to the simplest things here. At the Bu and Garth we never thought of locking the door at night, and during the day, at least in summer, it always stood open. Now my father was cribbed in a small flat on a stairhead; the door, when it was shut, automatically locked, and you had always to shut it when you went out or came in: it took him a long time to remember this. Beggars were perpetually ringing the bell, and we did not learn for weeks that you must not take a beggar in and give him something to eat, but must slam the door at once in his face. The perpetual climbing of stairs was bad for my father's heart; trudging the streets tired him, and when he returned from his excursions he was so exhausted that he had to rest in bed for a while. He began to long for a glimpse of the sea and the fields; but he died before he saw them again. One night, after talking cheerfully as he lay in the kitchen bed—some friends of Jimmie were in—he suddenly sat up and fell back again. I was sleeping in another room, and Clara came in and told me that my father was dead. Still half asleep, I cried angrily, 'It's a lie!' then burst into tears.

This was about a year after we came to Glasgow. I was by now an office-boy in a law office, where I got four shillings and twopence a week. I worked from nine to five in the pleasant, boring office, copying letters, addressing and stamping and delivering letters, and keeping a little petty-cash book. I wearied my heart out there; I felt, as I had done when I first went to school, that I was beginning a term of imprisonment, and began once more to move the hands of the clock on with my will. The clerks chaffed me because of my Orkney accent, and that made me grow more tongue-tied than I had been before. Of the business of the office I had no idea, and have no idea still.

Out of my salary I had to buy for a few pence a lunch at a neighbouring dairy; when that was done there was not much left; so that both for economy and health (exercise being necessary in a town, my brothers assured me) I walked to and from my work each day through a slum, for there was no way of getting from the south side of Glasgow to the city except through slums. These journeys filled me with a sense of degradation: the crumbling houses, the twisted faces, the obscene words casually heard in passing, the ancient, haunting stench of pollution and decay, the arrogant women, the mean men, the terrible children, daunted me, and at last filled me with an immense, blind dejection. I had seen only ordinary people before; but on some of the faces that I passed every day now there seemed to be things written which only a fantastic imagination could have created, and I shrank from reading them and quickly learned not to see. After a while, like every one who lives in an industrial town, I got used to these things; I walked through the slums as if they were an ordinary road leading from my home to my work. I learned to do this consciously, but if I was tired or ill I often had the feeling, passing through Eglinton Street or Crown Street, that I was dangerously close to the ground, deep down in a place from which I might never be able to climb up again, while far above my head, inaccessible, ran a fine, clean highroad; and a soundless tremor shook me, the premonition of an anxiety neurosis. These fears might come on me at any time, and then, though I lived in a decent house, the slums seemed to be everywhere around me, a great, spreading swamp into which I might sink for good.

I soon made a habit of escaping into the surrounding country in my free time, but even the fields seemed blasted by disease, as if the swamp were invisibly spreading there too. My nearest access to the country lay through a little mining village, where grey men were always squatting on their hunkers at the ends of the houses, and the ground was covered with coal-grit. Beyond this, if you turned to the left, there was a cinder path leading past a pit, beside which was a filthy pool where yellow-faced children splashed about. Tattered, worm-ringed trees stood round it in squalid sylvan peace; the grass was rough with smoke and grit; the sluggish streams were bluish black. To the right a road climbed up to the Hundred Acre Dyke, along which mangy hawthorns grew. The herbage was purer here, but all that could be seen were blackened fields, smoke-stacks, and the sooty ramparts of coal-pits, except to the south, where lay the pretty little town of Cathcart. These roads became so associated in my mind with misery that after leaving the south side of Glasgow I could never bear to revisit them.

My first years in Glasgow were wretched. The feeling of degradation continued, but it became more and more blind; I did not know what made me unhappy, nor that I had come into chaos. We had lived comfortably enough in Orkney, mainly on what we grew; but here everything had to be bought and paid for; there was so much money and so much food and clothes and warmth and accommodation to be had for it: that was all. This new state of things worried and perplexed my mother, and it gave each one of us a feeling of stringency which we had never known before. My elder brothers had already grasped the principle of this new society, which was competition, not co-operation, as it had been in Orkney. The rest of us too presently came to understand this, but my father and mother never did. Though we imagined that we had risen in some way, without knowing it we had sunk into another class: for if Jimmie and Johnnie had lost their jobs we should have had nothing left but a small balance in a bank, which was not a responsive, adaptable thing like a farm, but would soon have run out. We were members of the proletariat, though at that time we had never heard the name. Happily my brothers kept their jobs, and we did not have to become acquainted with the abyss over which we lived. Yet somewhere in our minds we were conscious of it. The old sense of security was gone.

The first few years after we came to Glasgow were so stupidly wretched, such a meaningless waste of inherited virtue, that I cannot write of them even now without grief and anger. My father and mother felt lost because they were too old, and I because I was too young. My brothers and sisters, having reached the age when adaptation becomes conscious and deliberate, stood the change better; but Willie, without our knowing it, had already succumbed. He often came from Edinburgh to stay with us for the week-ends, and took me round a great deal; we had struck up a friendship founded on our interest in books. He took me to the Zoo, the pantomime, the Mitchell Library, which I haunted after that, and tried to explain to me the law of this new society, which consisted, he said, in looking after yourself. His words were bitter; he may have already guessed that he was suffering from an incurable disease;

he was always tired and listless when he came to see
us; yet he went on studying law, spending his evenings
over his text-books. Then one week-end he came and did
not go away again; his office had given him sick-leave; a
doctor had told him that he had consumption. It was in
midsummer, and in a little while my two weeks' holiday
was due: Jimmie and Johnnie did not get theirs till later.
Willie needed country air, yet could not be left to go away by
himself, and as he and I were now fast friends it was decided
that we should spend the holiday together. We took lodgings
at Millport in the island of Cumbrae. Willie's disease must
already have been far advanced, for when, after the sail
down the Clyde, we arrived at the house where we were
to stay, the plump daughter of our landlady, coming into
the sitting-room, raised her hands in fatuous pity on seeing
Willie, and cried, 'Puir soul! How thin he is!' words which
stabbed him to the quick on that very first day, and were
like a sentence of death. There were negro minstrels and a
few bleak walks, and people perpetually dipping in the sea;
but all these things were far outside us; we saw them only
in flashes and as from a great distance. Willie was shut deep
within himself, impatient for a word of hope from outside,
yet angry if I ventured to utter one; I did not know what
to say to him; I scarcely dared to speak as we walked along
the little paths, seeing nothing round us, both of us thinking
of that invisible, deadly, and yet peaceable enemy quietly
working beyond our reach. Willie's face took on the look
of a man sentenced to death in the midst of life; it was
as if he hated everything that had the glow of health: the
flowers in the gardens, the fruit in the shop-windows, the
children paddling in the sea, even the sunshine, though that
was supposed to do him good. Sometimes, in a sudden fit of
hope, he would scoop up a little sea-water in his palm and
with an apologetic air swallow it, having read somewhere
that sea-water was a cure for consumption. But in a few
minutes his despair would return again, and then a terrible
impatience would seize him, a longing for a sign, a miracle,
which he knew could never come. At last he could not
endure Millport any longer, though our fortnight was not
yet ended. We set out in a steamer on a rough day; Willie

was sick, and in despair cried to me, as he lay in a chair, that he was dying; I stood beside him not knowing what to do. When we left the boat and got into the train he began to feel better; hope automatically returned, and he told me not to say anything about his words on the boat. At last we reached our house; as we entered the kitchen I was wearing a strained, nervous smile which I could not wipe from my face. A neighbour was sitting talking to my mother; she looked at Willie, then saw the smile on my face, and stared at me in wonder. I was sixteen at the time.

Willie did not leave the house after that. Soon he took to his bed, and as he did not have enough strength to shave, let his beard grow; the soft, young, curly beard seemed to set him apart. After he went to bed his weakness increased rapidly; a few days before he died he told my mother that he was reconciled with God. He told her at the same time that a few years before he had prayed night after night for many months for an assurance that he was accepted by Christ, but that no comfort, nothing but silence, had answered him. He had told nobody of his solitary struggle; at last he had given it up, and later he had grown indifferent. Now the assurance he had prayed for came spontaneously, when he did not expect it.

Willie's death followed within a year of my father's. For the moment our family, though shaken, seemed safe from any further danger. But ill-health seemed to hang over it. Clara and I were always unwell, though Jimmie and Johnnie, acclimatized by now, enjoyed good health.

Dissatisfied with my four shillings and twopence, I managed to get a job in an engineering office in Renfrew at eight shillings a week. I had to leave by the eight o'clock train now, and did not get home in the evening until seven. My work was hard, and the head of my department, a bluff, insensitive man, kept shouting at me for my slowness; I fell ill, and in a few weeks was without a job. My mother, anxious about my health, kept me at home for some time; I spent it, ungratefully, in a dingy reading-room in the Gorbals, where I pored over all sorts of academic reviews, *The Contemporary*, *The Nineteenth Century*, *The Fortnightly*, emerging half blinded each day when the place shut. The reading-room, being warm, was frequented by a crowd of poor, dirty men who smelled of sweat; the light was bad, the reviews were thumbed and tattered, and the sweat of that unwashed crowd seemed to have worked into the paper like a solution of misery. Why I chose that particular reading-room I cannot say, unless by now a sort of attraction to squalor, acquired during my walks to my work, had soaked into me. I remember nothing of what I read in that place except a series of examples of great English prose chosen by well-known contemporary writers, which I discovered in some bound volumes of *The Fortnightly Review*.

The same attraction to squalor drew me to the football matches on Saturday afternoon. Crosshill was a respectable suburb, but there were vacant lots scattered about it, chance scraps of waste ground where the last blade of grass had died, so that in dry weather they were as hard as lava, and in wet weather a welter of mud. On these lots teams from the slum quarters of the south side played every Saturday afternoon with great skill and savage ferocity. Fouls were a matter of course, and each game turned into a complicated feud in which the ball itself was merely a means to an end which had no connexion with the game. Some of the teams had boxers among their supporters; these men stood bristling on the touchline and shouted intimidations at the opposing players. I first saw one of these games shortly after I came to Glasgow; a brown fog covered the ground, and a small, tomato-red sun, like a jellyfish floating in the sky, appeared and disappeared as the air grew thicker or finer. I found later that more civilized football teams played in the Queen's Park recreation ground, and I began to attend them instead, and later still, when I was earning enough money to spare a sixpence on Saturday, I attended the matches of the Queen's Park Football Club. But there was a grimy fascination in watching the damned kicking a football in a tenth-rate hell.

After my few weeks at home I got a job as an office-boy with a publishing firm. Here I made friends for the first time; there were several other boys of my own age in the place. It was a kindly, unceremonious office, with many women in it and a few men. During my errands to the other departments I came to know a few people, women mostly, who took an interest in me and lent me books. I struck up a semi-hostile friendship with a timekeeper, a one-armed atheist, with whom I had long arguments on religion. I heard for the first time, too, of Socialism, but barricaded myself behind the classical arguments. Some one recommended me about this time to get a weekly paper called *Great Thoughts*. It was filled with a high but vague nonconformity, and tried to combine the ideals of revivalist Christianity and great literature. There were articles on 'aspects' of Ruskin, Carlyle, Browning, and the other uplifting Victorians, and a great number of quotations, mainly 'thoughts,' from their works and the writings of Marcus Aurelius and Epictetus. For some time this paper coloured my attitude to literature; I acquired a passion for 'thoughts' and 'thinkers,' and demanded from literature a moral inspiration which would improve my character: there were many 'thoughts' bearing on character, particularly in its aspect of 'self-culture,' in which the reader was encouraged to strike a balance between the precepts of Christ and Samuel Smiles. There was very little poetry among these extracts, and that mainly of an edifying kind, so that for a time I read nothing but prose, most of it being Victorian prose. Behind all this nobility and lip-service to beauty stood the Baptist, the Methodist, and the Plymouth Brother. These figures disquieted me, for I already felt a disharmony between their beliefs and these 'thoughts' which they apparently endorsed; yet I did not resolve my doubts, for I was myself entangled in revivalism: a short time after Willie's death I had passed through another spurious conversion by attending some meetings at a Baptist chapel. This time I did not experience the fine emotions which my first conversion had brought me; there was an adolescent impurity in my worship of Christ, who appeared to me as the Comforter, and as I hummed to myself,

> I heard the voice of Jesus say,
> 'Come unto Me and rest,'

I sometimes burst into tears. I carried about with me a pocket edition of the New Testament which I was always reading, tried hard to practise self-renunciation, and was always doing some useless embarrassing service for the people I knew. One or two of the other office-boys were also Christians and encouraged me in my priggishness, and a very bad novel about the early Christians and their meekness under Roman persecution completed my demoralization: I went about with the forgiving smile of a martyr about to be swallowed at any moment by a lion. What made all this still worse was the fact that intellectually I despised the man who had saved me; he was a black-haired, iron-cheeked Ulster commercial traveller who loved to use, quite superfluously, such trite phrases as 'the blue vault of Heaven' to impress his hearers; I suspected him, probably quite wrongly, of being a shady character as well.

I was ill all this time without knowing it. Presently a gland in my neck began to trouble me, swelling up in an unsightly way. I went to the doctor who attended our family, an old, morose, stupid man, who treated the gland electrically for some time with no result, saying every now and then, 'It's just like an egg. It's just like an egg.' Finally I had to be taken to the Victoria Infirmary, where, under chloroform, my neck was cut open and the poisonous stuff removed. For several weeks afterwards the wound was scraped at intervals, a painful process, then allowed to close. My job was lost, and I was told by the doctor that I must look for work in the open air.

During all the weeks or months that I was attending the Victoria Infirmary I did a good deal of reading. I managed to get hold of sixpence weekly to subscribe for the parts of *Chambers's Cyclopaedia of English Literature*, my subscription happening to begin with the Romantic Movement. There were articles on the various writers by well-known critics such as Swinburne, Watts-Dunton, and Gosse; there were abundant extracts, both in poetry and prose; and the period from Wordsworth to Swinburne and Morris became tolerably familiar to me. While working in the publishing office I had saved enough to buy one or two volumes of the Scott Library, which were sold at a shilling and sixpence at that time; these included a translation of Pascal's *Pensées*, and another of Lessing's *Laokoön*, which gave me a new standard of what a 'thinker' should be. I had also acquired a Shakespeare and a Milton, Emerson's essays, *Jane Eyre*, and a number of Hardy's and Meredith's novels in sixpenny paper-backed editions. *Chambers's Cyclopaedia of English Literature* brought me back to poetry again; I was enchanted by *The Solitary Reaper*, the *Ode to a Nightingale*, the *Ode to the West Wind*, *The Lotus-eaters*, and the chorus from *Atalanta in Calydon*. Before this rush of new poetry my religious moonings were swept away.

I looked about for outdoor work, but could find nothing for some time. A friend of Jimmie's knew a chauffeur who worked at a big house in Ayrshire; it happened that he needed an assistant to wash the cars, do odd jobs, and in any time left over learn to drive. His employer was a Glasgow business-man who had a big house in Kelvinside, and I was told to call there one evening. Mr M. received me kindly; he was an affable, unassuming man who seemed to be just as embarrassed by our encounter as I was, and after informing me that he treated all his servants well he muttered, '*Noblesse oblige*, you know. *Noblesse oblige*.' I did not know how I was expected to address him, but though he was clearly a kind-hearted man, I could not bring myself to call him 'sir'; the *Noblesse oblige*, too, seemed uncalled for, and I could not help thinking, as I listened, that *Richesse* would have been more suitable. As for the 'sir', I had been brought up to believe that it was sycophantic to use it; in Orkney it was considered undignified to address another man, however rich or noble or powerful, as 'sir'; this point of honour may seem absurd to English readers, but there was a virtue in it, bound up with other virtues of the Scottish character. It was the quality which made Scottish crofters refuse to uncover their heads before royalty, a thing which sometimes happened during royal visits to Scotland. After coming to Glasgow I had found it very hard even to learn the habit of raising my cap, for in Orkney we doffed to no one, man or woman, minister, teacher, laird, or prince. I remember one day in Kirkwall coming plump upon the Duke of York (who later became King George V) as he rode on a brown horse down a quiet street. He had come up to Orkney with the Channel Fleet, in which he was a commander. I was among a crowd of other boys, and we gazed in reverential curiosity at the Duke, but none of us even thought of raising our caps. This was not due to any lack of respect; it was simply a thing which did not enter our heads.

These scruples did not trouble me very much during the few months I spent at the house in Ayrshire. I did not see my employer more than once or twice, and he was quite kind and informal. The estate had large wooded grounds, and the stable buildings where I lodged were a good distance from the house. I was not a success as an apprentice chauffeur; I disliked the work of hosing the cars and polishing them with chamois leather; but there were long days when, the chauffeur being away, there was nothing to do, and I could wander about the place in a happy, vacant mood, occasionally poring over *Chambers's Cyclopoedia of English Literature*. All my time there is associated with Rossetti and Swinburne, and whenever I read,

> Under the arch of Life, where Love and Death,
> Terror and Mystery guard her shrine, I saw
> Beauty enthroned, and though her gaze struck awe,
> I drew it in as simply as my breath,

it brings back the spruce and larch woods, the stone-flagged courtyard of the stable buildings, the whistling of the fat coachman as he groomed the horses (for the house had a carriage as well), the harness-room smelling of oil and leather, the wet gush of the hose stripping away the mud from the mudguards, and the stench of soaking chamois leather. The hounds of spring course through that mixed landscape, and the butler, a tall, handsome, clerical man in black, walks benevolently among them, followed by a procession of housemaids, the intelligent one, the pretty one, the proud and handsome one, the old, sad, experienced one.

A short distance from the gate, across a little bridge, lay a village with gay strips of flowers before the cottages. Because I was reading Rossetti and Morris at the time, this hamlet turned into part of a Pre-Raphaelite landscape, which shows the power of wish-fantasy, for I have been back there since and found it a bare and squalid place, and the pretty flower borders shrunk to a line of weeds. That first winter I learned dancing in the village hall: Triumph, Petronella, the Flowers of Edinburgh, Rory O'More, quadrilles, lancers, the waltz. A dapper little man with side-whiskers put us through our steps. There were flirtations among the boys and girls, children of farmers and farm-labourers in the district, but the dancing-master made us observe strict propriety, and even tried to teach us elegant manners; we clownishly submitted. Though I had been only three years in Glasgow, I felt a townee among these rustics, who were not in the least like the country people in Orkney. They knew far more than I did about what Yeats called contemptuously 'the root facts of life'; for I had been so busy learning about so many other things that I had had no time to learn about 'life.' They were all realistic and Rabelaisian; they knew which girls in the neighbourhood were virtuous and which were not, and though they were hide-bound intellectually, in their actual contact with life they were far less puritanical than I was. I received many shocks to my feelings, nursed on Rossetti's poetry, but found that I got over them and easily made friends. These months were happy and peaceful; my health quickly recovered; I had my first few flirtations with girls, and made more of them than there was in them, as one does at that age, getting a great deal of pleasure and disappointment out of them. But I was clearly unsuited to become a chauffeur; my work, in spite of all I could do, did not improve; the cars did not have the faultless appearance which was required. I was told that I had better leave.

For some time I had been troubled by my mother's letters, saying that Johnnie was suffering from unaccountable headaches. Some months before he had fallen from a tramcar and had been knocked unconscious. Being hardy and used to knocks—he had taken up wrestling shortly after coming to Glasgow—he had made light of the accident and refused to see a doctor. It was late spring when I returned home; Johnnie was not visibly suffering, yet seemed to be changed in some way; his face, usually careless, looked watchful, as if he were listening to something inside his head. My mother and Jimmie were worried about him; the same fear which had followed Willie's homecoming was in the house again. Physically Johnnie seemed as strong as ever, but there was always that vigilant look in his face.

Soon after returning I got a post as junior clerk in the office of a beer-bottling factory at fourteen shillings a week, and now felt at last that I was helping to support the family. It was a cheerful, careless place, and as I had some responsibility in it I ceased to feel a prisoner. But Johnnie's headaches were always in my mind, and each evening I dreaded to go home for fear of what I might find. The doctors he went to gave him medicines of various kinds, but they did not seem to know what was the matter with him. At last one of them recommended him to go to the Victoria Infirmary to be kept under observation. This meant that he had to give up his job.

After Johnnie left for the infirmary an uneasy lull fell on the house. In a few weeks he returned again; he had grown fatter, and the attacks had not troubled him so much; but his watchfulness had increased: it was as if a little clock, inaudible to every one else, were ticking away in his head, and he had no attention for anything else. I fancy that at this time Jimmie already knew his brother had a tumour on the brain and could never recover; but he kept the knowledge to himself, since my mother would not have been able to bear it. The doctor at the infirmary had recommended Johnnie to go for walks, and Jimmie and I went out with him by turns in the evenings: it was a fine summer, every evening calm and radiant. The disease had begun to affect Johnnie's legs: his feet, flung out impetuously, hesitated and wavered in the air for a second before they returned to the ground again. When we came to tramlines he would look carefully to the right and the left, as if he were the leader of an expedition in a dangerous country, and then carefully walk across. We often went to the Queen's Park recreation ground and watched the football and cricket going on together there. As he watched Johnnie would forget his illness for a few minutes, but then, as he lumbered past the other young men running about in careless ease, a realization of his state would come back in a clap, as if for the first time.

He never looked at the people who passed him now, and I too, partly because I identified myself with him, partly because it seemed a point of honour to act as he did, paid no attention to them either. We walked through the cheerful, crowded streets on these summer evenings as detached and cold as monks.

As the summer went on Johnnie grew worse; the attacks strengthened methodically, as if a power beyond our knowledge or reach were performing some dreadful operation on him which could neither be hurried nor retarded; it was like the infallible consummation of an objective process. The agony grew so extreme that he begged for death; yet, past every conceivable point, the pain went on increasing with a mathematical acceleration. This lasted during all the autumn; we knew now that there was no hope; my mother and Clara, left alone with Johnnie all day, grew thin as ghosts. A specialist was called in, and merely confirmed that nothing could be done. At last, that winter, the end came. Afterwards, when the house was quiet again and Johnnie was lying in his coffin, I went into the shuttered room to take a last look at him. His was the first dead face I had ever seen; for months it had been distorted with pain, never at rest; now all the lines were gone; he looked distant and young, and seemed to be by himself in a solitude which I had never guessed at before; the coffin, lying on the trestles, looked as if it were floating farther and farther into an unknown world which was present there in that room, yet was more lonely and distant than the most distant star. It was a deep, momentary impression, filling me with dread and peace, a peace too annihilating to be held and accepted. My heart locked and bolted itself against that perfection; yet I was glad I had seen his face and the peace which had come upon it at last.

All autumn I had prayed, night after night, that Johnnie would get better. As the pain increased and he became a mere substance upon which it worked like a conscientious artisan, there seemed to be no sense in praying, and if there was a God I told myself that he was deaf or indifferent. There would have been a meaning in Johnnie's agony if, after it was over, he had recovered and become a new man, purged by suffering. But if he had to die in any case, what point could there be, I asked myself night after night, in that impersonal, systematic torture which as it went on wrecked in turn his body, his mind, and his spirit, overthrowing him totally and reducing him to a state worse than that of a crying child, so that he lost even a sense of humiliation at his agony, accepting this half-existence, this quarter-existence, as everything that there was. I could find no answer to that question, except that life was ruled by an iron law. When my mother, weakened by nursing Johnnie, fell ill too I prayed again, desperately, but quite without belief: my words were mere words. Without telling us my mother had been suffering for some time from an internal disease. At last she could endure the pain no longer; she too was taken to the Victoria Infirmary, was operated upon, and died a few months after Johnnie. The family now looked as if it had been swept by a gale. Only four were left: my two sisters, Jimmie, and myself; and as we were grown up—I was eighteen—we presently went our own ways.

I have hurried over these years because they are still painful and still blurred in my mind: I was too young for so much death. All that time seemed to give no return, nothing but loss; it was like a heap of dismal rubbish in the middle of which, without rhyme or reason, were scattered four deaths. I climbed out of these years like a man struggling out of a quagmire, but that rubbish still encumbered me for a long time with *post-mortem* persistence. The successive deaths had merely stunned me; I grew silent, absent, dingy, and composed. But my health crumbled to pieces again. During Johnnie's illness I had contracted a nervous ailment of the stomach; I suffered from a perpetual faint nausea and dizziness which infected everything—my work, my walks, my reading, spreading itself like a dirty film over them all. In the evenings after my work I went to one doctor after another, with no result, spending many a useless half-crown out of my fourteen shillings. At last a clerk in the office advised me to go to a slum doctor in the south side who, he said, was a first-class man, the only thing against him being that he was reputed to be a free-thinker. I went along to his consulting-room one evening in early summer. He was a neat, small, handsome, very well-dressed man with greying hair and a brown moustache. He treated me with the utmost courtesy, and did what none of the other doctors had done: he gave me a thorough examination and kept me under observation for several weeks, finding some excuse whenever I asked him how much I owed him. At last he prescribed a stomach-pump; every night I had to swallow a great length of rubber tubing and bring up all that was left in my stomach; it was very unpleasant, but I went on, for by now, encouraged by the doctor, I had begun to take an interest in my state, and felt I was intelligently collaborating with him. I went on with this for several months; the doctor still kept me under observation; at last he began to see progress, and I began to feel better. During the consultations we chatted together like conspirators, but never for long, for he was a very busy man; he generally dismissed me with a pawky saying of Mr Dooley, a popular philosopher for whom he had a great admiration. His patients were mostly very poor people whom, I feel sure, he never charged for his advice; he worked in the slums out of pure goodness; he was never discourteous; he treated me as a fashionable practitioner in the West End might treat a rich patient, and in the end charged me some ridiculously small fee, refusing peremptorily to accept more. Out of mere love and admiration I should have liked to go on attending him, but when I was cured he said good-bye firmly, telling me to take care of myself and not to let him see me again. I realized that I was only one of many people he had helped, and that he did not want to have his good deeds coming back to embarrass him and waste his time. He was an excellent doctor and a delightful man, and, in spite of his free-thinking, more like a Christian saint than any other human being I have ever known.

As I grew well the squalor of my first five years in Glasgow rolled from me. I was nineteen now; my health was good; I was earning sixteen shillings a week; and my evenings—I stopped work at six o'clock—seemed, with their freedom to do anything I liked with them, to be all that I wished for. The office was a cheerful place; Bob M., the head clerk, a noisy, impulsive man who had once been a good

athlete, swore at us in a fraternal way, and was not above
joining in a game of office football with loud, warlike shouts.
There were four of us: Bob, another clerk, myself, and
an office-boy. The firm had several horse-lorries, which
went their rounds among the public-houses of Glasgow and
the surrounding countryside. The lorry-men were mostly
farm-servants who had come to Glasgow to make better
money. By the time they returned from their rounds each
night they were generally tipsy, for it was good business to
have a drink with the public-house keepers. One or two of
them had been a long time with the firm, yet could still
hardly count; it was a diplomatic triumph to settle their
daily accounts; you had to convince them that you were
not trying to cheat them and dispense at the same time
with strict book-keeping principles, which they hated and
distrusted from the bottom of their hearts. Each of them
had a lorry-boy; these boys came mostly from the slums,
and were a bloodless, tattered, ferocious-looking crowd.
There was one in particular, a short, squat boy in a suit
too big for him, with a jacket coming down to his knees
and trousers sticking out in great circular creases around his
legs; he quite terrified me when he grinned, for he had only
three teeth, two in the upper and one in the lower jaw; but
I soon found that he was quite harmless. Now that I came
in contact daily with boys from the slums I lost my horror
of the streets I passed through every day; I walked through
them with a sense of experience. The firm supplied clubs
as well as pubs; these were mostly drinking dens, some of
them frequented by thoroughly bad characters. George, the
manager of one of them, often came to the office; he was an
unshaven, auburn-haired man with a hoarse voice, who had
once done time and always carried a revolver: he was a quiet
man, and had a great admiration for Charlie Peace.

Sometimes as I looked at George I thought of a gruesome
incident which had happened when I was working in the
publishing office. I was sitting one day in a dairy having a
snack, when a horse-faced, severe-looking man in a check
suit sat down at my table; there was nobody else in the
place. He stared in front of him for a while, then said, as if
to himself, 'Ay, it's a' ower noo.' I looked up indifferently,

and as if he were outraged at my indifference he went on,
'Oh, you ken naething about it! At Duke Street yonder'—he
jerked his thumb over his shoulder—'a man took the drop
this morning. Poor Bob! He was a good lad, and noo they've
got him.' I did not know whether he was telling the truth
or trying to frighten me. Now I feel pretty sure that he
was speaking of a real execution and that he was afraid for
himself, he was so sad and indignant.

Two other memories sometimes returned while I was
working in that office, but now my familiarity with George
and the lorry-boys made them less horrible. The first was of
a summer evening when I was walking down the Salt Market
and came upon a crowd at the end of a close. A muscular,
red-haired woman with her arms bare to the shoulder was
battering the face of a little, shrinking man and screaming,
'It's him that led me away when I was a young lassie, the
b—! It's him that put me on the streets, the b—! I might
have been a respectable woman if it hadna been for him, the
b—!' The little man shrank against the wall with his hands
over his face. He did not seem to have put them there for
protection, but merely out of shame, so that no one might
recognize the long-lost seducer of this woman. He looked
forlorn and shabby and old; I felt sorry for him, and did
not believe what the woman was saying: he did not look
like a seducer. I do not know how it ended, for the thud
of the big, red-haired fist on the man's face sickened me.
The crowd looked on without interfering.

The other memory was of a dull winter Saturday afternoon in Crown Street, another slum. I had been to see some
doctor. Again I came on a crowd. Two young men were
standing in the centre of it, and one of them, who looked
serious and respectable and not particularly angry, raised
his fist slowly every now and then, and, as if objectively,
hit the other man, who stood in silence and never tried
to defend himself. At last an older man said, 'Why dinna
you let the chap alane? He hasna hurt you.' But the serious
young man replied, 'I ken he hasna hurt me, but I'm gaun
tae hurt him!' And with a watchful look round him he
raised his fist again. I did not want to see any more;
but the scene and particularly the words of the serious

young man—the other said nothing at all—took hold of
my mind as if they were an answer to some question which,
without my knowing it, had been troubling me: perhaps
Johnnie's slow and painful death, during which, without
being able to return a single blow, he had been battered
so pitilessly. In both these memories there was the quality
of Scottish Calvinism: the serious young man's reply had
the unanswerable, arbitrary logic of predestination; and the
encounter of the red-haired woman with her seducer, when
both were so greatly changed that their original sin might
have been committed in another world, and yet lived on,
there in that slum, was a sordid image of fate as Calvin saw
it. Somewhere in these two incidents there was a virtue of
a dreary kind, behind the flaunted depravity: a recognition
of logic and reality.

I have had only two dreams which can be attached to
this time. The first vaguely recalls Johnnie's illness and
that one-sided fight between the two young men. In this
dream I saw a boxing ring where a big, strong man and a
little, wizened man were fighting. The big man raised his
first and knocked down the little man with perfect ease;
but the little man bounced up and came on again. This
continued, round after round. Then the big man began
to look anxious and played for a knock-out blow. But the
little man, very much battered by now, kept bouncing up;
nothing could stop him; and at last his little fists, light as
paper, light as moths, flicked the big man's face wherever
they liked. The big man could still brush them away with
a wave of his tired arm, as if they were buzzing flies; but
immediately they settled back again, pattering on his face,
flicking him, torturing him. At last the big man, completely
beaten, lay down in the ring, tears oozing from his eyes,
his limbs outspread, and let the little man do whatever he
liked with him. It was a terrifying and abominable dream,
the image of something to which I can give no name.

The other dream was a strange and beautiful one. Though
it was ostensibly about one of my sisters, it really went
back to my mother's death, the dream making some kind
of substitution. I dreamt I was sitting in my lodgings in
Glasgow, when my eldest brother appeared at the door

dressed in black. Without entering he said in a careful voice, as if he were uttering a secret, 'Come with me; she is dead.' I rose more in wonder than in grief and followed him. We came to a house which I did not know, and entered a great, high room. The smooth floor stretched away before me, and everything glittered in the light from two tall, curtainless windows which reached from floor to ceiling. Islanded in the centre of the room was a little bed, more like a child's cot than a bed, round which a few men in black clothes were standing. On the bed or cot, dressed in white, a young woman was lying dead. The mourners looked up respectfully when I appeared in the doorway, and stood back a little, so that I might take my place by the bedside. But instead—all this seemed to happen of itself, without my will—I walked over to the mantelpiece, which was near the door, leaned my elbow on it, and bowed my head on my hand. Standing like this with my back half turned to the others, I began to cry; the tears streamed down my face; this went on for a long time; I did not try to stop it. At last my tears ceased of themselves, and, as if the moment had come now, I walked over to the bed through the silent mourners. Sitting down on a chair, I looked at my dead sister. She was very pale; the lines of the nose and the chin seemed so fragile that a breath might dissolve them; the eyes were closed. As I looked I thought I saw a faint glow tinging her cheeks; it deepened, and in a moment she was burning in a fire. The glow appeared to come from within her; but I knew that it flowed from a warm, limpid, and healing point in my own breast. Her eyes fluttered and opened, she held out her hand, and I turned to the others, crying, 'Look! I have brought her to life!' But at these words a terrible fear came over me, and I hastily added, as if to blot them out and destroy them, 'Look! God has brought her to life!'

I dreamt this in Germany seventeen years after my mother's death, when my memory of her, which had once been unendurable, could be borne again, and she actually came to life in my mind. In the dream I wept for her the tears which I could not weep at her death, when life seemed to be ruled by an iron law, the only response to which was a stupefied calm. In Germany I was enjoying the first few months of leisure and freedom which I had known since I went to work at fourteen. I looked back on my life for the first time and tried to form an intelligible picture of it, reliving consciously what I had once lived blindly, hoping in this way to save something of myself. Some months before I had been psychoanalysed in London, and the analysis had violently thrown up a great deal of my past which I had tried to keep buried. By this time, too, I had come under the influence of a friend of mine, a remarkable man, who had rekindled my love of poetry and brought back my belief in the immortality of the soul. Probably all these things came into the dream.

But there is a great area of my life during my first five years in Glasgow with which I can do nothing: it lies there like a heap of dull, immovable rubbish. My holiday with Willie, and Johnnie's long agony, stand out from it; but the rest is mere grimy desolation. If I were a self-made man perfectly satisfied with what I had made I could find a meaning in these years, and congratulate myself that I am better, or at least better off, now than I was then. But the complacency which can do this shocks me, and when I read the self-told tales of successful men who wear their youth as if they were flaunting a dingy decoration, proud of having risen a little in the world, to be a little further above the slums, I feel ashamed. The knowledge that such years existed for me, and that they exist still for millions of people, is more than enough; and that a few men have escaped from them is at best a romantic story with a happy ending, while to the overwhelming majority the story ends as it began, and their lives remain to their death a waste of rubbish, second-rate and second-hand, raked from the great dust-heap. There has been a great improvement in the lot of the poor since the time I am speaking of, and that is one of the entirely good achievements of the century.

I climbed out of these years, but for a long time I did not dare to look back into them; at this time my walks in the country to the south of Glasgow became unbearable. It was my health, renewed by the slum doctor, that saved me. As if four of my family had never died, I turned away from death and all thought of serious things. I struck up a friendship with Sam K., the same young man who had told the minister that his five converts were precious in God's sight. He was a little older than myself, and, having lived all his life in Glasgow, knew it much better than I did, so that he became a kind of adviser and father-confessor to me. We went for long walks in the evenings and at week-ends, attended football matches together, and eagerly discussed everything that happened to us. When Sam began to walk out with a girl three times a week, a procedure known in Glasgow as 'steady wenching,' I walked out with her sister. But my affair did not last very long; Sam's went on. I did not see so much of him as before, and as about this time I began to become interested in Socialism, of which he disapproved, we presently drifted asunder, though without ceasing to like each other.

My interest in Socialism was wakened by Bob, the head clerk, who suddenly took it up with the same enthusiasm as office football. I was posted in the classical anti-Socialist arguments, which I had found in *Great Thoughts*; I was calm, and Bob was hot-headed; and after I had demonstrated the need for free competition all he could reply was, 'And what about the poor, bloody little children?' The whole office, and the lorry-men too when they were there, joined in against Bob; at last in despair he would exclaim, 'Oh, tae hell! You know nothing about it; you're a set of ignorant b—s! Why don't you read?' An old lorry-man who was always boasting of his feats at ploughing matches in his youth would chime in with, 'Wallace, the hero o' Scotland! He was the man for thae English hoors.' And he would strike up,

> 'The standards on the braes o' Mar
> Are up and streaming rarely,'

or, if he felt sentimental, an emigrant's song beginning,

> Fareweel, fareweel, my native hame,

bringing his great hand down flat on the counter.

Bob's advice to read at last impressed me. I got Blatchford's *Britain for the British*, and surrendered at once, crying over his statistics as I sat in the tramcar. I took

Bob's side now, and as together we could beat all-comers the discussions died for lack of opposition, though we went on challenging them. The slum boys were horrified by the thought of Socialism, which they associated with atheism; the lorry-men were merely indifferent, being convinced that Bob and myself were mad on this point, though sensible enough on every other. This did not injure our relations in the least; every one felt better after a thorough disagreement; for we discussed Socialism as if it had nothing to do with us, except when Bob brought in the 'poor, bloody little children.' We thought of it as something which could not be achieved in our time, but might come about in two or three hundred years, the important thing being to work for it now by converting disbelievers. Society was evolving towards it; when the evolution reached a certain point a revolution would painlessly follow: we carefully insisted that this revolution, which gave us an intellectual pleasure as the logical consummation of the evolutionary process preceding it, had nothing to do with 'bloody revolution.'

Bob, because of his position in the office, felt that he could not take any active part in propagating Socialism; but he encouraged me when I decided to join the Clarion Scouts, an organization connected with *The Clarion*, a paper run by Blatchford. It conducted each winter a series of Sunday evening lectures in the Metropole Theatre, the Lyceum of Glasgow, where well-known people spoke. I was still close enough to my religious upbringing to feel that it was faintly blasphemous to attend these lectures on a Sunday, but this only added to my enjoyment. After the lecture the speaker generally came along with us to the Clarion Scout Rooms, which were in a pleasant house in the West End near Charing Cross. Some of the lecturers, well known at the time, are now quite forgotten. There were Christian Socialists, atheists, advocates of free love, anarchists, and ordinary Parliamentarians with their eyes on the public, immovably respectable. I can remember Ramsay MacDonald speaking with great passion and saying nothing for two hours: even at that time he was distrusted. One evening Edward Carpenter took us into his personal confidence, describing how he had his clothes made in a special way, without any lining, so that he could wash them whenever he wanted: he seemed to expect his working-class audience to follow his example. Belfort Bax mumbled through a long and intricate paper on some aspect of historical materialism, never raising his eyes from the bundle of papers which he held before him. There was also a Madame La Forgue, a Belgian who starred herself as the most dangerous woman in Europe. She strode on to the stage in a great black cloak, which she swept from her shoulders with the flick of a bullfighter, displaying the lining, a deep, bloody crimson. She was exclamatory and incoherent; all I can remember of her speech is the end of a long hymn in praise of 'revolutionary, volupt-u-ous, fr-r-ee love,' which embarrassed even us, though we were accustomed to curious things. I listened entranced to all these lectures, Sunday after Sunday, equally pleased with the extravagant, the sensible, and the dull ones. After the meeting, when we adjourned to the Clarion Scout Rooms, I could be for a little while in the same room as these famous people, see them drinking tea and eating cakes like anybody else, perhaps even win a smile from them. I never dared to speak to them.

By now I was twenty-one, and though I did not know it, my conversion to Socialism was a recapitulation of my first conversion at fourteen. It was not, that is to say, the result of an intellectual process, but rather a sort of emotional transmutation; the poisonous stuff which had gathered in me during the past few years had found another temporary discharge. I read books on Socialism because they delighted me and were an escape from the world I had known with such painful precision. Having discovered a future in which everything, including myself, was transfigured, I flung myself into it, lived in it, though every day I still worked in the office of the beer-bottling factory, settling the accounts of the lorry-men and answering the jokes of the slum boys. My sense of human potentiality was so strong that even the lorry-men and the slum boys were transformed by it; I no longer saw them as they were, but as they would be when the society of which I dreamed was realized. I felt for them the same love as I had felt for the audience that night in Kirkwall when I returned from the penitent form, but it was a lighter, more hygienic love, by which the future had already purified in anticipation what it would some time purify in truth. For the first time in my life I began to like ordinary vulgar people, because in my eyes they were no longer ordinary or vulgar, since I saw in them shoots of the glory which they would possess when all men and women were free and equal. In spite of its simplicity, this was a genuine imaginative vision of life. It was a pure, earthly vision, for I had now flung away, along with my memories of my squalid youth, everything connected with it, including religion. It was false in being earthly and nothing more; indeed, that alone was what made it false. But I could not have seen it in any other terms then; my horror of my past life was too great. I realized for the first time how I should live with other men and women, and what I should look for in them, and, as after my conversion in Kirkwall, I seemed again to become invulnerable, so that no jealousy among those who were working along with me for Socialism, no weakness or vice, could disgust me or lessen the stationary affection I felt for all of them. It was a state which did not last for long; but having once known it I could sometimes summon it back again.

There are times in every man's life when he seems to become for a little while a part of the fable, and to be recapitulating some legendary drama which, as it has recurred a countless number of times in time, is ageless. The realization of the Fall is one of those events, and the purifications which happen in one's life belong to them too. The realization of the Fall is a realization of a universal event; and the two purifications which I have described, the one in Kirkwall and the one in Glasgow, brought with them images of universal purification. After that night in Kirkwall I felt that not only myself but every one was saved, or would some time be saved; and my conversion to Socialism had a similar effect. It was as if I had stepped into a fable which was always there, invisibly waiting for anyone who wished to enter it. Before, ugliness, disease, vice, and disfigurement had repelled me; but now, as if all mankind were made of some incorruptible substance, I felt no repugnance, no disgust, but a spontaneous attraction to every human being. I felt this most intensely during the first May Day demonstration I attended. That day is still enveloped in a golden mist, and I have no distinct memory of it, except that it was warm and sunny. I can remember the banners floating heavily in the windless air, their folds sometimes touching like a caress the heads and faces of the people marching behind them. I can remember a tall, dark, handsome man wearing a brown velvet jacket and carrying a yellow-haired little girl on his shoulder, and a pot-bellied, unhealthy man who walked beside me, and some middle-aged working-class women with shapeless bodies which seemed to have been broken into several pieces and clumsily stuck together again, and a crowd of well-to-do and slum children all mixed together. But what I am most conscious of is the feeling that all distinction had fallen away like a burden carried in some other place, and that all substance had been transmuted.

I do not know what value such experiences have; I feel that they should 'go into' life; yet there seems to be no technique by which one can accomplish the work of their inclusion. They stick out from my workaday existence, which I cannot lead without making distinctions, without recognizing that some people are wise and some foolish, some good and some bad, some clean and some dirty, and that, for instance, if I associate with dirty people I may catch a contagious disease and transmit it to my family or my friends. I admit the validity of psychological explanations of these states; my squalid years and my sudden escape from them in adolescence clearly contributed something to my condition. Yet that condition was so palpable and self-evident that these explanations, though I acknowledge their weight, have no genuine effect upon it, and in the end I must regard it simply as a form of experience. It is a form of experience which I have had oftener in dreams than in waking life, for dreams go without a hitch into the fable, and waking life does not. It has persistently recurred to me, as in the dream of the glorified murderers and the praying animals. The following is one of the clearest of these dreams. I dreamt that there had been great rains, and from a high peak I was looking down on a new, crystal river flowing through some pleasant, green, undulating country: I thought it was France. All along the river, whose course I could follow for hundreds of miles, the children crowded to the water and eagerly flung themselves in. Then the older people came, until the very old men and women were there, bathing in the river. While they were there a warning distant voice said, 'The harlots of France are bathing in the river,' and I realized that the harlots were higher up, somewhere near Lyons, I thought. At this I felt alarmed, for I thought that the prostitutes would infect the river; but then I knew that these waters could easily wash away every impurity and still remain pure. The thought of the harlots was merely a thought, an echo in my mind; I looked down in delight on the crystal river and the multitudes bathing in it, and drew as deep refreshment from the spectacle as if I, by mere looking, were being cleansed there too. A curious thing about the dream, which greatly intensified my delight, was that the bathers were not on the same scale as the river, but much larger, like those ships and cities and fortresses and effigies of Neptune which adorn old maps. The undulating country itself looked somewhat like a map, but through it flowed that great river of water, so living, so deep and pure, that an actual river would have appeared artificial beside it, as though it alone contained the original idea and essence of pure and cleansing and ever-flowing water.

As if only there could I find real food for my mind, I read now nothing but books pointing towards the future: Shaw, Ibsen, Whitman, Edward Carpenter—somewhat windy reading, except for Ibsen, whose *Emperor and Galilean* I preferred to all his other plays simply because it dealt with a prophetic society, a Third Empire which has since acquired very different associations. But the book which enchanted me most was a selection from the prose writings of Heine, with an introduction by Havelock Ellis. I came upon it in the summer after my first conversion to Socialism. That summer I caught whooping-cough, a piece of great good luck, for it took me back to my slum doctor, who as I grew better ordered me a month's holiday instead of my usual fortnight. I spent my holiday in Orkney at Skaill, the farm run by my Uncle Willie and his sister Sophie. There I passed my days lying in the sunshine among the little sandy coves and hollows, listening to the sea and reading Heine. His wit and irreverence and charm infatuated me, for behind them I was aware of a lyrical faith in the future such as I had never thought possible before. Tears came to my eyes as I read, 'Yes, I know that there shall come a day when all men and women will be free and beautiful and live on this earth in joy.' I read over and over again such passages as this:

> An enchanted nightingale sits on a red coral bough in the silent sea, and sings a song of the love of my ancestors; the pearls gaze eagerly from their shells, the wonderful water-flowers tremble with sorrow, the cunning sea-snails, bearing on their backs many-coloured porcelain towers, come creeping onwards, the ocean-roses blush with shame, the yellow, sharp-pointed starfish, and the thousand-hued glassy jelly-fish quiver and stretch, and all swarm and listen.

> Unfortunately, madame, this nightingale song is far too long to be set down here; it is as long as the world itself; even its dedication to Anangis, the God of Love, is as long as all Scott's novels, and there is a passage referring to it in Aristophanes, which in German reads thus:

> > Tiotio, tiotio, tiotinx,
> > Tototo, tototo, tototinx.

Heine's irreverence invigorated me, dispelling the last vestiges of my evangelical piety; so that the more outrageous he was the more virtue I found in him. I was delighted particularly by his description of his schooldays and his struggles with the Latin irregular verbs:

> But, madame, the *verba irregularia*—they are distinguished from the *verbis regularibus* by the fact that in learning them one gets more whippings—are terribly difficult. In the damp arches of the Franciscan cloister near our schoolroom there hung a large crucified Christ of grey wood, a dismal image that even yet at times marches through my dreams and gazes sorrowfully on me with fixed, bleeding eyes—before this image I often stood and prayed, 'Oh, Thou poor and equally tormented

God, if it be possible for Thee, see that I get by heart the
irregular verbs!'

This ironical paganism was like some substance which I
needed for my health, and though Heine renounced it
on the deathbed where he spent so many years, I was
not like him, suffering from spinal consumption, and his
words, though they touched me with compunction, passed
me by: I responded ardently to his youthful errors, and
ignored his mature knowledge. A passage such as the
following seemed an extravagant caricature of my own
attitude:

I was young and arrogant, and it gratified my self-
conceit when I was informed by Hegel that not, as my
grandmother had supposed, He who dwelt in the heavens,
but I myself, here on earth, was God. This silly pride had,
however, by no means an evil influence on me. On the
contrary, it awoke in me the heroic spirit, and at that
period I practised a generosity and self-sacrifice which
completely cast into the shade the most virtuous and
distinguished deeds of the good *bourgeoisie* of virtue, who
did good merely from a sense of duty and in obedience to
the laws of morality. I was myself the living moral law,
and the fountain-head of all right and all authority. I
myself was morality personified; I was incapable of sin,
I was incarnated purity . . . I was all love, and incapable
of hate . . .

Like many other divinities of that revolutionary period,
I was compelled to abdicate ignominiously, and to return
to the lowly life of humanity. I came back into the humble
fold of God's creatures . . . I am too humble to meddle,
as formerly, with the business of Divine Providence. I
am no longer careful for the general good; I no longer
ape the Deity . . . I am only a poor human creature that
is not very well; that is, indeed, very ill. In this pitiable
condition it is a true comfort to me that there is some
one in the heavens above to whom I can incessantly
wail out the litany of my sufferings, especially after
midnight, when Mathilde has sought the repose that she
often sadly needs.

The first picture came close to my wishes. I did not know that, having begun with this food, it would inevitably lead me on, as my state grew more and more difficult to maintain, to a more drastic stimulus: the writings of Nietzsche. For the time being I knew no measure; nothing now but Heine pleased me, for nothing else could keep me in my state of euphoria; and that state was so delightful that I could not bear to give it up, fearing that if I lost it I might subside into my old quagmire.

Heine is associated in my mind with the homely life of Skaill that year. The farm stood on a bay of fine white sand, next door to the church and the churchyard. My Uncle Willie, a gentle bachelor, worked the farm with the help of a farm servant who had grown as silent as himself. Our meals were eaten in a wordless dream. Sometimes my uncle would open his mouth and pay an oblique tribute to events by mentioning the name of some famous prize-fighter or murderer who had been filling the news. Then he would look up at me with his kind, remote eyes, and say reflectively, 'Cheffrey and Chonson' (for the *j* in Orkney was always pronounced *ch*). There would be a silence for a few minutes, and then the farm servant would look up in his turn and say, 'Cheffrey and Chonson,' or if he felt the need for variation, 'Chonson and Cheffrey.' My uncle had a number of these conversational gambits, and as he had once read *Guy Mannering* and had been greatly struck by the character of Dominie Sampson, to the surprise of strangers he often came out with, 'He flourished his arms and shouted, "Prodeegious!"' He was the gentlest and kindest man alive.

My Aunt Sophie was a very different character. She was the youngest of my mother's sisters, and when she was a girl had been pretty and flirtatious. But she had fallen into bad health, and was now a tough old woman with a wrinkled, piratical face and a stringy neck; she perpetually suffered from indigestion, which she described in detail, snatching my hand and clapping it to her flat stomach, and saying that that was where the knot was: could I feel the knot? She had a Rabelaisian tongue, and if she suspected I had been with a girl she would chaff me as roughly as a navvy, chuckling at my blushes. She was avaricious, but kind enough, telling me she must feed me up so that I might pursue the girls with more spirit. Her stomach was a standing theme for realistic description; she seemed to know every part of it separately, but it had two main features: there was the pit of her stomach where she often had a pain, and the legendary knot, which I thought of as an actual knot that would have to be untied. She was always taking patent medicines, sometimes several of them at the same time. She wrote to quacks who advertised in the papers, and read with a purely literary interest the strange dietaries they recommended for her. She would ask me, as one who knew the South (Aberdeen, Edinburgh, and Glasgow were all 'the South' to her), 'Boy, can thu tell me what this stuff they call plaice is?'

'It's a kind of fish,' I would reply.

'And sole, I suppose that's a kind o' fish too?'

'Yes.'

'Weel, I'll just hae to do without them.'

One day, after receiving a letter from one of her quacks, she hopefully asked me to draw a map of her stomach, giving me minute instructions, and clapping my hand to the place again to localize the knot. But the map was beyond my powers.

I had spent all my holidays, after that first one with Willie, in Orkney: it was my one happy fortnight in the year, when all my ailments and cares left me. I spent it partly at Skaill and partly in the house of John Ritch in Kirkwall: he had given up farming and gone back to tailoring. He was more handsome and urbane than ever; merely being with him gave me a deep pleasure, he was so good-looking and agreeable; the only saying of his I can remember is his epitaph on my father, his oldest friend. 'It can be said of Cheems Muir,' he said, 'that he was not only a *good* man, but an *inoffensive* man.' It seems to me the highest praise that could be given to anyone, especially as John Ritch used the word in the old signification, meaning that my father had lived without offence.

My Aunt Maggie was living in Kirkwall now, and I went one afternoon to see her: I did not know that it was for the last time. She had been earthly enough, if ever anyone was:

a soured woman who had had to subdue the rumbling of her stomach with great quantities of baking-soda, the sourness working there too. Now age had matured in her a gentle piety from which I instinctively shrank. When I entered she took my hand in her soft, boneless hand—for even her bones seemed to have grown gentle—and in a piercing voice tried to lead me to Christ. She was living by herself in a little room far back from the street; she asked nothing from life except permission to love without return. I felt shaken in my happiness by that absolute humility which made no claim and yet was so shockingly direct, and tried to withdraw my hand in pity and faint repulsion; but though she would have let it go at once if she had felt my longing to escape, her passionate desire for my salvation made her impervious to everything else, and she held my hand for a long time as she went on pleading with me to come to Christ, now, in the flower of my youth. The little room seemed to be far away from the world where I wanted to be; I was strong, and could easily have torn away my hand and left her; but the soft, impetuous stream of loving words hypnotized me, and I sat on in a sad, reluctant trance. I gave some half-promise at last, longing to escape and not wishing to leave her without some comfort. She died shortly afterwards, and I never saw her again.

Along with some good I had borrowed from Heine a quality which did not become me at that stage of life: a habit of speaking about everything ironically. This complicated my relations with my friends, who did not appreciate irony, especially bad irony. I became ruthless towards sentimentality, like so many people in their early twenties. The reason for this phase is comprehensible enough. It is that a young man is keenly aware of his feelings and at the same time unsure of them. His awareness of them makes him despise conventional emotion, which seems a caricature, and his unsureness makes him distrust deep emotion in case it should be false. He needs a standard of criticism, and, not having it, falls back on sarcasm. Heine had initiated me into the art of feeling and laughing at my feelings; but if one laughs long enough the feeling dwindles, and the laughter usurps its place, until there is very little left to laugh at, unless one manufactures it. My euphoria presently became altogether too impregnated with irony; I actually felt unhappy at times, and that was then a crime in my sight. My belief in the future, which once had made me love all mankind, now showed itself to be inhuman; but as I loved it above everything else I clung to it and let humanity go. I was not interested any longer in descriptions of suffering, for suffering had no place in the vision of mankind I still clung to, where all vice and weakness and deformity were transcended. Reading somewhere a passage from Nietzsche in which pity was condemned as a treachery to man's highest hope, I eagerly embraced it. The thought that the future did not lie with mankind at all, but with the Superman, seemed to be an answer to a question which I had not yet formulated, but whose approach had been secretly troubling me.

All this time I worked on in the beer-bottling office, went out on Sundays with the Clarion Scout Rambling Club, attended Socialist demonstrations and street-corner meetings, and went to Socialist dances. I had struck up a friendship with a likable, handsome young man, Tom M., who had been brought up in a free-thinking, Socialist family. We were both fond of country walks and dances, and disliked the singularity which some Socialists were fond of assuming. As Tom was a member of the I.L.P. I joined it too. Every Sunday evening we attended a speakers' class run by an old and experienced Socialist. Working-class mothers, dock labourers, suffragettes, and all sorts of other people attended the class. Each of us, after a few weeks' instruction, had to get up on a platform and address the others for ten to twenty minutes, after which we had to answer their questions.

With another young man, George L., I attended church literary societies, for he was convinced that the next stage was to convert the churches. He too had been brought up in a free-thinking home, but he had reacted against his upbringing by becoming a primitive Christian. He was a simple, opinionated young man with the empty face of a handsome cleric; one could not imagine him as anything but a bustling Christian; his face gave him no choice.

Having discovered Christianity all by himself, he was convinced that the churches knew nothing whatever about it. Unbelievers he tried to convert by arguments such as that 'God' really meant 'good,' or the principle of goodness, both words having the same root; and he would ask what possible objection they, as reasonable beings, could have to goodness. He discovered that the churches, on the other hand, had never realized that Christ was a socialist, and in his work in the literary societies he did his best to impress this truth upon them. It did not matter what the subject of discussion was—the pessimism of Thomas Hardy, the optimism of George Meredith, the wild flowers of the neighbourhood—George would somehow insinuate into it that Christ was a socialist, and that the churches in ignoring this were making a grave mistake. he invariably brought this out as if it were a striking paradox, for Christianity was still a novel creed to him, and some of its axioms, such as that God is love, seemed novel to him as well, very like the advanced ideas of Ibsen and Shaw. He loved any telling and terse phrase for its own sake, and the assertion that God is love was not an ineffable mystery to him, but merely a neat way of clinching an argument. He produced the tritest statement as if he had just hatched an epigram. He was so sure of himself in this triumphant triteness that any argument against him seemed to him merely an attempt to avoid the issue. A favourite phrase of his was, 'I have no use for *him*.' He had no use for Plato, Shakespeare, Montaigne, Pascal, Hume, Marx, and a host of other writers. He was so supercilious, entrenched in his claptrap, that all the literary societies came to dread him. I tried to retrieve his errors, but I got tired at last of hearing him saying, 'I told them,' for I realized that people dislike to be 'told'; finally I stopped attending him in his rounds. He was an unhappy young man trying to do what good he could with a few threadbare ideas, confident, or apparently confident, that he had the power and the intellectual equipment to convert the churches. All that he did was vitiated by an innocent vanity. He was such a perfect representative of a certain type found in all advanced movements that I am glad I knew him.

About this time I began to take *The New Age*, which had

just come under the control of A. R. Orage. Reading it gave
me a feeling of superiority which was certainly not good
for me; I can still remember with some embarrassment a
phrase of the editor to the effect that the paper was 'written
by gentlemen for gentlemen.' But it stimulated my mind.
It also sharpened my contempt for sentimentality, since,
except for Orage's own political and literary notes, the
tone of the paper was crushingly superior and exclusive,
and some of the contemporary writers for whom I was in
danger of contracting an admiration were treated there with
surprising rudeness. On the strength of this I acquired a
taste for condemnation to which I had no right, and when
any of my friends came to see me, filled with enthusiasm
for some new book, I could crush him with a few words,
though his enthusiasm was genuine and my condemnation
borrowed. But, in spite of this, *The New Age* gave me an
adequate picture of contemporary politics and literature,
a thing I badly needed, and with a few vigorous blows
shortened a process which would otherwise have taken a
long time.

I was still a member of the Clarion Scouts, and still went
out now and then with the rambling club; but presently I
began to ascend towards the more exclusive circles of the
organization, who were facetiously known as 'the intellectuals.' We regarded indulgently the antics of the rambling
club, but did not join in them, as they provided no
opportunity for rational conversation. We went for country
walks of our own, and discussed everything under the sun:
biology, anthropology, history, sex, comparative religion,
even theology, for we did not accept the superstitions of
the mob, such as that 'religion is the opium of the masses,'
some of us being inclined to think that the description
fitted Marxism itself better. We did not go to the Metropole
Theatre on Sunday evening unless some one of real importance was speaking; the mere propagandist or Member of
Parliament was beneath our notice. We followed the literary
and intellectual development of the time, discovering such
writers as Bergson, Sorel, Havelock Ellis, Galsworthy,
Conrad, E.M. Forster, Joyce, and Lawrence, the last two
being contributed by me, for I had seen them mentioned in

The New Age by Ezra Pound. Dostoevski, who was enjoying a vogue, roused a great controversy among us. I was deeply repelled by him, for he brought human suffering home to me in an uncomfortable way, and I still clung to the belief that pity was the deepest treachery to man's ultimate hope. Yet at the same time he fascinated me so thoroughly that I had to go on reading him, and though I felt I was drinking large draughts of poison, I swallowed in quick succession *Crime and Punishment* and *The Idiot*. Eglinton Street and Crown Street rose again at a Siberian distance, as if they had always been somewhere and would always be somewhere. I dismissed them, abruptly stopped my reading of Dostoevski, and in all the arguments over him remained hostile. His grimy world was too close to the grimy life I had cast behind me.

It was the first time that I had listened to or taken part in intelligent conversation. Up to now my mental life had been quite solitary, and though I was always reading and discovering new books to read, there was no one to whom I could talk of them. I lived two lives, a quite private life of intellectual discovery, and another in which the name of a book never escaped my lips and I was careful to behave like everybody else. Now that I could speak and listen freely I was filled with a deep sense of relief and gratitude. The other members of the group knew far more than I did about everything but literature; I had only a distant acquaintance with biology, anthropology, and history, and some of them knew these subjects well. The group was made up of school-teachers, civil servants, clerks, shop assistants, commercial travellers, masons, engineers, typists, nurses; we all demanded and set an intelligent standard of conversation; we were filled with faith in the future and felt that we were on the threshold of a new age, and the excitement of that knowledge quickened our minds and senses. It was the age of Shaw and Wells, by whom all of us swore except myself; for I had taken a dislike to Shaw, his picture of the future seeming to me a mere caricature.

I struck up a closer friendship with one member of the group, George Thomson, who was slightly older than myself and gave me much more than I could give him in return.

He was endlessly interested in history, and he was never tired of bringing up my large speculations on the future against the actual story of mankind. He was a humanist fascinated by the beginnings and development of things, a world which, as my eyes were fixed on ends, I had impatiently ignored. He delighted in poetry, which I had given up for some time on the excuse that the real song had not yet been sung, and that all the poetry of the past was the prolonged echo of a dead or dying world. Gradually I began to realize, as I listened to him, that in dismissing the past I was dismissing all knowledge and all life as life is known; but my realization of this was reluctant: the ghosts of Crown Street and Eglinton Street brooded over it, and behind them lay my first five years in Glasgow, which I could not face. I set myself to read history books, but that record of unsatisfactory approximations, that story of achievement which always turned out to be less than achievement, saddened me and undermined my faith, for if this was how history had worked in the past, how could it be expected to work differently in the future? A passage from Heine came to my mind, and I took it to George, who was also a great admirer of Heine. It was from the story telling how the Emperor Maximilian, as he lay in a dungeon in the Tyrol, was comforted by his sole remaining follower, his Court fool, Kunz von der Rosen.

'Even though thou liest there in fetters thy good right will arise in the end, the day of freedom draws near, a new time begins—my Emperor, the night is over, and the dawn shines outside.'

'Kunz von der Rosen, my Fool, thou errest. Thou hast perhaps mistaken a bright axe for the sun, and the dawn is nothing but blood.'

'No, my Emperor, it is the sun, though it rises in the west—for six thousand years men have always seen it rise in the east—it is high time that for once it made a change in its course.'

I do not know what answer George found for this with his quick mind versed in all the accommodations of history; but whatever it was it did not impress me then; Heine's ironical fancy was merely an excuse for me to laugh at my hopes and, having laughed, to cling to them all the harder.

This state lasted for about three years, and it would have collapsed or faded into a modified humanism if, as I found my idea of the future more and more hard to live up to, I had not come across Nietzsche. One day, feeling that my illusive world was beginning to crumble around me, I plucked up courage and wrote to Orage asking his advice; it was pure impertinence, for the only claim I had upon him was that I read him every week. He wrote me a long and kind letter describing his own intellectual struggles as a young man, and saying that he had been greatly helped by taking up some particular writer and studying everything he wrote, until he felt he knew the workings of a great mind. He had studied Plato for several years in this way, and he was now studying the *Mahabharata*, which he tentatively recommended to me. I took his advice to study a particular writer, but after some hesitation I chose Nietzsche instead of the *Mahabharata*; it was the choice most likely to maintain me in my suspended brooding over the future and the least likely to lead me to wisdom. I did not know German, but a complete English edition of Nietzsche had appeared under the general editorship of Dr Oscar Levy. The volumes were comparatively cheap. I bought them one by one and carefully read them in the evenings, marking passages and returning to them. This went on for more than a year. The idea of a transvaluation of all values intoxicated me with a feeling of false power. I, a poor clerk in a beer-bottling factory, adopted the creed of aristocracy, and, happy until now to be an Orkney man somewhat lost in Glasgow, I began to regard myself, somewhat tentatively, as a 'good European.' I was repelled by many things that I read, such as the counsel to give 'the bungled and botched' a push if I found them going downhill, instead of trying to help them. My Socialism and my Nietzscheanism were quite incompatible, but I refused to recognize it. I did not reflect that if Christianity was a 'slave morality' I was one of the slaves who benefited by it, and that I could make no pretension to belong to the 'master class.' But I had no ability and no wish to criticize Nietzsche's ideas, since they gave me exactly what I wanted: a last desperate foothold on my dying dream of the future. My heart swelled when I read, 'Become what thou art,' and 'Man is something that must be surpassed,' and 'What does not kill me strengthens me.' Yet it swelled coldly; my brain was on fire, but my natural happiness was slipping away from me as I advanced into colder and colder regions and found myself confronted with the forbidding thought of the Eternal Recurrence. I tried, when I came to Nietzsche's last works, *The Twilight of the Idols* and *Ecce Homo*, to ignore the fact that they were tinged with madness, for that was the orthodox Nietzschean standpoint; I did not quite succeed; yet I kept up the pretence. Even when in the midst of all this I was plunged again into squalor on a scale which I had never known before I still remained intellectually a Nietzschean. To support myself I adopted the watchword of 'intellectual honesty,' and in its name committed every conceivable sin against honesty of feeling and honesty in the mere perception of the world with which I daily came into contact. Actually, although I did not know it, my Nietzscheanism was what psychologists call a 'compensation.' I could not face my life as it was, and so I took refuge in the fantasy of the Superman. Already I was beginning to see that my job was at the mercy of any chance; yet I could look forward only to the life of a clerk; and when I thought that I might grow middle-aged and round-backed and grey at that work I was overcome with dejection. But this realization came only at rare moments, when, sitting in the tramcar after my work, I saw nothing but worried, middle-aged clerks sitting round me; and I quickly turned my thoughts in some other direction. A few years before, in my Heine period, I would have felt at least some pity for them; but now, after a year's association with the Superman, they merely filled me with horror. Without admitting it I was very unhappy, and dishonest as well. Apart from all this Nietzsche had ruined my feeling for good English, for many of the volumes were badly translated. When I first began to write, some years later, what I produced was a sort of pinchbeck Nietzschean prose peppered with exclamation marks. I should be astonished at the perversity with which, against my natural inclinations, my judgment, and my everyday experience, I clung to a philosophy so little suited to a clerk in a beer-bottling factory, if I did not realize that it was a 'compensation' without which I should have found it hard to face life at all. 'Be hard' was one of Nietzsche's exhortations, but I was not hard enough even to give up Nietzsche.

Years later, when I was being psychoanalysed, I had a dream about Nietzsche which contained a curious criticism of him and my infatuation with him. I dreamt that I was in a crowd watching a crucifixion. I expected the crucified man to be bearded like Christ, but saw with surprise that he was clean-shaven except for a heavy moustache. It was undoubtedly Nietzsche; he looked as if he had usurped the Cross, though like many a usurper he appeared simultaneously to be perfectly at home on it. He stared round him with an air of defiant possession, as if this were the place he had always been seeking, and had now, with deep astonishment, found—or, rather, conquered—at last; for he was like a man who had violently seized a position which belonged to some one else. His temples were so racked with pain that I could see the nerves twitching and jangling under the thin skin; his thick eyebrows were drawn down in a scowl, but in his eyes there was a look of triumph. I was bewildered by this dream, which seemed at such odds with Nietzsche's philosophy; yet it had the profound naturalness of a dream, the cross seemed to fit the man and the man the cross; and I slowly began to realize that Nietzsche's life had been a curious kind of self-crucifixion, out of pride, not out of love. This dream brought a dream of Nietzsche's own to my mind; I had found it described in Halévy's life. Nietzsche once dreamt that his hand had turned to glass, and in it was sitting a little frog which for some reason he had to swallow. He tried to swallow it several times, convulsed with nausea, but could not. As if I had now identified myself with him, I dreamt a little later, while I was still in Glasgow, a similar dream. I thought I was looking at my hand, when it grew transparent, so that I could see all the veins running and branching through it. As I looked I saw, writhing among the veins, a black devouring worm. I woke in a sick sweat.

The dream was a horrible indication of my state at a time when I considered myself beyond good and evil.

About the same time a change was happening in the office which greatly disturbed me. A foppish little old man with pink cheeks and a clipped grey moustache began to come about the place, and had long consultations with the proprietor and Bob in the room behind the office. Rumours began to go about that the firm was changing hands; Bob's temper became uncertain; we all dreaded that dapper, polite, smooth old man, and rightly, as it turned out. In a little while he assumed control of the firm; my first realization of it came one Saturday morning when I was making up the wages of the workmen. The new owner, who did not know one of them from another, asked to have a look at the wages book, and while I stood beside him he casually ran down the page with a pencil, putting a tick against every second or third name. Then he said, 'These men are to be given a week's notice to-day,' and walked out of the office. I had not realized before the power of an employer over his workmen. I knew all the men who were to be sacked. I went in distress to Bob, but he morosely shrugged his shoulders and told me to do what I was ordered.

Young girls were at once taken on to replace the men. Then one of the clerks in the office was dismissed, and a girl engaged in his place. I felt that my own turn would come next, and as I preferred to leave rather than be asked to leave I began to look out for a new job. At last I got a reply to one of my applications, with a request to call at an office in the town. It was a large, repellently clean office, very unlike the kind, dingy office of the beer-bottling factory. I was shown into a private room, where a tall, grey, weary-looking man and a small, eager, sharp-eyed man put me through a kind of third degree. I did not like them or the look of the office, but they told me that I was not to work in it, but in the office of the factory down in Fairport. I had no idea what would face me there, yet I was eager to leave the beer-bottling office before I could be given the sack. So I closed with the new job, and in pure ignorance walked into a new period of squalor.

CHAPTER FOUR

Fairport

When I left the office in Glasgow I had no picture of the job I was going to. I got out of the train at Fairport on a warm evening at the end of August. I had never been in the town before, and knew nobody there. For some time I stood looking round the station, which was sooty, like all stations in industrial towns, and had a damp, rotting look. As I stood there I became aware of a faint, insinuating smell. I paid no attention to it. I should have done so.

The job I took up in Fairport and kept for two years was a job in a bone factory. This was a place where fresh and decaying bones, gathered from all over Scotland, were flung into furnaces and reduced to charcoal. The charcoal was sold to refineries to purify sugar; the grease was filled into drums and dispatched for some purpose which I no longer remember. The bones, decorated with festoons of slowly writhing, fat yellow maggots, lay in the adjoining railway siding, and were shunted into the factory whenever the furnaces were ready for them. Seagulls, flying up from the estuary, were always about these bones, and the trucks, as they lay in the siding, looked as if they were covered with moving snowdrifts. There were sharp complaints from Glasgow whenever the trucks lay too long in the siding, for the seagulls could gobble up half a hundredweight of maggots in no time, and as the bones had to be paid for by their original weight, and the maggots were part of it, this meant a serious loss to the firm. After one of these complaints the foreman, an Irishman, would go out and let off a few shots at the seagulls, who would rise, suddenly darkening the windows. But in a little while they would be back again.

The bones were yellow and greasy, with little rags of decomposed flesh clinging to them. Raw, they had a strong, sour, penetrating smell. But it was nothing to the stench they gave off when they were shovelled along with the maggots into the furnaces. It was a gentle, clinging, sweet stench, suggesting dissolution and hospitals and slaughter-houses, the odour of drains, and the rancid stink of bad, roasting meat. On hot summer days it stood round the factory like a wall of glass. When the east wind blew it was blown over most of the town. Respectable families sat at their high teas in a well of stink. Many people considered that the smell was good for the health.

The workers in the factory were mostly Protestant Irish. The men were paid fourpence an hour, the women less. The grease of the bones worked into their clothes, their skin, their hair, and under their nails. They carried about with them everywhere the smell of sour fat.

There were old, faithful hands in the place who had spent their lives among the bones. They were morosely feudal, proud that they could speak their minds to young Mr C. without any risk of being sacked. They made free with the bones, humorously flinging them at one another as they sat at their midday meal in the bone-yard; the older ones cynically stirred their tea with a pointed dry bone. There were fights occasionally. Once when the factory was busy a dozen Irish Catholics were taken on, and quietly told not to say anything about their religion. But the Protestants soon smelt them out, and there was a great battle in the yard, with hurtling bones darkening the air. The Catholics, covered with blood and maggots, were hurriedly summoned to the office and paid off.

The firm was conducted on ordinary business lines. Old Mr C. came down from Glasgow several times a week. He was a clean, sharp-eyed, apple-cheeked little man with a wailing voice, who called all his workmen by their Christian names as a compensation for underpaying them. If the trucks were covered with seagulls he would come into the office, look at me reproachfully, and say, 'This will never do, Edwin. This will never do. Where's Robbie?' Robbie being the foreman. But Robbie always had some excuse, and by barefaced flattery and nothing else always sent the old man away pleased. Robbie kept two dogs in the office: a black retriever and a Skye terrier. They brought in rotten bones and fought over them, and then I had to separate them.

Except for making a return of the weight of the bones and enduring their stench during the various stages they passed through, I had nothing to do with the stuff out of which the firm ground its profits. Yet I could not stave off a feeling of degradation. At the beginning I fought against it by doing my work with strict accuracy, maintaining in it a cleanliness which did not exist in the bone-yard. But even that became impossible. When there was some delay in dispatching an order and Glasgow complained, no coherent explanation could ever be got out of Robbie, and I had to improvise one. The other clerk in the office, an older man who had hoped to get my post, jealously kept any knowledge he had to himself. Then the office-boy left to take up a better job, and the Glasgow office sent down a lad who had been found stealing, without letting me know about him. The money in the petty-cash box in my desk began to melt away; I told young Mr C. about it; he seemed to be strangely unconcerned. At last I said that I could not be responsible for the money any longer; old Mr C. was brought down from Glasgow; the office-boy, it seemed, had got hold of a key that fitted my desk; there was an edifying scene, and the boy was indignantly thrust out, dissolved in tears.

Under these difficulties my resolve to conduct my work as if I were in an ordinary office gave way. I became evasive and plausible like Robbie, let my work fall behind, gave vague and comforting replies to the complaints from Glasgow, and everything went well: I was acting as I was expected to act. The more completely I yielded to this weakness, the more my conscience pricked me; but it did not prick me effectively. I would waken in the night, remembering something I had not done, and realizing that my life had gone wrong. I would make up my mind to put things right next day, and apply for another job; but next day came and I did nothing. I applied for many jobs during the first six months, but after I had been a year in the place the letters almost stopped. I felt I should never get out of Fairport. These moments of anxiety and alarm were like stones cast into a stagnant pool, making a few ripples and releasing a faint, unpleasant smell, but doing nothing more.

Part of my degradation came from my relation to the head office in Glasgow. The head office was clean and methodical, and, worst of all, it was generally right. In Fairport we ground out the profits and committed the sins, and it was my job to answer for those sins without casting blame on the offenders. As the sins had begun long before I took up my post they had fixed in the heads of the Glasgow people the conviction that everything done at Fairport was done badly. The daily letters from the head office were accordingly written in a style of uniform insult. I fancy that at the beginning it was adopted out of desperation, for the workings of the Fairport factory were incalculable: if we managed to get an order out in time there was great rejoicing. The head office, on the other hand, was not infallible; for days, sometimes for weeks, it would overlook some glaring omission or blunder, and we would begin to hope that it had been forgotten: then one morning a devastating letter would arrive, from which we knew that some clerk in Glasgow had got into hot water.

I had to reply daily to these complaints. I never admitted that Fairport was to blame, for that was against the rules; but I could not retort to the head office in its own style either, except at the rare times when some one there made a mistake. We lived in Fairport in a state of chronic reprobation, always in the wrong, among the filth and the stench, grinding out the profits. The errors were not made by me, but I had to find an excuse for them and drearily lie them away every day, year in, year out. I ended by acquiring a habitual bad conscience, a constant expectation of being accused.

This was demoralizing enough, and was the origin, I fancy, of the vague fears which pursued me for years afterwards. Still more demoralizing was the mere effect of living among the dirt and stench—the stench in particular. But worst of all was a sort of objective shame that slowly settled within me like a grimy deposit. It was quite unlike the shame a man feels for wrongdoing, being mainly physical. I never had to touch the bones; but the stench from them was so insinuating that I came to believe that I smelt of them like the workers in the yard. I took baths, dressed with great care, and went for long walks on the hills in the evenings and at week-ends; but gradually I found all these precautions relaxing; I grew dingily absentminded, morose, and solitary. The dampness of the climate added to my misery; I always felt wet, and was always catching colds. I had occasional shabby affairs with girls. All the hopes that I had brought from Glasgow withered one by one. At last one night, as I was walking along the Clyde with a friend, I said casually, hardly knowing what I was saying, merely speaking my thoughts, 'If I don't get out of this place I expect I'll jump in there some night.' He gave me a startled look, and shortly afterwards managed to get me a post in an office near Glasgow. I shall be grateful to him all my life.

When one's life is going wrong in one way it seems to go wrong in every way. During my first few months I lodged with a strange collection of landladies. Before I came old Mr C. had got lodgings for me near the factory. They were in the house of a barber, a widower with two daughters who looked after him. On the evening I arrived the elder daughter showed me to the room where I was to sleep. It was a huge room with two double beds, a number of sofas and chairs and wardrobes, a washstand with a mirror above it, and a great unused table islanded in the middle of the floor. The room was so big that in spite of all this miscellaneous furniture it had an empty, forlorn look. I was told by the girl that I was to share one of the beds, the other three occupants of the room being apprentices in her father's hairdressing establishment. I decided not to stay for long.

There were two other, more mature barbers somewhere in the house, a son who played football, and a pious old bachelor who went every morning for a bathe in the Clyde, summer and winter, and could not resist patting the apprentice barbers on the head. They were curly-headed dandies who pursued the flappers on the esplanade every evening in a band, and came back boasting of their exploits. They hardly existed except when they were all together; they were jealous of any interference; they shared everything, their clothes, their ties, their jokes. Housed in that room with the three of them, I was in much the same position as the farmer's new cow among the old herd. They were not rude to me. But they could not make me out. They were like a music-hall troupe playing for their own amusement in a vacuum. I stayed in that fantastic place for two weeks.

My next lodgings were with a neat little maiden lady whom I scarcely saw from the time I went until the time I left. She must have watched my movements very carefully, for every morning when I came back from the bathroom my breakfast was on the table, as if it had appeared by some impersonal agency. My lunch and my high tea materialized in the same way; and if anything kept me late at the office I would find them still there, stone-cold. The only time the landlady appeared was on Saturday, to collect the money for my board. There was a low knock, the door opened, she stood beside it at attention with her eyes lowered, saying nothing, not even admitting that she had a lodger, while I began in a surprised voice, 'Oh, of course. That's right, isn't it?' handing over the money. All this circumspection was not due to shyness, but to fanatical propriety, for I learned that she was a popular church worker. As winter came on it appeared that she was stingy with coal. I met a fellow-boarder, an engineer, one evening in the passage, and he made a conspiratorial sign and came to my room. He too was troubled about the coal question, and told me that he had got into the habit of smuggling in under his coat lumps of coal and logs of wood from the shipyard where he worked. He generously shared them with me. Then one Saturday afternoon I returned unexpectedly from a walk, and found a venerable, white-bearded man sitting in my room before a blazing fire. I had never seen him before. The landlady hurried in, said in a breathless voice, 'This is my father,' and led the old man out growling to himself. I sat and enjoyed the fire, and that evening I told the lady I was going to leave.

But my third lodgings were no better. I was very shortsighted, and I had gone to inspect my new quarters in the evening, after it was dark. The landlady seemed to be a kind, comfortable woman. When I took my things along on Saturday afternoon I found that the windows of my new lodging looked out on the public cemetery, into which a hearse was passing in the cold rain. A fire was on in my room to welcome me, but the chimney was smoking. The landlady, sighing, sidled into the room and said, 'A terrible day! A terrible day!' I opened the window and let out the smoke, and made up my mind that I must leave this place too. But by now my resistance was weakening, and though it seems incredible to me, I remained in that place all winter. I soon caught a cold and had to stay in bed, while the landlady sighed round me. On the day I went back to my work the streets were deep in slush, but warmer weather seemed to be coming. The rest, and the feeling of spring in the air, gave me energy to seek fresh lodgings.

This time I made up my mind to look for them in the neighbouring town of Faldside, a summer resort on the sea, and at the first attempt I was lucky. I found a cheerful, well-run house with nothing but women in it: young Mrs Smith, her mother, a handsome, red-haired, muscular woman, and two little girls, Mrs Smith's daughters. My windows, at the top of a high block of buildings, looked straight out on the fifth and the Highland mountains. This pleasant house filled with feminine chatter should have helped to dispel my sense of guilt; but by now it had eaten into my mind and filled my dreams. Asleep, I turned to images of stagnation and decay. I dreamt of black, worm-eaten jetties, and of jumping into boats which crumbled and gave way at a touch, plunging me into soft, black, muddy water. But worst of all were my dreams about the maggots with their blindly writhing heads melting in the furnace into a soft, rich, yellow mass. Once, as from another world, I had a dream of my mother. She stood before me with her head bowed, so that I could see the parting in her thin hair, which seemed an image of her life of hard work, renunciation, and disappointment; and, looking at it, I took her in my arms and burst into such a passion of weeping that it woke me.

A few years after I left Fairport I wrote an imaginary impression of my life in the bone factory. I wrote it to rid my mind of its poison, but hoped that the impression would turn into a story. It did not. On re-reading it now

I find that it brings back vividly the feeling of those two years. I shall quote a part of it. The 'he' is, of course, myself, and was a device by which I tried, without success, to see my life objectively. I imagine myself going off for my annual holiday.

All the papers in his desk were neatly arranged: he gave them a last glance, let down the lid, and turned the key in the lock. The dusty afternoon sunlight filtered through the window-panes, making the office warm and still; from outside came the bright, shivering clash of wagons bumping against one another in the railway siding. They were still being unloaded; but in a little while silence would fall, broken only by the screaming of the seagulls wheeling over the bones with their rags of flesh. The birds squabbled over the rotting scraps, giving short, strident cries, covering the trucks like a feathery fleece, then rising and separating in wide circles and becoming dark and heavy in the air.

He changed his jacket and, going out, handed his desk key to the checkweighman.

'I'll see you in a fortnight, then? Everything's squared up?'

'Yes. So long.'

He set out for the station. He hastened downhill between the tenements, where the entries were choked with children squalling at play. In a cage outside a top-story window a canary was singing jubilantly; a few young men, fresh and razored and wearing mufflers, bristled on the pavement and stared at him; he had to get into the road. There was his train. He ran down the slope, out of the sun into the dark, clanging station; the train was moving out. He tugged at a carriage door and scrambled in. Just in time.

The train ran into the tunnel with a muffled snort; ran in more deeply, the engine moving far in front in the darkness. He closed his eyes. A fortnight: he was glad to get away. A little clean air, the sight of the sea and hilly country to wash away these piles of rotting bones and those rows of streets steeped in grease and smoke.

He had been in the town for almost a year. He remembered his first morning at the factory. His heart sank as it had done when he found himself first drawing nearer to the heart of that soft, sickening stench which he had sniffed as soon as he set foot in the town: a stench coaxingly suggesting corruption. Ten days before he had interviewed a washed, ruddy old man in a shining office in a town thirty miles away; nothing had been said then about dead animals' bones: he had simply been engaged as a book-keeper at two pounds a week.

He remembered the first days spent in fighting down his disgust. There was a whiff of obscenity in the stench which rose from the bones when they burned in the furnace, and the thick, oily smoke hung about in stagnant coils. On thunder-laden days the smell stood solid in the air, stirring slightly, fanning his cheek as with the brush of soiled wings; at those times it seemed to be palpable, permeating his clothes and coating his skin, and when he reached his lodgings he had to strip and wash all over until he felt clean again. Sometimes he fancied that the smell always clung to him, that it had soaked into his skin and went about with him like a corrupt aura. He had heard that the men and women who worked in the yard, unloading the bones and casting them into the furnace, never got rid of the smell, no matter how they scrubbed. It got among the women's hair and into the pores of their skin. They breathed it into the faces of their lovers when at night, under the hawthorn bushes outside the town, they found a few moments' sensual forgetfulness; they breathed it out with their last breath, infecting the Host which the priest set between their lips, and making it taste of McClintock's bone factory. A thing so tenacious and so vile had given him at first a feeling of mystical revulsion; but he had got used to it; he was almost immune now with the immunity of habituation.

But it was not until he had grasped all the details of the chemistry of which this stench was only the outward symbol that the sense of secret degradation had fallen upon him. First there were the bones, gathered by diligent hands all over the country, on farms, in back streets, in knackers' yards, from butchers' shops; amassed as if they were some precious ore, piled into trucks, and dispatched to the factory. There were bones of cows, oxen, swine, and horses, the last relics of well-tended herds which had browsed in the rich fields of Scotland. Sometimes by mischance a human bone, white and dry, an arm or a skull, would be found among them. But the animals' bones were always juicy and soft, though the fat had gone sour on them, and the marrow inside was beginning to rot. On some of them hung great clots of yellow maggots. which slowly heaved and turned in a heap, crawling over one another in a stagnant but ceaseless blind wave: eager anglers came to the factory and carried away tinfuls. On the maggots and the knots of decaying flesh the seagulls glutted themselves before the trucks could be unloaded. The trucks, one after another, were shunted as quickly as possible into the factory. He had never learned exactly what happened after that. There was some process by which the grease was extracted from the bones; and then the bones, clean and dry, were placed in the furnace and burned until they became black, until they disintegrated into dry, black dust—charcoal. The charcoal was sent to the refineries to purify sugar. So in neat iron drums of fat, in pure dry dust, the awful process of dissolution was violently ended by a clean and indifferent chemistry.

The chemisty was certainly indifferent enough, but its cleanliness was another matter. The dry, sterilized residue lay there at last, but the corruption was diffused in the air which people breathed; it was everywhere, yet beyond attack. There was no getting away from the smell, and everybody in the town was ashamed of it; ashamed as they sat round the supper table with the whiff of it in their nostrils; ashamed that it came in through their windows when they were entertaining visitors.

When the bell rang at midday the men and women sat down and ate their snacks among the bones. They could easily have gone elsewhere, but they would have carried the stench with them, so they stayed.

The train ran out into the sunlight. He let down the window and breathed in the sweet air. The wide estuary lay outstretched before him; a liner was passing up the river, shearing off sections of the hills on the opposite bank and sending out rows of little waves which came dancing to the shore. After its passing the hills lay more quiet in the evening light, and the transparent surface of the estuary smoothed itself out again. A seagull was perched on a buoy far out, a white speck on the suspended gulf.

He stared at it. The seagulls, the free birds screaming over the rags of rotting flesh, chained by desire to the vile trucks; the forsaken bones of dead animals with the stench of dissolution rising from them to betray their hiding-places in refuse heaps or flowering fields; the trucks piled with legs, ribs, skulls, rattling together, festooned by the yellow cable of maggots; McClintock's ostentatious villa with its ugly castellated towers, its spacious garden, the hothouse growing grapes and peaches; the respectable families at supper sitting in a well of stink left in the house by the east wind; McClintock's girls lying under the hawthorn bushes with their lovers, the odour of dead fat rising in sharp whiffs from their hair; and at the centre the stench secretly mounting at the onset of the fire, the fire that could not cleanse, the fire that was not quenched; and finally the clean, arid grains of charcoal: dust to dust. And this quiet arm of the sea, these hills, this pure air: what connexion was there between these things? Perhaps there was only a connexion on the indifferent plane of chemistry, where stench and filth were fortuitous combinations, where degradation was merely an imagination of another kind of consciousness. His mind reached out towards that pure world of chemistry; but he was deeply immured in his consciousness; chemistry could not help him.

At this point the sketch began to go wrong, and I shall not quote any more of it. It shows fairly conclusively that I had sunk into a very bad state. Yet I still went on reading Nietzsche, and into my images of the Superman now came the disquieting picture of a gigantic naked race rolling exuberantly among a hill of dead bones, so far beyond good and evil that my thoughts could no longer follow them. On the other hand, everything that was clean took on an unprotected, almost sickly appearance; the excursion steamers passing up and down the firth with their freight of sun-burnt holiday-makers looked dangerously fragile; the summer finery of the young girls seemed so evanescent that it filled me with apprehension, of what I did not know.

Before I left Glasgow I had had countless friends, but I had not realized that they were not ordinary people; I took their intelligence and sensibility for granted, and thought I should find people like them in Fairport. I soon realized my mistake. After several weeks of solitude I wrote a letter to the local paper suggesting the formation of a discussion club. My letter started a dribble of correspondence, and brought me into contact with a serious, spectacled young man and a dreamy, sentimental young man, who both scoffed at the idea that there could ever be a discussion club in Fairport. Then the correspondence got into the hands of the politicians; a meeting was called in a hall in Faldside; I turned up on the appointed evening and found a crowd of forty or fifty men there. I put my case for a discussion club, but the overwhelming majority were for a parliamentary debating society; I had to give in, and the Faldside Parliament was constituted. Like all similar societies, it was a piece of adult make-believe; we were extravagantly delighted at the chance of calling each other the honourable or right honourable member. The Liberals formed a Government, which was soon thrown out by the Conservatives; I acted as deputy leader of a small Labour group. We debated women's suffrage and unemployment insurance, which were then in the air; and as propaganda was the only excuse our little group had for taking part in these proceedings I was put up one evening to outline the Socialist remedy for society. As the debate was about real things it was a success, and every one spoke better than usual. But afterwards routine re-established itself, and the Parliament ground on more and more wearily, expiring, as far as I can remember, over a particularly tough budget.

The only profit I got out of the debating society was a friendship. After my speech on Socialism the Liberal Home Secretary, David P., a dark, handsome young man, came over to congratulate me, and we walked home together. After that we were close friends for many years, first at Faldside, then in Glasgow, then in London. David was the son of a well-to-do merchant in Glasgow, a very pious man with a strong sense of duty, who made many sacrifices for his religious beliefs. David had suffered from acute agoraphobia from childhood. His family did all they could for him in the light of the knowledge available at the time, and he often assured me of their kindness and unselfishness. They were evangelical Christians of the best type, but they did not understand his state, and regarded it as something which would have to be amended by discipline. At seven he was terrified by the thought that he had committed the sin against the Holy Ghost. When he went to school his journey each day was a torture; on coming to an open space he felt his breath leaving him. He fought against the obsession, but uselessly.

On leaving school David was sent to learn carpentering, as it was considered that he needed an open-air life. His real interest was in intellectual things, and particularly in social questions. He became an agnostic and a Socialist; his father, now concerned about him, decided that he should enter the Army. David went to Piershill Barracks, Edinburgh, and on his eighteenth birthday enlisted in the 17th Lancers, choosing that regiment because of the skull and crossbones on the regimental cap. In less than a year he was sent to the military hospital at Edinburgh Castle, from which he was invalided with valvular heart trouble and neurasthenia.

After a year at home he went to Canada, where he was an actor in a play called *Remorse*, a sailor on Lake Ontario, a waiter in a ten-cent restaurant, and a graphologist. His old illness returned, and, too proud to write home, unable to get work, he presently found himself starving. At last he collapsed in the street and was taken to hospital. Inquiries were made, and he was sent home a complete wreck. The only people in Canada who befriended him were the nuns at St Joseph's Convent in Toronto. Many years later, when he was a successful journalist in London, he wrote to the Mother Superior thanking her for her kindness to him. The letter was pinned up as an encouragement to the nuns to be merciful to poor men.

After he returned from Canada he hovered on the border-line for many years. Once when very ill the thought came to him, almost as if a voice had spoken, 'You have work to do which no one else can do. You must help to abolish war.' He remained true to this resolve ever afterwards, working for peace and founding an arbitration league which attracted the support of several well-known men.

At the time when I met him David was working for the local paper in Fairport. He was tall and strongly made, handsome and well dressed, and eagerly interested in every one he met. The only sign of his malady was a slight twitch of the head, which gave a distinction, a touch of mystery to his good looks, as a small defect often does. He was one of the most courageous, kind, and sincere people I have ever known; but his disability, which he concealed out of a sense of shame, had made him build up a system of little disguises and excuses, and turned him into an actor whose tricks sometimes deceived himself when he was required to produce them, though he laughed over them afterwards with sardonic enjoyment. As he was handsome and agreeable, women were attracted to him, and when they showed it the actor, the secondary David, could not resist going through his paces: he would come to me saying that he had made a fool of himself again. These affairs were quite harmless, but finally he made a vow that he would always travel to and from Fairport in a smoking compartment: at that time women never thought of entering such places.

David was filled with a love of humanity which I could not feel at that time. He would stop beside beggars and street-hawkers and have long talks with them; he could be perfectly natural with anyone; it was as if to him the class divisions did not exist, and he saw people simply as human beings. For this reason he was liked by all except the rigidly respectable, who were suspicious of a man who showed no sign of severity to poverty and vice. He did not know what censoriousness was; he never blamed anyone but himself. Even after his talks with beggars he always saw himself as playing a part, though the impulse which made him speak to them was perfectly sincere and perfectly in accordance with his nature. Though he was a Socialist, he liked to poke fun at the social revolution and the class struggle; yet if by some fantastic chance a revolution had broken out in Faldside he would have been the first to man the barricades: afterwards he would have laughed or groaned and decided that he had made a fool of himself again. His character was so natural and spontaneous that often he did not know when he was acting; and he would brood over some kind action of his, wondering if it were the real thing after all. He was a perfect friend, infinitely sensitive and understanding, eager to forgive and be forgiven. I do not know what I should have done without him during those two years.

Afterwards I made another friend, Bob S., a clerk like myself, who shamed me into joining the clerks' trade union and brought me in contact with the local Labour movement. I kept my friendship with David and him separate, knowing that they did not have much in common, and that they would not get on with each other. Bob was a reader of *The New Age*, and a man of remarkable character: the most single-minded, honourable man I have ever known. Like myself, he had picked up his education as best he could, and he was eager to apply it for the benefit of his fellow-workers; yet he never referred to them except in abusive terms, and pounced on sentimentality as if it were a deadlier enemy than Capitalism itself. In a debate he could be crushing, and one retort of his gives the flavour of his wit. 'I have a great respect,' he said, 'for the ideas of Christ and Karl Marx. My quarrel with the previous speaker is that he takes his economics from Christ and his religion from Marx.' His wit often nonplussed people, but he refused to adulterate it, and enjoyed their confusion. He was kind, generous, ruthless in argument, but scrupulously amenable to reason, admitting a mistake at once if it were proved against him. He, his younger brother Edward, and myself spent a great deal of our time plotting for the public good and the discomfiture of climbers and sentimentalists. We had not a single thought for our own advantage.

In spite of these friendships I was physically and spiritually in a bad way. My stomach trouble returned again, spreading the old, dirty film over my walks, my books, even my talks with my friends, to whom, out of a feeling of shame, I said nothing about it. I went to doctors and got various remedies which did me no good; one doctor, a big, brosy man, recommended me to take a large plate of porridge last thing every night to keep down the fermentation. I did this and suffered for it. As the second winter came round I caught a racking cough which would not leave me; I grew thinner and thinner, and at last had to take to my bed, where I stayed for several weeks. The doctor was afraid that my lungs were affected, but decided eventually that they were not. At last I tottered back to the office again, to the stench and the fighting dogs; old Mr C., who felt he had been getting no return for the salary he had been paying me all these weeks, was wounded to the heart, and gave me a sad, reproachful look.

During these months when I was tormented by my stomach and racked by my cough I had another Heine phase; yet this time, instead of helping me to recover, it merely weakened what resistance I had left. I had got hold of a collection of his shorter poems in the 'Canterbury Poets,' translated by a number of well-known writers. There is, as well as exquisite wit, a sickly, graveyard strain in Heine's poetry. It was this that attracted me now. I battened on tombs and shrouds. I cannot remember more than one or two of these poems now, though I knew many of them then by heart. There was one in particular beginning:

> Night lay upon my eyelids,
>   Upon my mouth lay lead;
> With rigid brain and bosom
>   I lay among the dead.

The dead man as he lies like this hears a knocking at his grave, and his sweetheart saying, 'Will you not rise up,

Heinrich? The eternal day is breaking, the dead have risen, the everlasting joys have begun.' The dead man answers, 'My darling, I cannot rise, for I am blind; my eyes are quite ruined with weeping.' His sweetheart exhorts him again, and he answers that he cannot rise because his heart is pierced by her sharp words, and his head shattered by the bullet he fired into it when she jilted him. At last her pleading moves him and he tries to rise. 'Then my wounds burst open, blood poured from my head and breast, and lo, I am awake!'

This poem, with its sickly lingering on death, took a deep hold on me. I identified myself with the dead man who knew so well that he was dead. Something in myself was buried, and I was only half there as I worked in the office and wandered about the roads. I felt that I had gone far away from myself; I could see myself as from a distance, a pallid, ill-nourished, vulnerable young man in a world bursting with dangerous energy. About this time, during a visit to Glasgow, I went to a music-hall one Saturday night. When the warm lights over the little sunk space where the orchestra played started out far beneath me I could feel energy flowing into me from these little, distant, inhuman points: it was a forlorn and solitary comfort. That was a sort of measure of my isolation. The world retreated from me with all its shapes; I found myself gazing at things, hillsides, woods, ships, houses, trifling objects in shop-windows, with a dry yearning. It was like a repetition of my state at Helye, but this time the cause of it was probably the intense effort I needed to shut my senses to the sights and smells of the bone factory; this had become a habit, so that I shut them as well to ordinary and pleasant things. Looking across at night at the lighted towns on the other side of the estuary, I felt an intense desire to be there instead of where I was, as if distance itself would give me relief and happiness.

My infatuation with Heine fed this mood, and when I read his poem about the pine-tree in the frozen north which dreamt of a palm in the south it was like a reflection of my own state. Some of the poems moved me by their imaginative power alone; the following one, for instance, of which I give a rough prose translation:

The night is wet and stormy, the heavens empty of stars; I wander silently in the woods, under the rustling branches.

A light glimmers from the lonely hunter's cottage; it must not tempt me, for things there are in a bad way.

The blind grandmother is sitting in the leather arm-chair, rigid and uncanny as an image, without opening her mouth.

The forester's red-haired son walks about cursing, and flings his musket on the wall, and laughs with rage and scorn.

The lovely spinner is crying and wetting the flax with her tears; her father's hound lies whimpering at her feet.

That still moves me as it did then, by the beauty and strangeness of the picture. But it was the poems filled with distance and isolation that really took hold of me and seemed to be specially meant for me. The word *einsam* ('lonely') recurs over and over again in Heine's poetry: the lonely cottage, the lonely man in his grave, the lonely pine-tree, and always the lonely Heine. I steeped myself in that sweet poison, and began to write lonely, ironic, slightly corpse-like poems, which I sent to Orage, who accepted them. I was twenty-six, and it was my first attempt at writing. When, a little later, I discovered Baudelaire, the shock of reading a man who was genuinely possessed by death, and not merely coquetting with the shroud and the tomb, cured me of that infatuation.

About this time *The New Age* was bringing out its proposals for National Guilds as an alternative to State Socialism, and on another plane of my mind, a clean, dry plane, I was an enthusiastic advocate of the new theories. In elaborating the idea of the Guilds Orage and his collaborators tried to combine the best in Syndicalism with the best in State Socialism. The Guilds, when they were formed, were to belong to the nation, but were to be controlled by the workmen employed in them; the bureaucrat was so far as possible to be eliminated. It was a clear and comprehensive plan for a workers' republic. The machinery for realizing it was there: the Trade Unions, which were incipient Guilds. The idea caught on; the Trade Unions were powerful at the time, the Shop Stewards movement was beginning. The outbreak of the European War did not destroy the movement; on the Clyde at least it grew stronger for some time afterwards, and a group there, of whom I was one, brought out a little monthly paper called *The Guildsman*, which had a respectable circulation. But the end of the War left the Trade Unions weak; Orage himself, under Major Douglas's influence, became convinced that nothing could be done so long as the monopoly of the banks remained unbroken, and the idea of National Guilds was forgotten. It was one of the most satisfactory plans for a Socialist State which have ever been attempted in this country. The real criticism of it is probably Carlyle's criticism of the Abbé Sieyès: that it is easy to make a constitution, the confoundedly difficult thing being to get people to come and live under it.

From Heine, the bones and the fripperies of shrouds and tombs, I escaped a little while after the outbreak of war, when my friend got me a post in his office. I took my stomach trouble and the remnants of my cough with me, and went on attending doctors, until I found a 'nature cure' doctor who actually did me some good. I was now twenty-seven, and among those who should be enlisting in the Army. In my state of incipient dissociation the prospect seemed to one part of me a matter of indifference, and to another a nightmare whose crest was curling to engulf me. At last, one winter evening, after wandering about the wet streets for hours and passing and repassing the Glasgow recruiting office, I went in, climbed the stairs, and found myself in a room filled with young men, well-dressed, ill-dressed, stout, thin, healthy, sick, confident. What brought me there, my own conscience or the universal suggestion that I should be there, I did not know. The room, when I entered it, seemed to be filled with dread and misery; whether it came from the other young men or from myself I have no idea: it seemed to be simply there, an element into which I had stepped, and which I now breathed and smelt. A young officer who seemed to be on the verge of a breakdown, as if the dread were sitting on his shoulders too, impatiently got us into line and told us to bare our heads and repeat the oath after him. A little distance from me a pale, round-faced young man with naked, staring eyes was standing with his head curiously bent; when the order was given to uncover he put up his hand and touched his cap hesitatingly, but without raising it. The young officer shouted at him, and at last he raised his cap, exposing a perfectly hairless skull: it was as if by a horrible conjuring trick he had taken off his cap and his hair at the same time. Every one looked away. The young officer blushed scarlet and stammered, 'I'm sorry, but you must obey orders here, you know.' As I went out I passed at the top of the stair an old officer in the uniform of a Highland regiment, sitting resting in a chair; he raised his eyes and gave me a look of profound, impersonal pity. Eventually I was not taken for the Army.

During the War I worked in a shipbuilding office. In the long tramway journeys from my lodgings in Glasgow to my work I began to teach myself French, of which I had only a smattering, reading straight through Molière and becoming infatuated with Stendhal, to whom Nietzsche had given his blessing. I read a great number of Socialist books as well, such as Hyndman's summary of Marx, and *National Guilds*, a book edited by Orage, which had just come out, and *Authority, Liberty, and Function*, by Ramiro de Maeztu, a Spanish writer who foreshadowed the Syndicalist State, and who was influencing Orage at the time. I remember one of the clerks taking Maeztu's book out of my hand when I arrived one morning, turning over a few pages, and then saying, 'Jesus Christ, Ned, do you *read* thae books?' But by this time I had grown so absent-minded, or 'dozened,' as one of the clerks called it, so absorbed in my own dissociation, that what would have been snubbed in anyone else as affectation or showing off was dismissed in my case with an indulgent shrug.

The National Guilds League had now been started, and a branch set up in Glasgow. The soul of the branch was

John Paton, a young draughtsman with a genius for ideas and action. He died many years ago; if he had lived he would have made his mark on the Labour movement and would have changed it for the better, for he had intellectual integrity, a clear conception of means and ends, brilliant practical capacity, and on the top of these a natural vitality and charm which no one could resist. Our little group was very busy during the winters: we made a thorough study of the book on National Guilds; we addressed meetings and brought out *The Guildsman*, for which Paton wrote the editorials. We tried to mitigate in it the exclusive note struck by *The New Age*. In summer we went out for rambles round Glasgow, and at one time contracted a passion for Chesterton's drinking songs, bawling out, 'Old Noah he had an ostrich farm' and 'God made the wicked Grocer' at the public-houses and tea-rooms with synthetic gusto, to show that we were good fellows, as intellectuals at that time felt constrained to do.

A great deal of my time was spent in an atmosphere of National Guilds; the members of our group became close friends and were always in one another's houses. At the same time, quite separately, I was carrying on a number of affairs with girls, which never went very far and never lasted for long: their number and their transience were symptoms of my neurotic state. They had started before I left Glasgow to go to Fairport, where for two years they stopped almost completely. Now they began again. All these affairs, some more, some less serious, were falsified by the fact that I was really puritanical while I thought myself 'emancipated.' They provided an almost continuous background to my life, a changing drama in which each new affair had all the excitement of an adventure and an escape. My main effort all this time, though I did not know it, was to escape from myself; my Nietzscheanism and my Socialism were escapes; but the most effectual escape was that series of absent-minded affairs with one woman after another, each of them leading nowhere except to another affair. It was a sort of illicit musical accompaniment to life. I was too deeply enclosed in my blind, inward unhappiness to know what I was doing, or to let a momentary pleasure escape me.

During my years in Fairport I had experienced now and then an anxious vague dread which I could not explain or attach to any object. Its real cause, I feel pretty certain, was my work in the bone-yard. This state now grew worse, or I became more conscious of it, realizing that it was bound up with my feeling of separation and yearning. Standing before a shop-window, or taking a country walk, I would waken with a start, conscious that for some time I had been staring at some chance object, a ring in a jeweller's shop, or a hill in the distance, with a dry, defeated longing. It was as if I could grasp what was before my eyes only by an enormous effort, and even then an invisible barrier, a wall of distance, separated me from it. I moved in a crystalline globe or bubble, insulated from the life around me, yet filled with desire to reach it, to be at the very heart of it and lose myself there. I was most subject to this state when I was by myself, but I sometimes felt it when I was with other people, so that my absent-mindedness became fantastic, and my friends, when they were out with me, would look round anxiously, as if they were afraid I would get lost. My state made me seek company with desperate eagerness; I was more sociable and more lonely than I had ever been before. I often woke in the night with this feeling of mingled longing and dread, and when I began to read Dante much later and came to the passage describing the souls approaching the river of Acheron I recognized my own state:

> e pronti sono a trapassar lo rio,
> chè la divina giustizia li sprona
> sì, che la tema si volge in disio.

'And they are quick to cross the river, for Divine Justice spurs them on, so that dread is transformed to longing.' But in my case it was longing that seemed to be transformed to dread: I stared at things for which I did not care a farthing, as if I wanted to attach myself to them for ever, to lose myself in a hill or a tiny gewgaw in a shop-window, creep into it, and be secure there. But at the same time dread raised its walls round me, cutting me off; for even while I yearned for these things I felt a hidden menace in them, so that the simplest object was dangerous and might destroy me. A memory of this state returns whenever I read Wordsworth's lines in *The Affliction of Margaret*:

> My apprehensions come in crowds;
>   I dread the rustling of the grass;
> The very shadows of the clouds
>   Have power to shake me as they pass.

A jagged stone or a thistle seemed to be bursting with malice, as if they had been put in the world to cut and gash; the dashing of breakers on rocks terrified me, for I was both the wave and the rock; it was as though I were both too close to things and immeasurably distant from them.

I remember my great relief one day when for a few moments this obsession left me and I saw things without fear, as they were. I was crossing the Clyde on a train one Saturday afternoon; a soft west wind was blowing, and the river was yellow and swollen with rain. I could feel that great volume of water flowing through me, flooding my veins with its energy, sweeping the fear from my mind. I woke now and then to such realizations, like a drowning man coming up for air. But I lived for most of these years in a sort of submarine world of glassy lights and distorted shapes, enclosed in a diver's bell which had grown to my shoulders.

It was during this time that I began to take up writing, still under the influence of Nietzsche. I produced a series of short notes or aphorisms which appeared weekly in *The New Age* under the heading of 'We Moderns,' and were afterwards published in book form; the book is now out of print, I am glad to say. In these notes I generalized in excited ignorance on creative love and the difference between it and pity, which I unhesitatingly condemned; I pointed out such facts as that humility is really inverted pride, and that the true antithesis of love is not hate but sympathy: whenever I hit upon a paradox which lay conveniently near the surface I took it for the final truth. My aphorisms, as they came from an inward excitement, excited some of the readers of *The New Age*; but the excitement was merely another escape, a lyrical refusal to come down to earth. I flapped bravely enough in the void, like Arnold's Shelley, but my wings were synthetic, and did not really fan the air. The perpetration of the book left me naked; the wings, having performed their act, fell from me; I felt the lack of them greatly, but was the better for it. After being unhappy for a long time without realizing it, I was now genuinely unhappy; and though I did not know it, there was a possibility of amendment for me.

While I was writing my aphorisms I came to know Francis George Scott and Denis Saurat. Saurat was then lecturing on French at Glasgow University. Scott was a school teacher at the time, and already writing those exquisite songs which will be remembered when the more popular music of our time is forgotten. He and Saurat were fast friends, continually visiting each other and discussing music and Saurat's system of ideas, which he had already thrown into the form which they take in *The Three Conventions*. Both men accepted me warmly into their circle, and two new worlds, the world of music and the world of intuitive speculation, opened before me. Saurat, with his eager generosity, found in my half-baked generalizations points of agreement with his own ideas. He read his dialogues to me one day, and they excited me with a sense of following a mind thinking ahead of me. I often read them still, moved again by some illuminating thought, but the total scheme outlined in them does not fit the framework of my own mind.

I knew very little about music when I met Scott. I had never seen a piano until I was fourteen or fifteen; the only classical music I had heard up till then was the Dead March out of *Saul*, played by a brass band in Kirkwall at the funeral of a sailor who had died there during a visit of the Channel Fleet. Until I was twenty-two or -three I had been interested only in evangelical religion, Socialism, and literature. My reading of Nietzsche had one good effect: his passionate love for music, his perpetual references to Mozart, Beethoven, Schubert, and, of course, Bizet, had encouraged me to attend the concerts of the Scottish Orchestra in St Andrew's Halls. These had sometimes bored me and sometimes moved me in a vague, undifferentiated way; I went on attending them more out of a sense of duty than a feeling of pleasure, being resolved to acquire 'culture' by hook or by crook. As I came to know Scott my preconceptions about music scaled away at the realization that this was a man who exercised actual musical power; I learned to listen to music as it was, still very uncertainly, but at least with an honest ear, and without worrying about Nietzsche's generalizations on what music 'should' be. For a time I took a more intense pleasure in it than in poetry, and could not have enough of it.

I do not know how widely Francis George Scott's songs are known; the best work is often the least advertised; and a composer who writes music for Scottish songs is at a crucial disadvantage, since his work is almost certain not to be sung by English singers to English audiences, though German, Italian, and French songs may pass as a matter of course. If Scott had written settings of English songs he would have been universally recognized as a musician of genius; but he was rooted in Scotland; his thoughts and feelings, his extravagance, his Rabelaisianism, his witty sense of form with its touch of excess, the form of Dunbar not of Spenser, were Scottish through and through. He was born to revive Scottish music, and in spite of every obstacle he has continued to do so, creating one masterpiece after another with hardly a murmur of recognition from his countrymen. His songs have a wide range, running from the wildest humour to a tender delicacy of feeling which, if it were not his own, one would call French. He had a deep admiration for France.

I was struck from the start by the contrast between Scott's explosive vitality and the extreme delicacy and grace of his songs. Like some other people from the Borders, he had a fine Caesarean head, cut so vigorously that you thought you could still hear the thud of the hammer on the chisel. He was blunt and uncompromising, yet delighted by the most fantastic notions, which he carried to wild lengths out of sheer enjoyment; then, without warning, he would make some remark which brought the whole structure down, while he listened with delight to the crash. Along with this he had the finest delicacy of feeling, which he showed to those who knew him well; but usually he was as explosive as Landor, whom he resembled in some ways, particularly in the combination of great vitality with the utmost perfection of form: I mean the exquisite Landor of the poetry, not of the prose writings. There was no musician in Glasgow with whom he would have deigned to discuss music; so he had to be content with Saurat, who knew a good deal about it, and myself, who knew very little, but was eager to learn. These days in Glasgow with Scott and Saurat were too delightful for me to attempt the impossible task of analysing their fragrance.

In the early winter of 1918 I met Willa Anderson, who had stopped at Glasgow on her way to London, where she lived. I wrote to her in the beginning of 1919 asking her if we could meet again. We met that spring, fell in love, and were married in summer. I was still a clerk in the shipbuilding office, and she was a lecturer in a women's college in London. I went down there in June. We got married at a registry office, had a short honeymoon at Sheringham, and returned again to our work. In September, after spending a few weeks at her mother's house in Montrose, we both went down to London without a job between us, with very little money, and with hopes over which our sensible friends shook their heads. If my wife had not encouraged me it is unlikely that I should have taken the plunge myself; I was still paralysed by my inward conflict. My marriage was the most fortunate event in my life.

CHAPTER FIVE

London

We set up house in Guilford Street and began to look for work. The weather was bright and dry, and the trees in the parks were putting on their autumn colours; the atmosphere had the suspended stillness which comes when the year is hesitating on the turn: a crystal density in which even the roar of the traffic seemed muffled and remote. We too existed in a suspended state, waiting for work, not really apprehensive, for we could not imagine the possibility of not finding it: the work was there, invisible for the present, and one day it would appear. When we were tired of looking for it we went to Kensington Gardens, and in complete idleness dreamt through the afternoons. At last, after we had been in London for two weeks and our money was running low, we both found work on the same day: Willa as a teacher in a cramming college, and myself as a clerk in an office where I had to make up little parcels from morning to night. Our work was hard and uninteresting, but we were glad to have it, and had no doubt that we should soon find something more suitable.

My fears still troubled me, and the feeling that I was plunged among several millions of people who seemed to be quite kind, but with a different kindness from that which I had been accustomed to, an alien, tangential kindness, disconcerted me. The mass of stone, brick, and mortar was daunting; the impersonal glance of the Londoner, so different from the inquisitive glance of Glasgow, gave me the feeling that I did not really exist; and my mingled dread and longing now turned upon itself and reversed its direction, so that as I gazed at an object or a face—it did not matter which, for the choice was not mine—I was no longer trying to establish a connexion with it, but hoping that it—whether animate or inanimate—would establish a connexion with me and prove to me that I existed. The vast solidity of my surroundings and my own craving emptiness threw me into a slightly feverish state, drove fear up into my throat, and made my lips dry, while at the centre of myself I tried to assemble my powers and assert something there, though what I did not know.

This was not a constant state, but came and went in the most disconcerting way. Willa's hope kept us going. We worked on, tired out every night, upheld by nothing but that hope, which was nevertheless so strong that the feeling these days give me in memory is one of happiness. In a few months we both went down with influenza and had to nurse each other, attended by a young Russian doctor, a friend of my wife, who lent us some money to recuperate in an hotel at Crowborough. As we got better we went for walks over the heath to the neighbouring villages; it was my first sight of the Southern English countryside, and I fell in love with it at once. In the hotel sitting-room we talked with gentle old ladies who were more strange to my Scottish eyes than a strange tribe; old ladies who did not seem to have made up their minds, like the ones I had known in Scotland, but to have had their minds made up for them by some curious, esoteric, masculine process. Among them, and attached to one of them, was a young man of extraordinary cold beauty. The morning before he left the hotel he abruptly began to talk to us—there was no one else in the room—and told us that he had discovered the secret of everlasting life. Existence, he explained, was an endless ring which by some disastrous accident had been broken. All that was needed, therefore, was to find the ends and join them, and this could be done by so controlling the chemical processes of the body as to produce a self-subsistent balance, an everlasting, living stasis. He had been experimenting for some years upon himself, and he had now reached this state. His looks and his composure were so godlike, and such a calm confidence radiated from him, that we were profoundly impressed. It was an extraordinary encounter, and I have often wondered since what became of him. We exchanged addresses, promising to write; but we never wrote, and now I have forgotten even his name.

Since coming to London we had been seeing Orage now and then. When we returned from Crowborough he offered me the post of assistant to him on *The New Age*; the salary was a small one, but my job would not take up more than three days a week, and would give me time to look for additional work. About the same time a large shop in the West End made Willa head of a continuation school for their work-girls. The post, unlike mine, was well paid, and when I got an additional job as dramatic critic for *The Scotsman* and occasional reviewing work for *The Athenæum*, then edited by John Middleton Murry, we were comparatively well off, and Willa's hopes were more than justified. We were working hard, but at work which interested us. We were meeting more and more people. My sense of being in an alien place wore off when I realized that at this or that address there was some one I knew, and my fears became more infrequent.

My adjustment to London was greatly complicated by something which happened shortly after I went there. For some years *The New Age* had been publishing articles on psychoanalysis, in which Freud's and Jung's theories were discussed from every angle, philosophical, religious, and literary, as well as scientific. The conception of the unconscious seemed to throw new light on every human problem and change its terms, and the False Dawnists (to use Hugh Kingsmill's phrase), of whom I was one, snatched at it as the revelation which was to transform the whole world of perception. Orage himself was deeply interested in it at that time, though later he came to regard it as a misleading path. He saw that I was not in a good state, and with the mixture of active benevolence and diplomacy which characterized him spoke about me to an analyst, a brilliant and charming man who one evening invited me round to see him. I went, not suspecting any plot for my good, was greeted kindly, and then asked some blunt questions which greatly shocked me. At the end the analyst told me that he would like to analyse me for the mere interest of the thing, and without asking for any payment. In spite of the fears that had been tormenting me for so long, I still did not admit to myself that I was a neurotic needing the help he freely offered me; but I had read a good deal about psychoanalysis, the experiment itself attracted me, and I accepted. I have been glad ever since that I did, and will always feel grateful for the kindness of the analyst.

The few months which followed were very painful. I do not know whether the experience of other people who have been analysed is the same as mine; perhaps the resistance which I put up was more obstinate than most, and this may have intensified my discomfort. For my new self-knowledge, as it grew, had to burst through that resistance, making great breaches and gashes in it, while I desperately tried to close them up again and preserve intact my old flattering image of myself. While my conscious mind was putting up this fight, my unconscious, like a treacherous spy, was enthusiastically working for the analyst. I had not dreamed for a long time; I had lain like Heine's dead man every night in a blank nonentity, and no ghostly hand had knocked on my grave. Now dreams began to come in crowds; every night I had more of them than I could keep count of; the notebook in which I jotted them down to take to the analyst was soon filled, and I had to begin another; there seemed to be no end to the inventive windings of my psyche. But as soon as the analyst started to interpret these dreams my resistance returned; I refused to admit their disreputable meanings, or agreed with a sceptical smile; yet after leaving him I was shaken with disgust and dread of myself. At last, by painful stages, I reached a state which resembled conviction of sin, though formulated in different terms. I realized the elementary fact that every one, like myself, was troubled by sensual desires and thoughts, by unacknowledged failures and frustrations causing self-hatred and hatred of others, by dead memories of shame and grief which had been shovelled underground long since because they could not be borne. I saw that my lot was the human lot, that when I faced my own unvarnished likeness I was one among all men and women, all of whom had the same desires and thoughts, the same failures and frustrations, the same unacknowledged hatred of themselves and others, the same hidden shames and griefs, and that if they confronted these things they could win a certain liberation from them. It was really a conviction of sin, but even more a realization of Original Sin. It took a long time to crystallize. It was not a welcome realization, for nothing is harder than to look at yourself. My whole world of ideas invisibly changed; the Superman, after attending me so faithfully, took himself off without a word after his appearance on the cross, and I could not see even a perfectly analysed human being as a Superman. My own analysis was never finished; it had to be broken off when my wife and I left London. It was not till nine months after that, when we were staying in Prague, that I knew how much good the analyst had done me: my vague fears, I realized one day, were quite gone.

The analysis was very painful, then, especially for the first few months; so much stuff gushed up from my dreams that the effort of facing it was a prolonged nervous and moral strain. I fell into a curious state, and had trances and visions. My unconscious mind, having unloaded itself, seemed to have become transparent, so that myths and legends entered it without resistance and passed into my dreams and daydreams. This happened a few weeks after the beginning of the analysis, and it began with a feeling that I had caught some illness; this in turn passed into a trance.

One evening after working in the office I came back at six o'clock feeling ill. I lay down on the couch in the sitting-room with my face to the wall. Willa was sitting at the table behind me, correcting examination papers for the cramming college; I listened to the sheets rustling as she turned them over, and they seemed to make a curiously loud noise in the room. Then my breathing too grew louder and—this is the only way in which I can describe it—deliberate at the same time, as if I were breathing because I had willed it, not because I could not help it: the first act or rehearsal of breath. I felt my breast rising and falling, and something pressing upon it which I flung off and drew back again. This turned into a great, dark blue wave of sea-water, advancing and receding. A dark blue seascape opened on the lighted wall before me, a dark blue sky arched over it; and as if I had slipped out of my body I was standing on the shore

looking at the waves rolling in. A little distance out a naked
woman was posted; the waves dashed against her, washing
up to her breasts and falling again; but she never moved;
she seemed to be fixed there like a statue rising out of some
other dimension.

Then everything vanished and I was at the bottom of
the sea, with the waves far above me. When I came up
again—all this time I was lying on the couch listening to
the rustling of the papers behind me—the sea and the sky
were perfectly white like paper; in the distance some black
jagged rocks stuck out of the stagnant water: there was no
colour anywhere but black and white. I began to swim at
a great speed (at this time I had not yet learned to swim)
towards the nearest rock. Round me countless creatures
were circling and diving, glass-coloured in the white sea:
long cylinders about the length of a man, without heads
or tails, mouths or eyes. I reached the rock and put out
my hand to draw myself up, when one of these creatures
fixed itself by the upper end, which seemed to have a little
sucker, to the middle of my brow just above my eyes. Filled
with rage, I kicked the creature with my bare toes; at last I
kicked through it, and it fell like a broken bottle into the
sea. All this time I had no fear. I pulled myself to the top
of the rock.

After this my memory of the dream is fragmentary for a
while. I think that it must have been an unbroken sequence,
but the pictures followed one another at such a speed that
I could not catch all of them. What I remember next
is wandering through a rough woodland country inter-
spersed with little brown rocks, where there were troops
of low-browed, golden-haired, silent creatures somewhat
like monkeys, while I saw in the distance a procession of
white-robed female figures slowly passing as if to silent
music. I wandered there, it seemed to me, for a long
time. I remember coming to what I thought was the green,
mossy trunk of a fallen tree; as I looked at it I saw that it
was a dragon, and that it was slowly weeping its eyes into
a little heap before it: the eyes were like brooches, ringed
blue and red and white, hard and enamelled, so that they
tinkled as they fell. All this seemed natural to me; each pair

of eyes as they fell appearing to be pushed out by other eyes behind them.

Here there was another break in the dream. The next scene was quite different. I was in a wild, rocky place, treeless and shrubless, and in the middle of it I came to an enormous white palace. The walls were high and windowless, and there was only one small door. I went up to it and pushed. The door opened at once, but when I took my hand away shut again, and would not open a second time. Then I saw a small opening, about three feet square, just beside the door. Creeping through it, I stepped on to the balcony of a great hall. Looking up, I could see the roof far above me; but downward the hall went farther than my eyes could follow, and seemed to sink deep into the ground. This lower part was covered with wooden scaffoldings, and was obviously under repair, though no workmen could be seen; the place seemed to have been deserted for a long time. I climbed on to the balustrade, raised my hands above my head, and dived. I had fallen head downward for a great distance, when my hand caught a beam of one of the scaffoldings, and I began to climb upward again, hand over hand, at a great speed, with the ease of an ape. I did not stop until my head was touching the ceiling and I could go no farther. Again I was filled with rage. I beat my head against the ceiling, which was thick and decorated with fine mouldings, and broke through it. Above, there was a broad terrace lined with cypresses; night had fallen, and the dark blue sky was glittering with stars. Tall, robed men were walking with melodramatic stateliness along the terrace, under the trees.

There was another break here, and when I caught the dream again I was standing beside a little mountain pool fringed with rushes. The sky had the whitish bruised look which it sometimes has before sunrise. As I looked at it I saw two little clouds like scraps of paper slowly floating towards each other, and for the first time I was afraid, I could not tell why. The two clouds met, blazed up, and turned into an angry sun. The sun began to revolve across the sky. As it revolved two serpents, one red and the other yellow, broke through its crust and began a furious locked battle. Still revolving, bearing the battling serpents with it, the sun burst into flames and in a moment turned to ashes. Black now, it went on wheeling across the paper-white sky. Then it stopped; its periphery trembled and quivered, and I saw that it was legged like a centipede. It began to come down diagonally towards me, walking on an invisible thread like a spider. As it came near I saw that it was a fabulous creature with an armoured body and a head somewhat like the prow of a sailing-ship, the head being partly that of a woman and partly that of a bird. Its body was jointed in the middle, and looked like two enormous tortoises one on the top of the other. I saw now that I was naked and holding a broad sword in my hands. I lifted up the sword, swung it over my shoulder, and struck the creature on the brow. The blow made no alteration. I raised the sword again and struck harder, but the stroke merely pushed the head back. In a fury I thrust the sword into the beast's side at the joint of the armour; then it turned its head and *smiled* at me. This inflamed my fury past all bounds; I twisted the sword round and round; the mail burst open; something with white wings, robed in white, fluttered into the sky; and the creature drew its torn mail round it like an umbrella shutting, thrust its beak into the ground, and shot out of sight.

I think there was another break here, though not a long one. The next I remember is seeing countless angels flying high up in the air, going through absurd and lovely evolutions, looping the loop, hiding behind the edges of clouds: the whole sky was filled with them. I watched an ordered formation of them flying over a still stretch of water, so that I could see them reflected in it as they passed above me in their flight. Then I was in the air, and when I was a little distance up some one took my hand: it was my wife. We flew up, now and then dropping extravagant curtsies to each other in the air, with a wide and light sweep, keeping our wings still. After a while I noticed that the wing on the shoulder next to her had fallen off, and looking at her I saw that the wing on her corresponding shoulder had disappeared too, so that we were mounting the air on two wings. After we had flown like this for a while we looked down and saw a great crowd ranged in concentric rings beneath us, and in the middle of it a gigantic figure clad in antique armour, sitting on a throne with a naked sword at his side. We flew down and settled on his shoulders, and bending behind his neck kissed each other.

When this waking dream, or trance, or vision ended I was quite well; all my sickness had gone. I astonished Willa by telling her about it; we discussed it for a long time, and then I wrote it down in my notebook along with my other dreams. Next day was the day for seeing my analyst; I handed the notebook to him, and there was a long silence. At last I asked him what he made of the dream, and told him that I had been awake the whole time, conscious of the light of the lamp and the rustling of the papers behind me. He said something about its being a myth of the creation, and warned me that my unconscious was far too near the surface for my comfort and safety, and that I should hurry to put something substantial between myself and it. The advice seemed sensible, but not of the slightest use to me; I knew of no substance which I could suddenly improvise as a buffer against myself; I might as well have been told to add a cubit to my stature. We agreed that it would be best not to analyse the dream, after I had tentatively suggested that it seemed to point to immortality, and he had retorted, 'Aha! That would flatter your vanity nicely, wouldn't it? Very nice to think that a revelation has been specially arranged for you!' And he indicated the sexual symbolism of the dream, which by this time I could read for myself: the tubular animals, the two-handed sword, the dragon shedding its eyes. Yet these things, though obvious enough, did not seem applicable to the dream, which was unearthly, or rather unhuman, and so in a sense unsexual. I tried to give him an idea of the vividness and rapidity of the pictures, more exhilarating than any I had ever found in actual life or in poetry, each detail perfectly finished before it melted in an instant into the next. I could not tell him how long the dream had lasted; it might have been half an hour, it might have been no more than a few minutes. But I felt that it took up far less time than the time required to put it into words.

It was decided, then, that we should not discuss the dream

and the curious circumstances in which I had dreamt it: this
might be more fitting at a later stage of the analysis. But
similar dreams or walking trances followed, especially when
I was about to fall asleep. There are not many of these, for
I soon discovered that I could stop them or let them go on
at will. In one of them I dreamed, in this semi-awake state,
that I was in a small circular room hung with red velvet, with
a cushioned seat running round the walls. The smallness of
the room, and the red hangings and furniture, for everything
was red, oppressed me dreadfully; but what troubled me
most was that I was quite alone and at a great height.
How I had been lured there I did not know, but cunning
and treachery of some strange kind had been involved in
it. Suddenly I realized I was in a star, millions of miles
from every one I knew, and that the circular room was
really the inside of the star. Its smallness, and particularly
the oppressive softness and elegance of its furnishings, the
cushioned softness of a padded cell, filled me with such fear
and forsakenness that I could hardly breathe. But worst of
all was the dreadful sensation of height. I searched the walls,
and at last saw, as if it were my salvation, a small window. I
went over to the window and opened it, then climbed on to
the sill and looked down. Far below I could see a little bank
of cloud touched by a faint radiance, and I knew that on the
other side of it was the earth. An overpowering longing to
be down there came over me. I lifted my hands over my
head and dived. I remember nothing after this until I cut
through the cloud and caught sight of the earth still so far
beneath me that I could see all one side of it. I saw that it
was a great grey ball completely covered with ice. I was quite
near it before I realized that I should be broken to pieces
by my fall, and at that my soul shot out of my body and
hung on the air a little above the ground, watching my body
hurtling down. I saw it striking the ice and lying outspread
and shattered: I looked at it objectively, with a touch of
pity, but with no fear. After a while a black, smooth-skinned
animal somewhat like a walrus, but much bigger, came out
of a hole in the ice, went over to my body, and sniffed it.
The great beast looked sad and kindly, but after sniffing
my body ate it up in a businesslike way and went back into

the hole again. I waited still, hanging on the air, for I knew that something else would happen. And after a while I saw myself coming out of the hole, reborn, with a sun-coloured serpent wrapped round my breast, its head resting on my shoulder. As I walked on new grass sprang under my feet and on either side of me.

I realize that this dream, like the first one, would have to be put down to naïve spiritual vanity if it was really invented by me and did not 'come' to me, as I felt at the time it did, and as I feel still: it was not 'I' who dreamt it, but something else which the psychologists call the racial unconscious, and for which there are other names. Some of my remaining dreams were not so flattering. In one I was in a primitive boat with two other men somewhere in the Far North, and we were fending off a grotesque roaring sea-beast, half fish and half animal. I struck at it with a clumsy oar, but it snatched the oar in its teeth and pulled it out of my hands. My terror broke off the dream at this point; my last picture is of the boat and the three of us in it with no weapon against the enormous beast but our hands.

Another of these waking dreams, a mere picture, was still more terrifying. I saw myself standing at the entrance to a pass in mountainous country, and a group of men standing round me. I was unarmed and they were armed, and there was no pity in their faces. The sun was setting; the spears glittered red; and I knew that this was my last hour.

All these waking dreams I took to my analyst, who was now growing concerned about me. I told him again that I could let them go on or stop them, and asked him what he advised me to do. He strongly advised me to stop them. I did as he bade me, and my waking dreams ceased at once, and have never come back again. I doubt now whether I was right in stopping them; I feel that if I had let these visions continue they would have ceased at their own time, instead of at mine. On the other hand, I may have been too close at this stage to the border-line between sanity and insanity; but I do not for a moment believe it. The analyst was concerned for the health of my mind, he was trying to bring me back to normality, whatever that is, and I do not see what other advice he could have given me.

I did not know at the time what to do with these mythological dreams, and I do not know yet; I used the trance for a poem, but a poem seems a trifling result from such an experience. The analyst himself never returned to it again, and his theory that the dream was a myth of the creation does not satisfy me; for while the first part of it points back to the beginning of things, with the first large breathings, the undifferentiated creatures, and the absence of fear (as if consciousness had not yet begun, and fear with it), the last part extends beyond time altogether; and the battle with the wheeling sun, which, after running through all its revolutions, becomes the sphinx, is the last battle with time, after which time, having gathered its torn mail around it and vanished into the grave which timelessly waits for it, releases the spirit into eternity. A discernible pattern certainly runs through the dream, but if it is anything it is the pattern of man's evolution and ultimate destiny, not of the creation: the whole dream is concerned with our beginning and our end. On the other hand, there are things in it to which I can attach no clear meaning; the whole episode of the palace, half above and half under the ground, is quite incomprehensible to me. The sun in its revolutions and transmutations is a fantastic image of time, and that is probably why its first appearance evoked my first sense of fear. The woman or statue at the beginning, whom I saw when I was still so far from human consciousness that I could swim among the headless, eyeless sea-creatures without fear, as if I were one of them, seemed to belong to another millennium, and to be a prophecy of a remote future age; as if, long before the existence of mankind, the animal soul were dreaming of it and yearning towards it. The female figures passing in the distance in their white robes, while I wandered among the golden-haired animals, had the same mysterious prophetic air. The longing to fling myself down from a height (which comes into both dreams) is immediately associated with the analyst's exhortations to come down to earth, to accept reality; but it also brings to my mind images of the Fall and of the first incarnation, that of Adam, and another image as well, which is my image of timeless human life as the intersection and interpenetration of a stationary beam falling from heaven and the craving, aspiring dust rising for ever to meet it, in denial or submission, in ignorance or comprehension.

Und Einer steht darunter
Sein Leben lang.

If I had more credulity, or more faith, or perhaps more knowledge, I might accept as a truth this intuition that long before man appeared on the earth he existed as a dream or a prophecy in the animal soul; but I do not have that credulity, or faith, or knowledge, so that while there is a sense in which I accept the trance as a revelation of truth, my mind, accustomed to deal with a different kind of experience and apparently fitted only for that, questions each separate detail, finding riddles and discrepancies and reminiscences. The armoured figure on the throne with the naked sword by his side was clearly a picture of Jehovah, the God of battles; the angels were the conventional angels of the Christmas calendars, except that in movement they were so wayward and divinely frivolous, expressing the very extravagance of complete liberty. Their conformity to the established notion of an angel, instead of making them unreal, made them more convincing, giving them the actuality of a rare species of which one has often read, about which there has been some controversy, and which one now sees with one's own eyes. On the other hand, the dragon and the sphinx seemed to be completely self-created; so far as I know there was no subject-matter in my mind from which I could have fashioned them. And the whole atmosphere of the dream was strange and astonishing: its exhilarating speed, its objective glory, above all its complete lack of all that is usually meant by human.

When I dreamed this dream I had already got over the worst of my infatuation for Nietzsche, and after a period of dismissing immortality as an imputation on earthly life and the purity of immediate perception I had tentatively begun to believe in it again. So that the dream did not actually convert me to that belief. But it very much strengthened and at the same time modified it. Some light is thrown on my state of mind at this period in a letter from a new friend of mine, John Holms, who reported to Hugh Kingsmill his first encounter with me. We met for the first time in Glasgow one Sunday morning in the summer of 1919 as I was setting out for a walk in the country. Hugh Kingsmill, whom I already knew, had brought Holms along to see me, but afterwards had to leave for Bridge of Allan. Holms wrote:

I had a delightful afternoon with old Muir; we wandered about the country from two till nine—talking incessantly. . . . Metaphysics almost all the time. Of course, his whole outlook is purely Nietzschean—there is really no one else. But though he is a bit limited, he feels it all so intensely that one does not mind.

Talking about the tragic view and so on, and the happiness to be got out of misery, he admitted that owing to his bloody life he may have tried to believe what he does—but justified himself, of course, on the line of W. James's *Will to Believe*, which makes it perfectly true for him. The really interesting part of it is—as he probably told you—that he was brought up by intensely religious people, and that at fourteen he was 'saved,' and went through perfectly genuine ecstasy, though of a very hysterical kind, for several weeks. The keynote was resigning his will to Christ—i.e., the denial of his own individuality, and of any responsibility. By the way, beauty never influenced him at this time at all. The next two years were more and more unpleasant, the ecstasy, which was at bottom only artificial stimulation, not won at any price, having faded, and the unnatural life and mental outlook withering him up. Then came Nietzsche, whom he read straight through, with the inevitable result. He now looks back on the time of his 'salvation' with absolute spiritual nausea. He won't even walk near the country he used to frequent then. It is extraordinarily interesting, entirely confirming by experience my purely intuitive nausea at all that kind of thing. The result is, of course, that any kind of mysticism annoys him. Unity with beauty or anything else he won't have at any price, because it means surrendering his personality. He far prefers the idea of Nietzsche's eternal return to the union which is at the heart of every mystic's vision, and the longing for which is one's—mine, at any rate—deepest emotion when moved by beauty. The two ecstasies are, of course, as far apart as heaven and hell. The most obvious distinction is the sense of beauty, which is absent in the one, but implicit in every word of the real mystic. The first tries to get there by renouncing all exertion—an attempt at premature birth—whereas, like everything else in this bloody world, it can only be won by using all one's energies at extreme tension, in the effort to attain complete expression. And, according to all the mystics, Christ included, the supreme height of individual self-expression, and union with the universe, are one. Energy is the royal road to rest.

E.M. is explained by his nationality just as much as by his life. I am sure Muir has never experienced profound emotion through beauty—he has read very little poetry. Their habit of mind is moral and metaphysical. Any writer not concerned with the universal, or with moral problems from a metaphysical point of view, he is inclined to wash out. Swift, for instance, he at first shrugged at, and then grudgingly conceded to be good. His virulence about Pater surprised me—simply, at bottom, because he was concerned with nothing but beauty, and [Muir] would not take even that from life.

It was an extraordinarily lovely evening; not a breath of wind, the hedges covered with roses, the heat quivering in all the distant valleys . . . I hadn't caught my emotions as a child so often and so vividly for a long time, but Muir would have little of it. He wanted a roaring gale to inspire him and to fight with physically. So obviously to that type of mind the idea of the absolute as rest, as union with beauty, or whatever you like to call it, is merely boring. W. James, up to a point a very acute intelligence, is just the same. My own belief in the absolute—interpreted even in the widest possible sense—wavers considerably; and I am almost entirely convinced that our personality as we are conscious of it at present ceases to exist. Muir only understands the absolute with his intellect—i.e., by the words with which one tries to explain it, which, of course, is impossible. Logically I can pull the absolute to pieces as well, and in as many ways, as anyone else can.

. . . He said that, though his views on immortality were not settled, he was inclined to believe in the eternal survival of personality, which strikes me as horrible, and also, luckily, as absurd—and that not merely from the will to 'disbelieve.'

I am the half-way house between him and you. With all my metaphysical leanings, I have a lot of Shakespeare and Rabelais, and I found it impossible to talk to the old man freely about women. When I mentioned them once or twice he was apparently quite sympathetic, but really in a totally different world of thought.

That, I suspect, is a true description of me as I was during that last year in Glasgow; a better description than I myself could give. Holms saw, as I was incapable of seeing then, that my belief in the ideas of Nietzsche was a willed belief, and that in my struggle to maintain myself against fantastic odds personality had become my last desperate defence. But I never realized that I had pushed my belief in personality to the repulsive length of believing or wishing my personality to live for ever. Holms's remark that I would not take even beauty from life makes me realize that my struggle for survival was harder than I thought; so that the union of which he spoke probably appeared to me as a surrender, an ignominious acceptance of a world where all I could become was an ageing, round-backed clerk. My life since fourteen had been a struggle; I could not accept anything that weakened me or appeared to weaken me in that struggle; and union, no matter with what, doubtless seemed to me a sort of treachery. Here my mingled longing and dread came in again, concealing from me the fact that the results of acceptance are strength and faith, not weakness. My belief in the deathlessness of my personality was merely a projection of my will, an idea without imaginative content, consisting of 'the words with which one tries to explain it,' which, as Holms said, was impossible.

My trance gave me an inkling that my personality at least

was not and could not be immortal, unless immortality was another name for hell; and when I tried to conceive what was enduring in me beyond the second-rate, ramshackle structure which I had built with time's collaboration, I could not see it in terms of any form or substance for which time had a parallel; in time form and substance are synonyms of separation and bondage, and what the soul strives for and is made for is boundless union and freedom. I realized that immortality is not an idea or a belief, but a state of being in which man keeps alive in himself his perception of that boundless union and freedom, which he can faintly apprehend in time, though its consummation lies beyond time. This realization that human life is not fulfilled in our world, but reaches through all eternity, would have been rejected by me some years before as an act of treachery to man's earthly hopes; but now, in a different way, it was a confirmation of them, for only a race of immortal spirits could create a world fit for immortal spirits to inhabit. This was, of course, an enormous simplification, but it saved me from the more monstrous simplification that 'religion is the opium of the masses,' and that our hope of ultimate union and freedom is a mere mirage leading us away from the concrete possibility of achieving union and freedom in a human society. The theory that the soul is immortal was not invented as a pretext for keeping the rich from being made uncomfortable, or to provide texts to quote against the class-conscious workers in the late nineteenth and early twentieth centuries.

While these things were becoming clearer to me I went on working for *The New Age*, still writing articles of a Nietzschean cast. My relations with Orage were somewhat uneasy at first, and this was my fault. In Glasgow I had contracted a sort of reverence for him, and it was strengthened by his great kindness to me when I went to London. At the same time my 'personality,' hardened by my long struggle for existence, shied at the very idea of discipleship; yet that idea was suggested to me by my great respect for Orage, the difference in our ages, his superiority to me in experience and knowledge, and my position as his assistant. He was a man who naturally attracted disciples. In some cases he became accustomed to the relation; in others it bored him, though he was so courteous that he patiently endured it. I might have been the better for becoming his disciple for a while, but my 'personality' revolted; perhaps there was something more in my resistance than the mere resolve to remain myself as I saw myself. The struggle was not so much a struggle with Orage as with myself; it was I who wished to be a disciple, and I who revolted against the thought of being a disciple. Orage was uncannily sensitive; he felt that I was rebelling against him or some idea of him, and he did not know what to do with me. He had begun by advising me in all sorts of ways, and if my attitude to him had not been so complicated his advice would have been of great help to me; but when he saw that it was not taken he grew sparing of it, and that disappointed me still more. I ignored his advice out of sheer absent-mindedness; but absent-mindedness is generally a disguise for obstinacy. On the other hand, I felt that Orage did not take the nature of my gifts into account at all, or even recognize my limitations. He wanted to train me to write the 'Notes of the Week,' which he had himself written almost without a break ever since he had taken over *The New Age*. He could make himself do whatever his mind told him he should do; he had trained this power systematically. But I was capable of doing only one thing, which was to write what I thought, in my own way. I did not have Orage's intense interest in politics. I did not possess real political intelligence, and although in Orage himself this would merely have inspired him to acquire an interest in politics and create in himself a political intelligence, in me it had the opposite effect; I thought that if I yielded I should be unfaithful to what talent I had. Orage at last gave up his attempt to get me to write the 'Notes of the Week,' and uncomplainingly continued them himself. But he often looked at me with perplexity and a touch of impatience. When I met him again later on, after his years of discipleship to Gurdjieff at Fontainebleau and in the United States, our relations were far easier and friendlier; yet I felt that I never knew him intimately.

Orage was one of the most brilliant talkers I have ever listened to, particularly on the border-line where conversation meets discussion. He did not have the lyrical imaginative power of Æ, who was a great crony of his, or the rich spontaneous genius of Hugh Kingsmill, or the first-hand reality of John Holms. His mind was peculiarly lucid and sinuous, and could flow round any object, touching it, defining it, laving it, and leaving it with a new clarity in the mind. From a few stammering words he could divine a thought you were struggling to express, and, as if his mind were an objective clarifying element, in a few minutes he could return it to you cleansed of its impurities and expressed in better words than you could have found yourself. This power was so uncanny that at first it disconcerted me, as if it were a new kind of thought-reading. Sometimes the thought was not quite the thought I had had in mind, and then I was reassured; perhaps, indeed, it was never quite the same thought, though it came surprisingly close to it. He was a born collaborator, a born midwife of ideas, and consequently a born editor. His mind went out with an active sympathy to meet everything that was presented to it, whether trifling or serious; and his mere consideration of it, the fact that his intelligence had worked on it, robbed it of its triviality and raised it to the level of rational discourse.

As a man he lived on the plane of antique virtue, and like Plutarch's heroes roused admiration not so much for his inborn genius as for his conduct of his life, his formulation and control of his endowments. Consequently, his life had a style, like his writings: a style achieved by a conscious discipline which he concealed from the world, letting it speak for itself. First thoughts did not excite him, as they excited me, except to the formulation of second thoughts; and all his life, it seems to me, was spent in an effort to find a second thought, perhaps a second personality, which would satisfy his idea of virtue and knowledge and conform to his taste. He had an extreme faith in the power of man to create out of himself by conscious discipline the image which lies buried in him; and I remember his once saying to my wife and myself that if he were given a child of five, no matter what its 'gifts' were, he could make a genius of it. He had dealt with himself in the same faith, and ever since his youth had taken up and followed creeds which seemed to provide a short-cut to intellectual and spiritual power. He had been a theosophist, a member of a magic circle which included Yeats, a Nietzschean, and a student of Hindu religion and philosophy. He was convinced that there was a secret knowledge behind the knowledge given to the famous prophets and philosophers, and for the acquisition of that knowledge and the intellectual and spiritual power it would bring with it he was prepared to sacrifice everything and take upon him any labour, no matter how humble or wearisome or abstruse. It was this that made him throw up *The New Age* a few months after I had left it, and put himself under Gurdjieff's direction at Fontainebleau. I was in Prague at the time, and he wrote to me saying how sorry he was that I was not in London, since I too might have listened to that remarkable man. I know nothing of the school at Fontainebleau except by hearsay, and when I met Orage several years later he seemed to be the same Orage, except that he was a little younger and wittier. In *The New English Weekly*, which he started some months after his return, he took up political writing again; but this time he did not succeed in gathering the younger writers around him, as he had done in *The New Age*. He returned to a generation which was strange to him, a generation political in a way which repelled him, encased in a watertight time philosophy, impervious to the spiritual battle which he had waged all his life, a generation which rejected such things, calling them 'mysticism.'

During these first few months in London he tried to start my wife and myself in the practice of yoga, counselling us to recite morning and evening for five or ten minutes, 'Brighter than the sun, purer than the snow, subtler than the air is the Self, the spirit within my heart. I am that Self, that Self am I.' My wife treated the suggestion ironically, but I tried for a little while to carry it out without the requisite faith. He advised us also to run over everything we had done each day before going to sleep at night, all our errors and offences clearly, but without exasperation or discouragement, and afterwards to meditate on some abstract quality, such as courage or love or beauty, emptying our minds of all our preconceptions about it and waiting for it to enclose us and sink into us. These counsels were wise, but we did not follow them, or followed them only for a little while; and it gives some idea of the greatness of Orage's character that he himself observed such disciplines, and far more austere and difficult ones, for the greater part of his life. He did not speak of it; he disliked solemnity and false seriousness; outwardly he was a man of the world, witty, urbane, often malicious, as Æ could be too, another man who had his secret disciplines. But the effect of Orage's extraordinary spiritual effort, sustained for so many years, could be felt by anyone who met him; it gave him an unspoken ascendancy, a charm (in both senses of the word) which was peculiar to himself. In spite of my complicated feelings towards him, I ended by surrendering to that charm, recognizing that it was his legitimate right.

The New Age had passed its brilliant peak when I joined it. Ezra Pound was still writing for it; I did not see very much of him, but enough to share his spontaneous kindness to writers. Dmitri Mitrinović, a tall, dark, bullet-headed Serbian with the lips of a Roman soldier and an erratic, soaring mind, had a great influence on Orage at this time, and contributed an extraordinary weekly survey of world affairs to *The New Age*, written in an English of his own, filled with energy, but difficult to understand. He was a man for whom only the vast processes of time existed. He did not look a few centuries ahead like Shaw and Wells, but to distant millenniums, which to his apocalyptic mind were as near and vivid as tomorrow. He flung out the wildest and deepest thoughts pell-mell, seeing whole tracts of history in a flash, the flash of the axe with which he hewed a way for himself through them, sending dynasties and civilizations flying. He and Orage broke off their connexion after Orage put himself under the direction of Gurdjieff; they remained friends, but each went his own way. Mitrinović was often in our house; he would arrive with a large bottle of beer under each arm and talk endlessly about the universe, the creation of the animals, the destiny of man, the nature of Adam Kadmon, the influence of the stars, the objective science of criticism (for he held that it was possible to determine the exact greatness of every poet, painter, and musician and set it down in mathematical terms), and a host of things which I have since forgotten. After I returned to London several years later I saw him once, but we had changed so much during the interval, each in a different way, that we could not resume our old relations. Or it may have been that the world itself had changed too much.

For in these first years after the War, in spite of the disillusionment everywhere, in spite of *Ulysses* and *Eminent Victorians* and *Crome Yellow* and *H. S. Mauberley* and *The Love Song of J. Alfred Prufrock*, the circle which surrounded Orage still lived in an atmosphere of vast hopes. Orage himself had an exact enough conception of the state of society, and saw the dangers which lay ahead, and his hopes existed on a different plane; but in Mitrinović the apocalyptic disasters which had overtaken Europe merely engendered apocalyptic expectations; since history itself had become incredible the incredible was now the rule. About this time Orage lent me a book called *The Rosicrucian Cosmo-Conception*, by an obscure American writer, telling me that if I did not read it too critically I might get something out of it. Mitrinović lent me simultaneously a French book whose name I have forgotten, which described the history of man since his birth in Atlantis, when he was a headless emanation with flames shooting from his open neck; and he too told me that if I did not read it too critically I might get something out of it. The Rosicrucian book described in the style of a country newspaper all the spiritual dominations, principalities, and powers, giving the exact numbers and functions of each. I asked Orage what authority the author had for this information, and Orage gave the only sensible reply to such a question, which was that I should have to decide about that for myself. I said then that I could not believe a book so badly written could be a revelation, for a man who had seen the angelic orders in their glory would be forced to speak the language of inspiration. I cannot remember how the discussion ended, but Orage did not lend me any more of that kind of mystical literature.

The French book was written on the assumption that, as man's year is made up of 365 days, so the year of history, or of all mankind, is made up of 365 years. On this computation man was, I think, a schoolboy during the great age of Athens, and adolescent at the time of Queen Elizabeth; I remember this because of the proof given in support of it—that at this time he began to take up smoking. The French author had come to the conclusion, working on this unit, that man would presently come of age, and that afterwards things would go much better. I mention this book because it expressed, somewhat extravagantly, Mitrinović's way of looking at human life, and also something in Orage's secret philosophy which he carefully kept in check, but to which he could not help giving way every now and then. As mankind was a great man to Mitrinović, mightily growing through the vast years of history, so the different races and nations were parts of that great man, all with their separate functions, which in their inter-working made up the synthetic instrument of his soul. Germany, Russia, France, China, England, were such functions, and when they grew bloated or atrophied great disasters were brought about. It was a colossally simplified view of history which justified one in foreseeing any calamity and in nursing any hope.

I met Janko Lavrin too at this time, and was captivated by his charm. Through him we came to know some painters; we attended studio parties, and were soon acquainted with so many people that we could not find time to do our work. It was this that made us leave London after two years for Prague, at Janko Lavrin's suggestion. Janko knew most of Europe. Born in Slovenia, he had attended the universities of Vienna, Prague, and Oslo; he had been military correspondent for the Russian newspaper *Novoyé Vremya* on the Montenegrin front during the War; he had visited Mount Athos, had stayed in monasteries in Finland, had made walking tours in the Caucasus, and hiked to Persia; he had been everywhere, and his stories of his wanderings enchanted us. He advised us to go to Prague as being in the middle of Europe, and as having the best beer and the best ham that could be found anywhere. We did not return again for four years.

But my chief friend in London and for many years afterwards was John Holms. After the meeting which he

described in his letter we met often in London, where he
was passing through a very bad time over a love affair.

He was ten years younger than myself; he belonged to a
different class (he had been to Rugby and Sandhurst); and
he was of a different nationality. On his father's side he
was partly Scottish and partly Irish; on his mother's he was
descended from John Ferrar, the brother of Nicholas Ferrar,
who founded the religious community of Little Gidding
in the seventeenth century. He had been intended for the
Army, and had joined a battalion of the Highland Light
Infantry at the end of 1915, when he was seventeen. He
won the Military Cross during the War, but I only came
to know this indirectly and by chance years after I had
met him; I think he regarded the distinction as slightly
comic and disreputable. He was captured by the Germans
in 1917, and spent the rest of the War as a prisoner, a year
at Karlsruhe and seven months at Mainz; it was during
this time that he began his lifelong friendship with Hugh
Kingsmill, who was also a prisoner of war then.

Holms was tall and lean, with a fine Elizabethan brow and
auburn, curly hair, brown eyes with an animal sadness in
them, a large, somewhat sensual mouth, and a little pointed
beard which he twirled when he was searching for a word.
At Rugby he had been a prize athlete, but there was a
strange contrast between his instinctive certainty as a physical being and the lethargy and awkwardness of his will. In
his movements he was like a powerful cat; he loved to climb
trees or anything else that could be climbed, and he had all
sorts of odd accomplishments: he could scuttle along on all
fours at a great speed without bending his knees; walking,
on the other hand, bored him. He had the immobility of a
cat too, and could sit for long stretches without stirring; but
then he seemed to be filled with a boundless melancholy,
as if he were a prisoner shut deep within himself, beyond
rescue. His body seemed to fit him for every enjoyment,
and his will for every frustration. Though his sole ambition
was to be a writer, the mere act of writing was an enormous
obstacle to him: it was as if the technique of action were
beyond his grasp, a simple, banal, but incomprehensible
mystery. He knew his weakness, and it filled him with the

fear that, in spite of the gifts which he knew he had, he would never be able to express them: the knowledge and the fear finally reached a stationary condition and reduced him to impotence. He was persecuted by dreadful dreams and nightmares.

His mind had power, clarity, and order, and, turned on any subject, was like a spell which made things assume their true shapes and appear in their original relation to one another, as on the first day. His talk often gave the same impression; it was clumsy and without surface brilliance; he often could not finish a sentence; but through it walked and lumbered the original ideas of things, with their first dark or radiant lineaments. His talk had an extraordinary solidity which made even the best serious talk seem flimsy or commonplace. It was always first-hand and objective, except when he was speaking of certain great writers with whom he could not help indirectly comparing himself.

He clung with the same childish pertinacity to certain lines of poetry, especially those which gave him a private delight or what he called 'a thick feeling of horror.' When I knew him first he was always repeating,

> 'A deep despair hath humanized my soul,'

for he felt that his soul had been humanized by the love affair which had caused him so much misery in London, and that it needed to be humanized more. He had been persecuted by fears, but longer than myself, ever since his childhood. He found an expression for them too in Wordsworth, and would often intone in his grave sing-song,

> 'My former thoughts return'd: the fear that kills,
> And hope that is unwilling to be fed'

(he had a particular admiration for the second line), and,

> 'They pity me, and not my grief.'

Whenever a new line caught his fancy he would bring it out lovingly, and I remember one summer evening, Holms sitting in a garden chanting,

> 'Why liketh me thy yellow hair to see
> More than the boundës of mine honesty?'

It was an evening filled with calm yellow radiance, and the 'yellow hair,' in that light, took on an unimaginable richness. The very first day that I met him he started to quote Donne (whom I did not know at that time) as we returned from our long summer day in the country. We were leaning over a gate of a field, and as the scent of hay rose in our nostrils, he recited,

> 'And while our souls negotiate there,
> We like sepulchral statues lay;
> All day, the same our postures were,
> And we said nothing, all the day.'

Perhaps haunted by some remote resemblance between the rounded haycoles and old rounded graves, he went on to the opening verse of *The Relic*, stopping in delight over 'the last busy day' and the picture of the resurrected soul waiting by the lover's grave to 'make a little stay.' For the last half-hour we had been meeting a long line of courting couples moving in the opposite direction: as we leaned on the gate they went on passing us, a millennial procession in the calm evening light. Perhaps it was this that recalled to Holms Traherne's 'orient and immortal wheat, which never should be reaped, nor was ever sown,' for he began to recite the passage, which moved me more deeply than Donne. He held Traherne's and Vaughan's and Wordsworth's theory of childhood, which was bound up with his belief in immortality; in time he converted me to it, or rather made me realize that my own belief was the same as his.

His knowledge of his genius and its frustration made him wretched and sometimes sardonically critical when he saw the second-rate acclaimed. This roused his thwarted ambition: unlike myself, he was very ambitious and perpetually measuring himself against other writers, alive and dead, for he would not let even the dead lie easy. His despair with his life sometimes made him think of going into a monastery; whether this was a serious thought or a fancy I do not know; but his excellent physique and his keen pleasure in all bodily things, including food and drink, were too much for him.

His goodness—and he had a natural goodness and a sense of goodness as a simple, self-evident thing which I have never known in any other man—was intrinsically bound up with these things. It was so natural that sometimes it made one feel the Fall had never happened, and that the world was still waiting for the coming of evil. These good hours always brought a sense of abundance, of numerous herds, rich fields, full streams, endless food and drink—all things gladly fulfilling the law of their nature—and was like a return to Adam's world. They were hours of affection and enjoyment (things which always went together with him); he clung to them with the childish persistence which had been left alive in him, as if he hoped to stop time so that they might go on for ever: this clinging to them adulterated and corrupted them. He was without any trace of puritanism, but he had a dark sense of evil, a profound conviction of sin due to the feeling that he was an immortal spirit caught in the snares of the world and ignominiously enjoying its bondage while rebelling against it. His inability to express his genius gave intensity to this feeling, greatly deepening his sense of guilt, which grew with his increasing realization that he would never become a writer.

Holms was the most remarkable man I ever met. No one who knew him so intimately could help being influenced by him, but the influence was a natural result of our friendship; he did not try to influence me; he did not have that weakness or vanity. I recognized that his mind was far more powerful than mine; but it lay so perpetually open to me, was put so freely and almost objectively at my disposal, that I did not feel any trace of jealousy or envy at the thought that this was his mind and not mine. It had the quality which Joubert attributes to Plato's mind: you could live in it, walk about in it, take your ease in it. Consequently Holms had enormous reserves of patience, for patience is the ultimate proof of strength and consciousness of strength. My own impulse when I listened to some statement which seemed to be untrue was to contradict it; but Holms used the Socratic method and patiently followed the argument to its conclusion, apparently as interested in the pursuit as if it were leading him to some great truth. I cannot analyse now the effect he had upon me, for it was produced by his whole nature, not by his mind merely. One of the things he taught me was to see things with my own eyes, to take them seriously even when they seemed in the highest degree strange or improbable, and on no account to dismiss them because of some idea or preconception. In saying that he taught me to do this I do not mean that he did so deliberately; I learned it simply by having free access to his mind. Our minds were completely open to each other.

Holms was not a personality, like Orage, but what I can only call a 'nature,' to use Goethe's word. I do not much admire personalities, and that may have been partly why I did not get on with Orage at first. A personality is too obviously the result of a collaboration between its owner and time, too clearly *made*; and no matter how fascinating or skilful the workmanship may be, ultimately it bores us. Orage was much more than a personality, but he kept that 'more' to himself as if jealously guarding his real strength, and it was his personality that he turned to the world; he was too proud of it. Holms had hardly any personality at all; when he impressed you it was by pure, uncontaminated power. If he had lived to middle age he might, in his frustration, have become a personality, for he had a trace of vanity in him, and perhaps every one who deliberately shapes himself into a personality has somewhere a deep frustration and a saving vanity. For this reason we end by making allowances for the man of personality, circumspectly coasting round him, forgiving him many things which we should not forgive a genuine human being, even acquiring a sort of appreciation of his quality as a thing *made*, his own creation. To show the irreducible second-rateness of a man of personality one has only to think of Holms's words in his letter to Hugh Kingsmill: 'The supreme height of individual self-expression, and union with the universe, are one.' If the soul is immortal and the personality is not, obviously our real task is not to cultivate but to get rid of personality.

CHAPTER SIX

Prague

In the summer of 1921 we both flung up our jobs in London and went to stay for a few weeks with Willa's mother in Montrose. In the beginning of August we set out from Leith by the Hamburg boat. The passage was rough, and every one was sick until on the second morning the cliffs of Heligoland, rising and falling, plunged past, and we were sailing between the flat green fields on either side of the Elbe estuary. At Hamburg a charming old customs officer raised his hands in dismay when he heard where we were going, and implored us to stay in Germany, which was a civilized country. We knew only a few words of German; but the old man was patient, and after advising us again to stay in Germany patted us on the shoulder and passed us through.

At the hotel in Berlin we were given a room with a dais, as if we were royalty. We would have preferred a cheaper one, but our German was inadequate, we were tired, and we intended to stay only for one night. After resting we hired a droshky to drive us along Unter den Linden, where we stopped at a little outdoor *café* and were astonished by the plainness of the women and the unsightly shaven heads of the men; by misadventure we must have chanced on a rich, exclusive *café*, for the people walking about the streets looked quite different. The stiff, plain women and shorn-polled men gave an immensely strong sense of character, not so much individual as collective, the character of a strange tribe obstinately different from other civilized tribes, with a defiant, almost savage corporate eccentricity, but otherwise without distinction. During our time in Germany we never came into contact with that particular class again; they were insignificant numerically, but powerful, as history has proved since. It was curious that we should have run straight into them on our first day in Germany.

Next day we started for Prague. I can remember only one thing about the journey: a procession of some kind which we passed near a town in the north of Bohemia. There were men in dark clothes and women in bright dresses carrying purple banners, and they were walking along the bank of a still stream which reflected them upside down. I have forgotten the name of the town. The distant figures, the bright dresses, the clear river, the silence—for there was no music—made everything like a dream, and it has lingered in my mind ever since. In the corridor a little later I heard an English newspaper correspondent saying that Beneš was the coming man.

In Prague everything was strange to us. We had no knowledge of the language, and only a little German. We found lodgings in the house of a woman who could speak English and was a member of the Prague Y.W.C.A. (called the Eevka), but on the first night we found that our rooms overlooked a tramway line, beyond which was a railway line, beyond which was the Vltava and a fleet of flat-bottomed barges with powerful sirens plying up and down it night and day. We stood the din for a little while, then moved into the house of Pani Mala on the Nabřezi Legii, which looked out on a higher reach of the river. Pani Mala was a kind, handsome and charming woman, and we stayed with her for the rest of our time in Prague. She had a pretty daughter of nine or ten, and an ancient mother, who appeared only on rare occasions. There was a maid called Marie who said, 'Ruku libam' ('I kiss your hand') every time she entered the room. She actually kissed the old mother's hand every morning. There was a very fat poodle called Brouchek, or 'Little Beetle.' It was a pleasant, kind and good house, in which every one, from Marie to the old mother, seemed to be happy.

Our windows looked out on the Vltava and a water-tower which had been erected there by Wallenstein. Opposite was a sluice over which the waters of the wide, shallow stream slid continuously with a faint reverberation. For the first few weeks, while the heat of the summer lingered on, the river had a golden sheen broken only by the heads and oaring arms of the swimmers who cut through it perpetually from midday until sunset. The crowds in the streets of the town gave out a fine energy and confidence. Everything seemed new.

While I was in Prague I wrote some impressions of it for *The Freeman*, an American review, now defunct, of which Van Wyck Brooks was the literary editor. As these impressions are more vivid than my memory of them I shall quote them.

On the Petřin Hill there is a small iron erection, two hundred feet or so in height, built in imitation of the Eiffel Tower. From the top of it one can see on clear days the environs of the town for twenty miles. The prospect, especially in autumn, is intensely dismal. To the horizon the air seems to be filled with fine, impalpable dust which casts, even on the sunniest days, a dirty shadow over the parched fields stretching in a hard, whitish plateau as far as the eye can reach. Here and there rises a decrepit line of trees, and an abrupt scar of white rock projects at intervals from the plain. On the other side the towers and spires of Prague surge up through the smoke.

But when you take a walk over these crumbling fields you presently discover a new country full of greenness. The landscape, which seems an unbroken waste from the Petřin, is diversified by little hidden dells. These gullies generally descend without warning, almost like cliffs. The houses, painted yellow, red, and blue, climb up their sides until the sheer rock puts a stop to them. Every available square foot of soil is laid out in terraces, and in the afternoon sun sturdy old men and women are busy upon them. You climb by a winding path to the hot upland, where nothing but a goat or two can find sustenance, and once more the gully is swallowed up in the unbroken contour of the plain.

The banks of the river are charming, and up to the beginning of winter a fleet of excursion boats, small, efficient craft, carry all sorts of freightage to a distance of a few miles on either side of Prague: old women with baskets full of mysterious personal goods strapped on their backs; young misses returning to their summer villas from

their music lessons in Prague; retired grey-haired officials
out for a solitary trip; fat business-men who sit apart wrapt
in calculation; gendarmes going on unaccountable errands;
and foreign tourists, full of curiosity and patronage. The
old women, their bundles unstrapped and piled on the
deck around them, gossip with that air of democratic
fraternity which old women of the working class, of all
human beings, seem most completely to possess; but as
soon as the boat reaches their town they are already on the
gangway, and begin to trudge on their way without looking back. Among them there are magnificent old women,
cheerful and stalwart, broad-shouldered, carrying immense
burdens with a careless air, decisive and capable, with the
honour and freedom of poverty in all their gestures. I have
watched them often at the market-stalls and in the streets,
and I have found nothing in Prague more beautiful.

Prague, like the country round it, reveals its beauty in
detail rather than in general plan. There is, of course,
the wonderfully romantic view from the Most Legii over
the river to the Hrad, crowned with its cathedral and
surrounded by a chaos of palaces and churches surging
up to it out of the Mala Strana. The little hill itself
has from a distance the appearance of a single piece of
architecture daringly executed; the streets of palaces rise
up like a confused but solid pyramid, and on the top is set,
square and secure, the immense castle, while over it soars,
as the final crown of the edifice, the cathedral of St Vitus.
At all times it is beautiful: in the morning, when through
the sunny mist it hangs insubstantial over the river; in
the afternoon, when every line stands out clear and bare;
and at night, when it becomes a solid shadow against the
luminous sky.

When you go through the streets of the town itself you are
continually surprised by lovely or quaint old houses, but the
sense of spaciousness is gone. The streets are narrow. The
very squares are small, and palace is hidden behind palace
with an effect of rich overcrowding. The Mala Strana is a
sort of museum of palaces and churches, a museum without
a plan, where costly things are jumbled together as if they
had been left lying about by a gigantic but absent-minded

collector of antiques. They are mostly in the baroque style, and it is to their advantage that the baroque, itself a too luxurious and overcrowded style, can stand this method of presentation. Outline is lost, for the palaces press in upon one another so closely that you can never get far enough away from them to see them properly. From the narrow, steep lanes, mere trickles of cobble between precipices of masonry, shadowy courts filled with baskets, barrows, and all sorts of rustic implements open out. Here and there a fruit or a tobacco stall appears between the crumbling pillars of a monastery. From the top of the hill you look down as from a cliff on the red roofs of the Little Town, and farther away on the smoke-draped towers of the Great Town. The castle itself is a solid, spacious building containing about a thousand rooms, among which President Masaryk, when he took up his official residence, found with difficulty, I have been told, one containing a bath: a charming commentary on the aristocratic simplicity of his predecessors.

At the foot of the hill, in an unfortunate position, lies the huge palace of the renowned Wallenstein. It stretches along the full length of a street in which municipal trams run now. The great general caused twenty-eight private houses to be pulled down to provide a foundation for it. The architecture is undistinguished. Wallenstein was a Bohemian, and, considering the baffling part which he played in the Thirty Years' War, he is a puzzle to Czech writers. They would like to claim him as a great Czech, and are tempted to repudiate him as an adventurer. Some historical investigators try to interpret him as a long-waiting but unsuccessful Czech patriot (he certainly had the notion of re-establishing Bohemia as an independent nation with himself as king); while others simply set him down as a man with a boundless thirst for power: the old Bohemian historian, Palacký, after standing motionless before his statue in Vienna, delivered himself abruptly of the brief verdict 'Blackguard!' Public offices are now ensconced in remote corners of his enormous palace.

You become aware of the vitality of the republican idea in Prague as soon as you enter it. Whether you walk the streets or sit in the *cafés* you hear politics being discussed; it seems as if the whole people, old and young, after being denied all their life any voice in their political fate, had resolved to enjoy an orgy of self-government. They argue about politics, interests, grievances, new acts, with measureless gusto: they enjoy their very difficulties because of the freedom with which they can discuss them. Their political ardour bursts out everywhere: in the *cabarets* and the *cafés*, where there are always two portraits, one of President Masaryk and one of President Wilson, staring at each other from opposite walls or hanging amicably side by side; in the *sokols*, or gymnastic clubs, which in the old days of oppression did so much to encourage the Czechs in their struggle against Austria.

The Czechs are shrewd, enterprising, and resourceful in all practical matters. I spoke of their practical temper to a professor at the Prague University, an intelligent man and a patriot; and I was immediately aware of the inadequacy of my ideas about them. The Czechs, he told me, are misunderstood from both sides. They are misunderstood by the Russians because they have so many of the virtues of the West, and by the Western peoples because they are, in spite of everything, essentially Slavonic. More than any of the other Slavs, he said, they have the moral passion which is associated with England and America. In their intellectual lucidity and their quick wit they resemble in some ways the French. They are the branch of the Slav people which stretches most saliently into the heart of Europe; they are the first Westernized Slavs.

These reflections were set down when my impressions of Prague were fresh. Actually the life of Prague had a somewhat improvised air; this was inevitable, since it was new and not yet properly organized; but the very improvisation gave it extraordinary vigour. The theatre was particularly lively and progressive; less than two years after the War Prague had probably the most brilliant producers and actors in Central Europe. The Vinohrady Theatre, one of whose producers was Karel Čapek, performed during the winter we were in Prague plays by Sophocles, Shakespeare, Molière, Racine, Goldoni, Alfieri, Ibsen, Strindberg, and Chekhov, in addition to plays by Czech dramatists such as Čapek himself. The standard of production was high. In addition to the Vinohrady there was a National Theatre, which performed both plays and operas, a German theatre, and a small experimental theatre. There were numerous *cabarets*, with first-rate Rabelaisian comedians. There were orchestral and chamber concerts almost every night. At all these places you found an admirable mixture of classes, old peasant women with shawls sitting side by side with fashionably dressed girls. There was a feeling of nationality and a feeling of equality, and the two things went together. There were also, of course, social distinctions and snobberies; but the feeling of nationality could on occasion sweep them away. And on every side there was an abundance of energy and hope such as we had not known in London or in Scotland.

We had been given a number of letters of introduction by Paul Selver before we left London. These were mostly to writers, who all treated us with the greatest kindness. When we set ourselves to learn Czech they showed surprise and gratitude: they were not accustomed to such consideration for their language. Our teacher was a Polish lady, a pale young woman with iron-grey eyes, hair tightly combed back, and a grim expression. Willa made enough progress to read one of Čapek's plays in the original, as a reward for which he presented her with another that he had just written. But I never got very far, and stopped when I reached the stage where I could buy things in shops and order food in restaurants. After a few weeks our lessons had an interruption. Miss X had till then come to our lodgings, but now she announced that she could not do so any longer; we must go to her flat; she refused to give any explanation. Next day we went along to the address she had named. Her flat was on the third floor of a big block of buildings. We knocked at the door; Miss X opened it, put her fingers to her lips, beckoned us in, and silently shut the door after us. The room was filled from floor to ceiling with furniture; there were several wardrobes and chests of drawers on top of one another, many tables and chairs, a few bookcases, and two or three beds. Through the middle of the room a narrow trickle of passage led to the window, where three chairs were standing close together. Miss X explained to us that all these things had been left to her by her mother, who had recently died, but that her father and her brother were wicked men, and if she left the room for too long she was afraid they would force the door and carry away her belongings. The lesson began; we wandered through the history of Pan Novak and Pani Novakova and their children, told in the Czech of the infants' reading-book; but we could not fix our attention on their doings; the room was very cold; the dark furniture frowned down on us; and Miss X seemed to be absent and disturbed. On the mantelpiece, whose sharp edges were cutting into my shoulder as I sat clamped in my chair, there was an object which looked like a small gun-shell. To ease our constraint Willa asked if it was a souvenir of the War. Miss X burst into tears and stammered, 'It is my mother's ashes.' She cried for a while on Willa's shoulder, and a few days later told her the story of her life, which included a love affair involving the seduction of a priest. After this we became friends, but our lessons suffered.

We saw a great deal of Karel Čapek, who lived a few minutes' walk away from us in a rambling old house with a large garden hidden away behind it. Though he was about the same age as myself, he was already round-backed; the brightness of his eyes and the flush on his cheeks showed that he was ill. He knew only a little English, and we only a little German, so that we had to converse in an absurd mixture of the two. He was always busy, always merry, and always supplying us with tickets to the Vinohrady Theatre. He often talked of the hardships the people of Prague had suffered during the War, and though he never said so, I imagine that his own health was undermined during that dreadful time. The attitude of the Czechs to the War was expressed in the common saying, 'The worse things become, the better'; they knew that they could not win their independence except by the defeat of Germany and Austria. Čapek seemed to be known and loved by every one, and when we walked along the street with him every second or third passer-by would shout, 'Oh, Karlíčku!' the equivalent of 'Hullo, Charley!' as if the mere sight of him filled them with pleasure. This warm, easygoing contact could only have been possible in a comparatively small town, and it was the first thing that made me wish that Edinburgh might become a similar place.

Our first few months in that Prague which no longer exists were happy and care-free. We had a great deal of leisure, for living was cheap and I could make enough to keep us comfortably by writing two articles a month for *The Freeman* and a weekly article for *The New Age*. It was the first time since I was fourteen that I had known what it was to have time for thinking and daydreaming; I was in a foreign town where everything—the people, the houses, the very shop-signs—was different; I began to learn the visible world all over again. In Glasgow the ugliness of everything—the walks through the slums, the uncongenial work—had turned me in upon myself, so that I no longer saw things, but was merely aware of them in a vague way. In Prague everything seemed to be asking me to notice it; I spent weeks in an orgy of looking; I saw everywhere the visible world straight before my eyes. At this time too I realized that my fears were gone; there was nothing to spoil my enjoyment of this new world which had been created simply by travelling a few hundred miles and crossing two frontiers. Willa and I explored the surroundings of Prague and made excursions up the Vltava, where the leaves of the cherry-trees were red against the silver stubble of the fields. We went on the river-boat to Velky Chuchle and Mala Chuchle, walked in the woods and stopped at little country inns, where we had tea with rum. Everywhere we were struck by the independence of the people.

For the first few months we did not try to meet any English people, though we knew there was a fairly large colony in the town; we liked our solitude of two, and we wanted to see all these new things with our own eyes. As winter came on it grew very cold; by the middle of December the river was frozen. On the theory that walking in cold, bracing weather was good for the health we set out one afternoon for a walk in the country. Pani Mala looked surprised when she heard of our intention, but, assuming that British habits were different from hers, she said nothing. All I remember of that walk is a snow-covered field on the outskirts of Prague dotted with big crows, and a black-bearded Jew in a long, black, fur-trimmed overcoat and a fur cap walking rapidly across it to a little cottage; he walked as if he were walking on a city pavement, not through snow a foot deep, and this gave his progress a curious nightmare effect. The sky was shrouded, the snow dead white, the crows and the Jew glittering black. It was so cold that the longer we walked the more chilled we grew. At last we turned back, went into a *café* at the end of our street, and drank great quantities of hot tea with rum until we felt warm again. When we came out a wind had risen, and it was so cold now that we had to go into doorways to breathe. That was a particularly cold winter, we were told. The river remained frozen until the beginning of March.

During the winter we came to know the English colony. Some of them were giving English lessons, some studying Czech; the others were mainly connected with business concerns or the Embassy. A dancing class was started where the Czechs and the English met twice a week. We joined it, and after that we heard all the gossip which flies through a foreign colony, the members of which are slightly suspicious of one another for living out of England: there is never any convincing argument for living out of England. We became members of the English community, attended dances, and took part in Carnival when it came round. But we still had three-quarters of every day to do what we pleased with.

After the New Year the cold grew less intense, and every morning after breakfast we went to the Kinsky Park, which was still deep in snow, to feed the birds. This was a favourite occupation of the Prague people, and the gardens were consequently swarming with finches, sparrows, blackcaps, blue tits, and woodpeckers, which were so tame that they would sit on your finger and peck crumbs or fragments of nut from your hand. At the end of February Holms appeared for a few days enveloped in an enormous long brown overcoat, in which, with his red hair and red beard, he looked somehow Russian. He made a great impression on the English colony, who kept trooping to our lodgings to have a look at him. A young Englishman from the Midlands who had written part of a novel which, so far as I know, has not been finished yet, dropped in while Holms was there, carrying a copy of *Ulysses*, which had just come out. Like many aesthetes from the North and Midlands of England, he was both very sensitive and very shrewd, a cross between Aubrey Beardsley and Samuel Smiles. He was small, dark, thin, malicious, and very plucky. He had once had a Platonic affair with Gaby Deslys while he was working in a store in London, and amused us with stories of how she concealed him when her lovers came to visit her; she would send him to the pantry to have a good meal while she entertained the suitor of the evening—a really humane act, for he always looked underfed. We both came to like him, but after a while we lost sight of him; the English colony did not know what to make of him.

As the winter was ending Willa caught bronchitis, and we called in a doctor who lived above us, a handsome Austrian. He had attended the same university as Otto Weininger, the author of *Sex and Character*, who, he said, had been cruelly tormented by his fellow-students, and actually involved in a sham duel staged to make him look ridiculous. The doctor related all this objectively, without showing pleasure or disapproval. He had an extraordinarily calm, disillusioned, and yet pleasant manner. The War had killed his ambition; he did not think that the battle of life was worth waging; all that remained to him was a sense of honour. He had left Vienna because it was no longer the Vienna he had loved before the War. He had no political convictions, and if any reference was made to politics he looked disgusted: he gave me more strongly than anyone else I have ever met the feeling that he had come to a place from which there was no turning back, the place which Franz Kafka says must be reached; but in the doctor's case it did not seem to be the right place, even though he would never turn back. He did not like Prague, which as an Austrian he found provincial; but he had no intention of leaving it. He had come to terms with a completely unsatisfactory state of things, being convinced that life itself was completely unsatisfactory. Yet he was a kind and honourable man. We saw him at intervals; he was always pleasant and distant, like an amiable damned soul speaking to tyros who were not yet either saved or damned.

In early March the ice on the river broke, and came down in irregular blocks, some of them as big as a dancing-floor. When they reached the sluice opposite our window they heeled up like large pieces of furniture and plunged under the water, coming up again several yards downstream. The seagulls played a great game with them. They perched on the blocks and sailed down the river, rising when they came to the sluice, flying upstream again, perching on some other block, sailing down again, rising again. This went on for hours.

We left for Dresden about the end of March, and from the start loved the fine, spacious city. There during the hot, idle summer I seemed at last to recover from the long illness that had seized me when, at fourteen, I came to Glasgow. I realized that I must live over again the years which I had lived wrongly, and that every one should live his life twice, for the first attempt is always blind. I went over my life in that resting space, like a man who after travelling a long, featureless road suddenly realizes that, at this point or that, he had noticed almost without knowing it, with the corner of his eye, some extraordinary object, some rare treasure, yet in his sleep-walking had gone on, consciously aware only of the blank road flowing back beneath his feet. These objects, like Griseldas, were still patiently waiting at the points where I had first ignored them, and my full gaze could take in things which an absent glance had once passed over unseeingly, so that life I had wasted was returned to me.

> And with ane blenk it come into his thocht,
> That he sumtime hir face befoir had sene.

In living that life over again I struck up a first acquaintance with myself. Till now, I realized that I had been stubbornly staring away from myself. As if I had no more choice than time, I had walked with my face immovably set forward, as incapable as time of turning my head and seeing what was behind me. I looked, and what I saw was myself as I had lived up to that moment when I could turn my head. I had been existing, to use Holms's phrase, merely as something which consisted of 'the words with which one tries to explain it'; so that when at last I looked back at that life which, whatever I might think of it, was the life I knew best, it seemed to me that I was not seeing my own life merely, but all human life, and I became conscious of it as a strange and unique process. In turning my head and looking *against* the direction in which time was hurrying me I won a new kind of experience; for now that I no longer marched in step with time I could see life timelessly, and with that in terms of the imagination. I felt, though I had not the ability to express it, what Proust describes in *Le Temps Retrouvé*. 'A moment liberated from the order of time' seemed actually to have re-created in me 'a man to feel it who was also freed from the order of time.' But as this kind of looking required the use of the imagination it wakened my imagination, sluggishly at first. I did not feel so much that I was rediscovering the world of life as that I was discovering it for the first time.

I was thirty-five then, and passing through a stage which, if things had been different, I should have reached ten years earlier. I have felt that handicap ever since. I began to write poetry at thirty-five instead of at twenty-five or twenty.

CHAPTER SEVEN

Interval

I finished the first part of this book thirteen years ago. Since then there has been a great war and a succession of revolutions; the world has been divided into two hostile camps; and our concern has ceased to be the community or country we live in, and has become the single, disunited world: a vast abstraction, and at the same time a dilemma which, as it seems, we must all solve together or on which we must all be impaled together. This world was set going when we began to make nature serve us, hoping that we should eventually reach a stage where we would not have to adapt ourselves at all: machinery would save the trouble. We did not foresee that the machinery would grow into a great impersonal power, that we should have to serve it instead of co-operating with nature as our fathers did, and that as it grew more perfect we should become more powerless and be forced at last into a position not chosen by us, or chosen in blindness before we knew where our desires were leading. The generation to which I belong has survived an age, and the part of our life which is still immobilized there is like a sentence broken off before it could be completed; the future in which it would have written its last word was snatched away and a raw new present abruptly substituted; and that present is reluctant now to formulate its own sentence, from the fear that what it has to say will in turn be cut short by yet another raw present. I can see myself walking about in that first age and in the one which succeeded it, I can measure the difference between them, and feel the doubt which the present throws upon the past, suggesting that what once appeared innocent—a harmless excess of liberty, perhaps, a naïve trustfulness—may have been the stuff which a Hitler or a Stalin would later on manipulate for his ends. I cannot see even the life of Orkney as I saw it when I began this book, for remote as it seemed from history, it was already making for or being driven towards the present we know. The process which produced this universal effect seems, looking back, both blundering and inevitable: good and evil, our hopes and our fears, our dreams and our sober calculations, equally helped it on; as if nothing we could have done could have prevented us from reaching the exact point where we are now. Yet this feeling of inevitability, if we were to submit to it, would make our life perfectly empty; we should become conscious ciphers in a historical process whose intentions are not ours but its own; and our thoughts, our affections, our most intimate life, would be mere illusions to amuse or distract us.

I do not believe in the inevitable and the impersonal, these twins which always go together; yet they have come so powerfully into our lives that we have to make a conscious effort now to resist them. This was not so forty or fifty years ago; then there was no preoccupation with the inevitable or with its corollary the unitary world; this has sprung up since, enfeebling our individual power to live. It has made easier the growth of creeds which deny the significance of life: the creed of pure power which Spengler expressed when he said that 'Man is a *beast of prey*; I shall never tire of saying that': the creed of power directed towards an end in the future, which was formulated by Marx: creeds later to be put in practice by Hitler and Stalin. According to them everything is inevitable; yet one is still free, it seems, to choose inevitability. Those who reject it stand outside, insecure, delivered to the mercies of freedom and chance, with only their lives intact.

Our sense of the inevitable has been greatly strengthened by the changes which science has brought about. When at fourteen I went to Glasgow I was assured that the life of that city was the 'inevitable' development of a life, very like that of Orkney, which had existed in many other places in Scotland for many generations. Glasgow was undeniably there, and if I compared it with Orkney it certainly seemed to have advanced far into the future; in looking at it I was indeed looking at the future. The citizens of that future world seemed to me then very precise, docketed and quaintly dogmatic compared with the Orkney people, and its life continued only because every single workman and functionary fitted exactly into his own tight and narrow niche, observed his allotted hours, cleverly caught the tram which would take him just in time to his work, and so on: a life evidently requiring great care and arrangement. The men who embodied it—I came to recognize them by sight, for they were always in the tram-car which I caught to take me to the office where I worked—had a more compact and concentrated appearance than the Orkney farmers; as if they had been made over again for their specific occupations, and shrunk in the re-making; and this gave them a curious anonymity which it took me a long time to penetrate. These things are relative; the look of a man conscientiously doing a small job impressed me as strange then because it was outside my experience; it would not strike me now. Yet that humble anonymity may for all I know have been the germ out of which grew the terrible impersonality which thirty years afterwards could declare an absolute division between men according to their race or their class, and treat those who fell on the wrong side as if they were scarcely human. The specialization of labour and the crystallization of suburban and working-class habit must have made it easier for Hitler and Stalin to announce their gigantic segregations and set the Jews and the bourgeoisie beyond the reach of pity, until they could be used in any manner required, merely as bodies capable of reacting to certain stimuli under physical or mental torture, of saying yes, of obeying any suggestion made to them, and sometimes of believing, apparently in all good faith, things which they, knew to be false.

This terrible impersonality is the mark of the last twenty or thirty years, and it is sometimes justified by the inevitability of the historical process. Yet it diffuses itself even without that support, for it has established itself in practice and has the prestige of established things; we can be appalled but we cannot any longer be surprised by it; we accept it as a fact, even if we accept it in no other sense. By chance I have come close to it, and in a later chapter I shall describe its workings on men and women who were treated, quite impersonally, as the subject-matter of history. It is a relief to say that they did not all surrender themselves spiritually to that process, but under the most extreme pressure maintained their imperious need to live their own lives.

CHAPTER EIGHT

Dresden and Hellerau

This awareness of the direction in which the world is moving, which came to me so belatedly, casts doubt on my memory of these years in the early 'twenties when my wife and I lived in Dresden and Hellerau. Yet they still seem to me among the happiest of my life. We lived by ourselves in a town pleasantly strange. Everything seemed good, the houses, the streets, the people, because we were disposed to find them so. The Saxons are not a handsome race, but I was not looking for beauty, and when I encountered it in some chance face it was so unusual that it surprised me, and awoke a sense almost of alarm. There was so much of life which I had not accepted and felt the need to accept, that what I wanted now was the ordinary as the reassuring, given substance of life—round faces and blank blue eyes and comfortable bodies—and here they were in plenty, more consoling than any more carefully finished sketch of the human form could have been. These people were like a race still in the making, and quite content to be so, affirming without knowing it that the material out of which mankind is shaped has a simple natural virtue. When we went out for our mid-day meal at some nearby restaurant and saw Saxons converging upon it with greetings of 'Guten Appetit' or 'Mahlzeit,' the simplicity of that salutation, that blessing on the stomach and its doings, though the mere observance of a convention, moved us genuinely. It confirmed and blessed the rite of eating.

In Dresden we lived in an agreeable, silent vacuum, except for the talk of our garrulous landlady Frau Mütze, who was always asking us to get a nice English husband for her pretty daughter. Now and then we met John Holms and his wife, who had turned up shortly after our arrival. We lodged on the top floor of a large insurance building in the Old Town, and looked down on a square and beyond it, through a fringe of trees, at the Elbe. Except for the time I spent in writing my articles for the American *Freeman*, on which we lived, we had our days to ourselves. We employed them in learning German, and reading German poetry, and seeing the sights, and visiting cabarets, and attending concerts with the Holmses. The Germans whom we met were friendly, perhaps all the more so because they could practise their English, after long disuse, on us as accommodating patients. They did not show any bitterness at the defeat of their country, or any envy at our good fortune in being on the winning side. All this seemed now in a sense pointless, and it was assumed that they and we were above such considerations. I think that at that time the Germans sincerely wished to be reconciled with the world.

The Dresden we knew then, that spacious, handsome city, has since been destroyed in a war of which we never dreamt. Hitler was already collecting a small group around him in Munich, but in Dresden and Hellerau we never heard his name or knew that he existed. We knew nothing either, after living some months in the town, of the many families ruined by the war and the inflation: old people whose life-savings had disappeared as through a hole in a sack; comfortable families reduced to bewildered poverty. We became aware of these things only a year or so after we went to Hellerau. There, as we came to know almost everyone in the little community, we realized the difficulty they had in dealing with each day as it rose. But Dresden looked ambiguously prosperous; the people were well-dressed, the shops well-stocked, the places of entertainment filled: not a sign of ruin hiding in its respectable burrows.

We lived there in ignorance, not looking ahead. In spring we watched the sweet-smelling lime blossom coming out on the trees bordering the streets, and in summer spent a great deal of time on the banks of the river, sun-bathing among the seal-like Saxons whose skin was tanned to a Red Indian brown: a pleasant, vacant life without a trace of boredom, for everything round us was strange. My wife began a play, and I attempted one or two poems, with indifferent success. Holms tried to make up his mind whether Wagner compared with Beethoven could be called a great man, and whether love satisfied or love unfulfilled was the better inspiration for the artist, Wagner standing for the first and Beethoven for the second. He spoke of a long poem he had in mind on the metamorphoses of the animals, in which the various species would be shown emerging pictorially in the course of a long magical process, by an enormous speeding up and simplification of time. But the lethargy which weighed upon him did not lift long enough for him even to start. To begin, to find a fulcrum for the lever which would raise him to the point he would be at, was the problem that he was never able to solve.

One autumn evening, as we were waiting at a tram stop, we ran against A.S. Neill, who was an old friend of my wife. He told us that he had started an international school at Hellerau and begged her to come out there and help him. After thinking it over for a few days she agreed, and a fortnight later we moved to the house of Frau Doktor Neustätter, five minutes' walk from the school. She was an Australian married to a Bavarian doctor who worked in the Ministry of Health in Dresden. She helped Neill with his work.

The people we knew in Hellerau made up a small community gathered round an euryhthmic school which Jacques Dalcroze had built there and had forsaken after the war. It was a spacious building, with a theatre and lecture rooms and dancing-halls and tennis courts. The central part was now used as a school of dancing, one of the wings housed Neill's international school, and the other a school for the Hellerau children. We all had our mid-day meal each day in the Schulheim. The dancing students, mostly young women, were drawn from most of the countries in Europe; the common language was German. My wife taught in Neill's school every morning. The students were often in Frau Neustätter's hospitable house in the evenings, and we came to know them all.

All this was thirty years ago, and with one half of my mind I can look at it historically, while the other half still sees it as I saw it then, wrapped in its own illusions. We lived, it seems to me now, in a climate of 'new ideas,' and looked forward to a 'new life' which would be brought about by the simple exercise of freedom, a freedom such as had never been formulated before in any terms, since it too was new. We were, or thought we were, without 'prejudices.' We 'accepted' everything, no matter what it might be. We were interested in psychoanalysis, not as a scientific method but as a magical process which would deliver us from our inhibitions and leave us with a freedom all the dearer because it was beyond our imagining. We did not know that the climate in which we lived was already growing colder, or if we did we took care to keep it at its level of liberal warmth. While the inflation was spreading around us like a dry rot, we thought only of a potentiality which would, almost without our lifting a finger, painlessly realize itself and deposit us in a new existence. Our desire for that new state, which was so clearly good since it was all freedom, seemed to give us a foretaste of it. To dream, and to dream 'scientifically,' of such things as techniques triumphantly employed, prejudices dispelled, complexes dissolved, was to us a sort of activity which could achieve its end only by a wise suspension of all effort. A life without an obstacle, activity without endeavour, desires which would spontaneously exhale into universal freedom: that was our dream. Actually our desires did not behave in this way, nor indeed, with the sensible part of our minds, did we expect it; in our conduct we observed the usual conventions without noticing it, and were annoyed when anyone violated them, for it caused, to our surprise, all sorts of inconveniences. We felt free without practising freedom; we merely talked; and to talk freely gives an illusion of freedom hardly to be distinguished, except by an intellectual effort, from the reality. We discussed everything.

How much I was immersed in that atmosphere I cannot say, perhaps more than I realized. Reading some of my articles for *The Freeman* written about that time, I see that I was very little concerned with the truth of what I said; I was simply letting my mind range freely among 'ideas,' as if that were a sufficient end in itself. I had started the habit in Glasgow, where ideas were so scarce that any, good or bad, was a treasure to be prized. I had afterwards come under the influence of Orage, the most intelligent merchant of ideas of his time. But in Hellerau my imagination was beginning to waken after a long sleep, and the perceptions it promised were so much more real than those with which I had been trifling, that these no longer excited me. Some of them vanished altogether and were as if they had never been; others transmuted themselves into imaginative forms, particularly those which touched the ideas of innocence and reconciliation: Eden and the millennial vision of which I had dreamt as a child. The atmosphere in which our little community lived, with its affirmation of a freedom of mere wish and thought, had indeed in it something which faintly evoked the image of Eden and the prophecy of the time when the lion would lie down with the lamb: a nonsensical Eden, no doubt, and a sentimental lion and lamb, but touching as things genuinely felt. My image of Eden was associated with these naturally good and charming people, and the innocence with which they used their supposed freedom. They have been scattered long since to their own countries or exiled to others; they have grown into the real world, and the life they lived in Hellerau, which they could not have continued to live in any case after a certain age, has quite disappeared from the world. Some of them probably died in the gas chambers, and among them one or two who had such a genius for happiness that I still cannot imagine them as being anything but happy.

This provincial dream was fostered by its surroundings. Hellerau—I had better speak of it in the past tense, for the war may have destroyed it as it has destroyed Dresden—was a little garden city, the first of its kind, and the model, I believe, of the English ones. It had been originally intended for craftsmen, and was pleasantly secluded among sweetbrier hedges and in the midst of pine woods. The small population when we went there were no longer chiefly craftsmen; government officials from Dresden and faddists of all kinds had settled in the place. But all of them had acquired a distinct character which would not have been found in any other small German town, a certain amenity and mazed tolerance. They met in the evenings at a little tavern on the edge of a pine wood to drink and converse or, in summer, to dance outside in the courtyard.

In other parts of Germany, particularly in the large cities, the freedom we amateurishly cultivated had been pushed far beyond any bounds we could imagine. It was the age of Expressionism and the New Objectivity. The Expressionists carried freedom to a point where it lost all meaning and became an elaborate torment. They were driven by a need to pour out the last dirty dregs of the mind, as if it were a duty to appal themselves and their readers; one could hear in their works the last hysterical retchings, perhaps the death-rattle of freedom. The New Objectivity set out to describe things as they were, and it too was involved in the nightmare, for the state of the large cities was as horrible as the visions of the Expressionists. But in Hellerau we did not know of that terrible and apparently real freedom which assumed that since everything was possible everything was allowable; and we could continue our dream.

The German landscape, as I have said, helped to foster it. There was something in the appearance of the woods which seemed to invite nature-worship, and from nature-worship to worship of our own nature, which we were modestly practising, was an easy step. The trees solicited us to be natural, since they were natural, to be young, since they renewed their youth every year, to be child-like, since we could easily feel as we wandered among them that we were children of nature. The German poetry we read added to this mild enchantment. The poems of childhood in particular, so numerous and so unlike those of Vaughan and Traherne—poems of natural not of heavenly innocence—softly persuaded us that it was sweet not to grow up.

What I am trying to describe is an enchantment. It was so strong that it could transmute and use for its ends the most recalcitrant material, such as the ideas of Freud. The child of nature, the companion of the woods and streams, would enter into a still more perfect communion with them when he had resolved his complexes.

The worship of nature was a powerful cult in Germany in these years after the war. There were a few nature and self-worshippers in Hellerau: I remember a thin dusky man who always seemed to be working in his garden, clad in nothing but a loin-cloth, eye-glasses and a wrist watch, and always with the serious air of one making an important, if misunderstood, demonstration. The self-worship took more elaborate forms. As I sat one evening in Frau Neustätter's garden I saw a tall handsome man in flowing robes, a fillet round his head, passing majestically with a beautiful subservient young woman on either side. I never saw him again, and hardly know whether he was a visiting prophet or an apparition. But in the week ends the simple-lifers, the direct worshippers of nature, came out from Dresden and crowded in the woods. They called themselves the Wandervögel; they neither smoked nor drank; instead they carried guitars, and sang German songs, and kindled ritual fires, and slept, young men and women together, in the woods. The war had made them poor and wakened in them a need to be with harmless unwarlike things like trees and streams, and to move freely through peaceful spaces. Most of them, I have been told, were carried away later by the gospel of Hitler. They had nothing but simplicity and a belief that smoking and drinking were evil to protect them against him.

There were, outside the Schulheim, some people with a different philosophy of life. I met one day a stiffly polite, stiffly superior, apparently rich young man who had just returned from a visit to the circle in which Stefan George, the poet, passed his life. He told me that George was the only hope for Germany, and that I should not be distracted by the simple antics of the Wandervögel. (The Wandervögel eventually turned out to be more powerful than the poet.) I had not read George at that time and did not know that he was a great poet in spite of his curious ideas. On the young man's advice I bought a book on him by Gundolf, a member of the circle, and was repelled by its mixture of superciliousness and reverence, in which the reverence was so plainly based on the superciliousness. George was a man of proud spirit, with a devotion to the art of poetry unique in Germany in his time; but he could follow it only in seclusion, and he had been imprisoned for a long time within the circle he had summoned to guard him: it cut him off from life. When he escaped from it into his earlier memories he could still be a great poet; as it was, he went on shaping himself in his self-imposed privacy until he became incapable of shaping experience. It was greatly to his honour that, when the Nazis began to court him as one who had also dreamt a dream of a Third Empire, he would have nothing to do with them. He went into exile and before his death gave orders that he should be buried with his face turned away from Germany. I mention him because at the time he had power over a small but influential group of intellectuals.

In a sort of friendly detachment there lived in Hellerau an impoverished Junker, Ivo von Lucken. He had lost all he had in the inflation and lived in a little basement room in the Schulheim which he never let anyone enter, I think because of its extreme bareness. He gave lessons in Spanish and was paid by his students, at his own request, in parcels of food, pounds of rice, pats of butter. He was a high-nosed, hawk-faced man of an extraordinary sweetness and courtesy, so innocently simple that he would tell the most embarrassingly absurd stories against himself; most of them were about his time in the army during the war, when he never seemed to have carried out an order rightly, or managed to make his uniform fit him. As he spoke of these things a look of surprise would settle on his face, for he could never account for the strange difficulties that beset him during that time. He was interested in poetry and goodness, not at all in politics. He knew most of the living German poets and had himself written poetry of which nobody seems to have taken any notice. But that did not in the least disturb him; his devotion to the poetry of others was too great, and his own vanity too small. Although he had lost all his money and lived in great poverty, I never heard him make any complaint. He was tubercular, and his lodging in the basement must have been very bad for his health; but to him this predicament was simply a fact to be adapted to his style of life—a style created out of a complete lack of pettiness and a refusal to recognize the existence of time. My wife and I often tried to wile him to have a meal with us, but he would never admit to himself that he had any need of one, and only once or twice did he consent, with an air of elaborate carelessness, and then, as a point of private honour, would eat very little. He had one desire, which he often came back to, though with the detachment of one speaking of a dream: he wanted to go to Spain. It is unlikely that he ever had his wish. When I think of all the people I knew in Hellerau, I feel that he for one could never have gone across to the Nazis: his innocence would have saved him. Indeed he lived with Hölderlin more than with any living man, and he was more pleased when he succeeded in making me begin to understand that great poet than when he got a parcel of food from his students. I cannot remember that he had any 'views'; I think he had only devotions. Of all the people in Hellerau he was the poorest, but also possibly the happiest.

I have often wondered how many of the people I knew then, and which among them, went over to the Nazis ten years later, when Hitler came to power. I know of two who stood out: one, a Gentile, was shot by the Nazis; the other, a Jew, was shot a decade later by the Russians when they occupied Dresden.

We left Hellerau in 1923, when the inflation was making life intolerable and the guilt of appearing responsible for it, however indirectly, was more than we could face. I remember the days of mourning, mourning rather than bitterness, when news came that the French had sent 'black' troops into the Ruhr. The mourning in a little turned sour as the inflation made life impossible. A year or so after we left, when a Communist majority came to power in Saxony, Neill had to give up his school and move what was left of it to Austria. By then people had become so desperate that they were willing to listen to Hitler or Thaelmann or anybody. We tried to salve our consciences in the last few months by taking our German friends in relays to Dresden for a good meal. But we felt at last that we had no right to be in the country.

In the year and a half before things worsened I was beginning to write poetry. I had no training; I was too old to submit myself to contemporary influences; and I had acquired in Scotland a deference towards ideas which made my entrance into poetry difficult. Though my imagination had begun to work I had no technique by which I could give expression to it. There were the rhythms of English poetry on the one hand, the images in my mind on the other. All I could do at the start was to force the one, creaking and complaining, into the mould of the other. I have come to realize since then that Pound and Eliot were wise in regarding the first stages in the writing of poetry as a sort of apprenticeship, to be learned like any other. I know now what Eliot means when he says that Dante is the best model for a contemporary poet. But I did not know then, nor did I even like Eliot's poetry: it took me several years to recognize its great virtues. I had caught from John Holms a devotion for Wordsworth, but Wordsworth is not a poet to be imitated, and if the thought had occurred to me then, I would have regarded it as presumption. I began to write poetry simply because what I wanted to say could not have gone properly into prose. I wanted so much to say it that I had no thought left to study the form in which alone it could be said.

I certainly knew far too little about myself; yet I feel now that, in spite of the troubles brought about by my ignorance, I was more fortunate than the young poet (I was not even young) who knows too much or thinks he knows too much about poetry, and can solve with ease the technical problems which I could not solve at all. To think of poetry like this makes it a simple and business-like, and may make it almost a clever thing. I wrote in baffling ignorance, blundering and perpetually making mistakes. I must have been influenced by something, since we all are, but when I try to find out what it was that influenced me, I can only think of the years of childhood which I spent on my father's farm in the little island of Wyre in Orkney, and the beauty I apprehended then, before I knew there was beauty. These years had come alive, after being forgotten for so long, and when I wrote about horses they were my father's plough-horses as I saw them when I was four or five; and a poem on Achilles pursuing Hector round the walls of Troy was really a resuscitation of the afternoon when I ran away, in real terror, from another boy as I returned from school. The bare landscape of the little island became, without my knowing it, a universal landscape over which Abraham and Moses and Achilles and Ulysses and Tristram and all sorts of pilgrims passed; and Troy was associated with the Castle, a mere green mound, near my father's house.

I do not know whether in others the impressions of the first seven years of their lives remain so vivid and lasting, or if it is good that they should. In any case we need a symbolical stage on which the drama of human life can play itself out for us, and I doubt whether we have the liberty to choose it. The little island was not too big for a child to see in it an image of life; land and sea and sky, good and evil, happiness and grief, life and death discovered themselves to me there; and the landscape was so simple that it made these things simple too. In his youth my father had known witches in the island of Sanday, from which he came, and often spoke of them. My Aunt Maggie used to tell a story of a cruel mother who starved her little daughter by baking for her every day a stone covered with a thin layer of dough, and made her sleep in damp sheets so that she might fall ill and die. Aunt Maggie would recite the lugubrious little song the child sang to herself.:

> I wiss me dame was hame
> And I had pickéd me stane,
> I wiss me sheet was weet
> And I laid doon tae sleep.

I listened entranced to this story, and fitted its cruelty unreflectingly into my picture, never doubting that it had a right to be there. The witches and the cruel mother, the honest ploughman and the good minister, had an equal and justified place in my world. In recollecting these years in Wyre I recovered an image of life more complete than I had known in all the years between.

This naîve acceptance lasted for a year or two after we left Wyre and my father moved to the farm of Garth, some four miles from Kirkwall. I was returning from the Kirkwall Burgh School one summer afternoon when I caught up with a cart driven by a neighbouring farmer. He invited me to climb in at the back, and I found myself beside a very pale young man who smiled to me and then stared at something which he alone seemed to see; for he never looked at the fields and the distant sea where so many things were happening. The farmer glanced round and said, 'This is my son, home from Leith.' Then he turned away again and nothing more was said until I got off at the end of the path that led to our house. When I got there I told my mother about the young man; she looked grave and made no reply; but later in the evening I heard her telling my father about the neighbour's son and saying that he had 'come home to die.' The words were simple and yet strange, and dying became a sad and deliberate act which could be accomplished only in its own place, and for which careful provision had to be made. I learned later that the young man had 'fallen into a decline' as it was still called in Orkney, and that he was in the last stages of it.

A few weeks later, standing at the end of the house, I watched the funeral procession moving along the distant road. There were six men in front carrying the coffin on their shoulders, and behind them a long line of men in black clothes. Presently they reached the edge of a hill and one by one disappeared. But I stood for a long time afterwards looking at the white empty road, the hills and the sea, and what thoughts were in my mind then I shall never know; they were certainly tinged with sadness, but at the same time suffused with wonder and a simple acceptance of wonder. The fields were empty out of respect to the dead. It was a calm bright summer day and the hills and the sea hung suspended in light and peace.

These distant memories returned to me in Hellerau, but I scarcely knew that my image of the world had changed. I went on writing a poetry of symbols drawn from memory without realizing that I was doing so. I continued to do this for ten years before I became aware of it, and then only when it was pointed out. I fancy that the longer a poet writes the better he knows what he is doing: it is an advantage and a danger. An advantage, for the task of a poet is to make his imaginative world clear to himself. A danger, for that world in becoming clear may grow hard and shallow and obscure the mystery which it once embodied. We do not know enough about such things.

We left Hellerau in the spring of 1923 for a little town in Italy where Holms and his wife had rented a lodge which they wished us to share, as it was too expensive for them.

CHAPTER NINE

Italy and Austria

The lodge was a small box divided into three compartments: a bedroom for the Holmses, a bedroom for us, and a tiny kitchen. It was set flush on the main road leading to the town of Forte dei Marmi. The Holmses had chosen the room looking out at the back on a large straggling garden and a vineyard; as newcomers we were left with the one facing the road. The house was so cramped that four people could just fit into it by a skilful avoidance of movement. We arrived in May; it was already getting hot, and as June and July and August followed everything grew steadily hotter. There were moments of strain, only faintly eased by Holms's immobility, which seemed specially made for the heat and our cramped quarters. In the mornings my wife and I were pestered by peasant women carrying baskets of sardines and tomatoes and carrots to the town. They would stop before our window at five o'clock and cry 'Signora! Signora! Signora! Signora!' until my wife awoke and shouted at them to go away; but they would continue their bargaining for quite a long time in the hope of lightening their burden for the mile's trudge to the town. They were indomitably reasonable and very persistent.

We had our meals in the garden and used the house as little as possible. A calm and beautiful young Italian girl, Teresa, came to cook for us every day. Her complexion and hair were of almost the same golden colour, and where they met were like two substances differing from each other only in their texture. She had a stocky body, a regularly classical face, and the thick ankles which the Etruscans loved to give their statues. She dealt imperiously with the little charcoal stove on which she cooked our meals, flapping a straw fan before it with the air of one who would stand no nonsense, and treated us with the indulgence due to harmless and helpless foreigners.

The Italian landscape is not, like the German, one which solicits you to become a child of nature; it has been cultivated too long and has been too thoroughly steeped in human life. That summer I could not come to terms with it or with the combination of nature and art which the Italians embody in their lives and the contour of their faces. Coming for the first time to the South, I was repelled by the violence of the colours, the sea like a solid lake of blue paint, the purple sky, the bright brown earth: to my unaccustomed eyes the contrasts seemed crude and without mystery. Everything certainly was strange enough, yet so definite that the strangeness was no sooner felt than it was arrested by the complete finality of every shape I saw. I think I could have had little sense of form at that time. At any rate I saw many fine buildings in Pisa and Florence and Lucca, but except in Lucca every palace or church was irrecoverably cut off from the part of myself in which I could feel as well as see it. The insects too, a different race from any I had known before, troubled me by the intensity of their life, and I found myself watching them with the attraction and repulsion I had felt as a child in Orkney, staring at a worm writhing in the heart of a dandelion.

The little town of Forte dei Marmi, the port of the marbles, was about a mile away. To the east rose the Carrara mountains with their marble quarries, and between them and the town stretched a flat plain which not long before had been a marsh and still had a dank look and smell. The road to the quarries was deep in marble dust, and along it shambled great white oxen dragging blocks of hewn marble to the town. The beautiful gentle beasts with their wide brows, their great curving horns and soft eyes, evoked a pastoral landscape far older than the one through which they moved. They had the look of creatures walking in a dream from which they never woke as they dragged the creaking carts along the road.

A path led through the vineyard and the tangled garden to a flat sandy beach. We bathed twice a day in the tepid sea and lay on the sand until the sun dried us. A drowsy content, a placidity as of dreaming amphibians, filled our bodies and drugged our minds as we walked back through the sunflowers in the garden to tea under the pergola. As the summer advanced the houses on either side were occupied by holiday-makers, the beach became fashionable, and the price of everything rose. The sands were crowded with upper-class Italian families, and fat men stood in the lukewarm sea without moving, for hours, with parasols held over their heads. The crowds were like a picture which we observed without curiosity as we lay basking in the sun.

I think we should have come to know Italy better had it not been for Holms. He had been in Italy before; we were newcomers, and he could not resist the temptation of acting as a benevolent Virgilian guide and making us see everything with his more expert eyes. His tone at these moments was indulgently authoritative, and I still hear him, as he gazed at a particular effect of light one calm evening, saying pensively, while he plucked at his beard: 'It's pure Leonardo da Vinci.' He was always eager for agreement at these moments; when anyone confirmed his momentary perceptions it doubled his own pleasure in them, so that sometimes I could scarcely resist the unspoken solicitation. But his predigested Italy, of whose authority he never had a doubt, came between us and the Italy we wished to see for ourselves.

As it was, we observed the 'humours' of Italian life, amusing only because they were new. Our weekly visit to the bank in Forte dei Marmi was a recurring comedy. We had become friendly with the cashier and had helped his children to build sand-castles on the beach. But that did not keep him from staging a sham battle over the exchange of our British currency every time we called at the bank. He would begin by saying, 'I must ring up Pietrasanta,' Pietrasanta being the chief branch of the bank in our district. Then he would go into another room, pretend to carry on a telephone conversation, and return saying: 'Pietrasanta tells me—' naming a figure ten lire less than the official one. We would protest; he would appeal to any people who chanced to be in the bank, complaining that his wife and children would starve if he gave way to our cruel demands. At this we would name a figure ten lire more than the right one, he would take up the challenge, and at last, to everybody's satisfaction, we would get our money at the current rate and leave amid showers of good wishes.

But we knew nothing about Italy. The first time we had a real glimpse of it was during a few days' walk with the Holmses among the Carrara mountains. We had spent the first night in a little hostel far up on one of the slopes. Next morning we had not gone far when a heavy shower came down, drenching us. Presently we came upon a solitary farm and decided to ask for shelter. The farmer, a mild-eyed, bearded man, invited us to enter and led us into a large kitchen. There he introduced us to his wife and his two daughters, who had the faces of people who live much alone and within themselves. We must have seemed very foreign to them, but they showed no surprise; they might almost have been expecting us. The wood fire on the open hearth had burned low and we were wet and cold. After a glance at us the farmer left the room and returned with a long trumpet-shaped instrument. Standing upright before the fire like a herald, he set the small end to his mouth, rested the other on the hearth, and blew; the fire leapt up. We asked his leave to dry our clothes before it, his wife came in bearing great bowls of coffee, and we settled down to talk in our stumbling Italian. Presently as I looked round the kitchen it seemed to me that the walls were hung with a thin black muslin veil which swayed gently whenever the door opened. I looked again and saw that it was made up of flies torpidly clinging to one another. The strange artificial pattern which they formed, and their almost touching dependence on one another, made them into a humble neglected image of resignation. We went on talking at courteous intervals, our clothes dried, our minds were rapt in a Biblical peace. When we left to go we offered the farmer a little money for his entertainment of us, but he mildly and firmly refused. Standing at his door as at the gate of a little castle, he sent us his blessings on our journey. The gentleness and dignity of that family in that lonely place, the veil of flies hanging from the walls, bemused us as we walked on, and I became dimly aware of a good life which had existed there for many centuries before medicine and hygiene identified goodness with cleanliness. The veil of flies seemed to throw into relief the delicacy and purity of these faces bred by a tradition so much older than ours, and embodying virtues which we had forgotten.

My wife and I had another glimpse of that more real Italy when we attended the annual celebration of the Black Christ at Lucca. The statue, of black wood worn and polished smooth by time, was said to have been miraculously floated from Palestine to a port in Italy, and then conveyed to Lucca. When we arrived the town was filled with peasants from the surrounding country who had come to have their rings and keys touched by the Black Christ and blessed for the coming year. It was a day of sorrow for the death of God and of reassurance for the year to come. A procession formed; one by one the peasants passed before the image of Christ, handed their rings and keys to the priest, kissed the toe of the image, and passed on. On the stone floor of the church old peasant women were kneeling in prayer, their faces streaming with tears as they gazed at the statue of their Lord. At the same time, not far off, a fair was in full swing, with booths displaying giants and dwarfs, clowns and conjurers. This was an immemorial part of the solemn day, and it seemed to us in no way incongruous. In the evening the results of a lottery were announced to the crackling of fireworks.

Lucca was small enough for us to feel at home in it. Florence was different. We went there in August, and the heat did not give us any respite to enjoy the beauty of the city. Also, I was persecuted by a dream which visited me every night. We were staying in a hotel which had once been a palace, and my dream might have been the resuscitation of an event which had once happened there, if such things do occur. In the dream I was a young man of twenty, dressed in what seemed to be a renaissance costume, a closely fitting suit of black. I was waiting in a dark archway for the approach of someone; it was late in the night; the moon was up, but I was hidden in the shadow of the arch. Presently I heard a man's footsteps growing louder; as he passed I leapt out, filled with rage from head to foot, a sort of possession, and plunged my dagger into his breast. The warm blood spouted out, covering my hand; this always wakened me.

Why I dreamt this dream, and why it came back night after night, I cannot think. Nothing resembling it had happened to me before or has happened since. The recurrence became so alarming that at last we had to leave Florence.

In September the weather broke in a few days of rain and the air became cool. We gazed in delight at the mud and the pools of water on the road. The Vendemmia came on, and the market-women ceased to pester us in the mornings; everyone was busy in the vineyards. Before each house great clusters of grapes were set out on trestles, and as we passed we had to eat a few from each, so that the wine harvest might be blessed. The young men sang late into the night as they wandered the roads, keeping us from our sleep; but early next morning they were busy in the vineyards again.

That first visit to Italy was a curiously external affair. We parted from the Holmses in October and left for Salzburg.

We had spent over two years in wandering about Europe, but we had no desire to return home. We lived simply; our belongings went with us in two suit-cases. I had spent a fortnight in Salzburg during the summer, attending the music festival there with my old friend Francis George Scott. I wished my wife to see it too. It was late autumn when we arrived, but the days were still mild though the leaves had turned. We got lodgings with a woman who pestered us with her inquisitiveness and was never able to understand why we had come to live in Salzburg. I think she suspected, all the time we were there, that we were not really married, though she never dared to broach the subject. She had a son who appeared at intervals making a great outcry and asking for money to extricate him from his latest scrape; he was a mixture of boisterous good spirits, cunning and malice more commonly to be found in Germany than in Austria. His visits always left his mother in a state of apprehension: what would he be at next? We could not tell.

In that lovely provincial town we became acquainted with a thing which was to cause the extermination of five million people twenty years later. In a *café* we came across a little local paper called *Der Eiserne Besen*, the Iron Broom. It contained nothing but libellous charges against local Jews, set down with great rancour. We read with astonishment of ritual murders still happening, and of curious Jewish perversions, described in detail, of which we had never heard. A little time afterwards we met some intelligent Austrians who maintained against all we could say that Ramsay Macdonald and Bernard Shaw were Jews: they must be, for they were subverters of society. And in a bookshop where I went one day to buy the poems of Walther von der Vogelweide, the proprietor, who was embarrassingly grateful for my interest in German poetry, became rude when I asked him for the poems of Hugo von Hofmannsthal; he said roughly that he did not stock them. I could not understand his sudden incivility, and only after I had left did I begin to realize that he must have thought it presumptuous for any Jew, or anyone partly Jewish, like Hofmannsthal, to write in German. We had known that there was a Jewish problem, for we took the newspapers, but we still thought of the Jews mainly as people we had read about in the Old Testament. Our landlady's son would have laughed heartily over the stories in *Der Eiserne Besen*.

In Salzburg, and during the time we were wandering about Europe together, my wife and I were our own chief company, and perfectly content to be so. We shared a common experience whose double reflection, thrown from one to the other, composed itself into a single image. That was our greatest pleasure. Yet, in the thirty years since, these impressions, which gave us so much pleasure then, have faded, and when I try to resurrect them now everything becomes insubstantial. And yet I had loved the little place enough to write a story about it two years after I left. Remembering this, I decided to have a glance at the book again; I had not read it for twenty years. I found that it did not tell me much about Salzburg but a great deal about the mingled excitement and fear which we feel on setting foot in a town we have never seen before. The story is about a young half-witted boy called Hans, and Salzburg is seen through his eyes with the simplicity of one who does not understand what he sees. Obviously in presenting his fragmentary picture of the town I was resurrecting my own, for our first impressions of a new place are very like the first impressions of a child come

new into the midst of new things. In any case these are
some of the sights which struck Hans in his first terrified
walk with his father through the town: the darkness of an
archway; the deafening clatter of the streets; two gigantic
horses with shining harness; dogs running about; the white
faces and black clothes of the crowds, the people farther
away looking like dolls; streets suddenly twisting to the right
or the left, the powerful circular slew of the houses giving
them a pitiless look; dust and scraps of paper revolving in
corners. These things were more vivid to me when I wrote
the story than others which intrinsically would have been
more worth remembering; but though when they returned
they brought back these secondary images with them, they
remained in a different region of reality. Such impressions
are so strong, perhaps, because they confront us anew with
the terrifying artificiality of the clothed human form, the
terrifying naturalness of animals, the movements of the dust
filled with a memory beyond memory, the strangeness of
shape itself. They move us more strongly than beauty and
seem to precede beauty and summon it to follow them; if
it obeys everything is transformed; if it refuses everything
falls back again into nightmare. These things tell us—what
we usually forget—simply that we are here and that there
are many here with us.

But as I read of these sights which caught the terrified eyes
of Hans, the town gradually began to return and come near.
The Kapuzinerberg reappeared with the twelve stations of
the Cross which changed for us with the brightness or
darkness of the day and the fluctuations of our moods. In
rain the wood looked soft and crumbling and the figures
painted on it seemed to be weary of their stations: Christ
under his burden, and the brutal faces of the Roman
soldiers, now blurred and weakened by time. In bright
autumnal days the slanting light irradiated every detail; the
blood flowed like a sunset river from the Saviour's side,
the soldiers stood by in pity, acknowledging the sad duty
that compelled their presence. When, passing the stations
of the Cross, we climbed the hill, the town lay beneath us
neat and small, washed in centuries of air: the Castle on its
rock, the Cathedral and St Peter's looking like curiously

shaped chess-men, the toy trees in the Mirabellen Gardens, the narrow green river rushing with miniature rage under the bridges, and far away, in a world by themselves, the jagged peaks of the Bavarian Alps. I have another image of the Cathedral, quite different. We were returning one early winter day from a walk over the flat roads to the north of the town; darkness was falling, and as we drew nearer the Cathedral rose high above the houses and the distant mountains, until it seemed to stand side by side with one tall peak; but the church, which had looked like a toy from the Kapuzinerberg, dominated the mountain. I remember too, while we were walking one day on the Mönchsberg—a smaller hill on the opposite side of the river—looking down on a green plain that stretched away to the foothills, and watching in the distance people moving along the tiny roads. Why do such things seem enormously important to us? Why, seen from a distance, do the casual journeys of men and women, perhaps going on some trivial errand, take on the appearance of a pilgrimage? I can only explain it by some deep archetypal image in our minds of which we become conscious only at the rare moments when we realize that our own life is a journey.

In December, with the snow deep on the ground, we decided to go to Vienna, which promised a spacious area of dryness and warmth scooped out from the cold white landscape. My wife had written to Neill, who had now taken his school to the top of an Austrian mountain, asking him for the address of a hotel in Vienna where we could put up while we looked round for private lodgings. He recommended a place which he said was clean and reasonably cheap. When we came down on the first evening for dinner we noticed that there were a great number of Jewish people at the tables, and decided that there must be many Jews in Vienna. Next morning, a Saturday, we rose late for breakfast, and sitting in a little enclosed veranda looked out on the street. The shops were all shut; the street was very quiet; the windows in the drab line of houses showed no faces behind them; little groups stood at the street corners in peaceful conversation; and we realized that they were all Jews. The scene was curiously foreign, indeed more strange than any other we had looked upon in our travels. We had never seen so many Jews together at one time; they had always been thinly scattered among a Gentile crowd; and the fact that they now seemed so foreign made us dimly understand the half-superstitious feeling which produces Antisemitism. Only after a while did we realize that this was the Jewish Sabbath and that it was not desertion but peace that lay on the street. But the feeling of strangeness remained: the little groups were like crowds distributed for effect on a stage; perhaps the fact that we were sitting in the enclosed veranda as in a box in a theatre, looking out through glass at the pre-arranged spectacle, added to the effect of distance and unreality. Among the groups were old men with long ritual curls and dressed in caftans. But the strangeness was not merely in the clothes. It took us a little longer to realize that we were in the Jewish quarter.

We stayed in the hotel for a few days. The Danube canal separates the Jewish quarter from the main town and to leave it you have to cross a little bridge. Walking either way we met nothing but Jews and were conscious how cut off was the life of that populous but restricted quarter and how different from that of the rest of Vienna. This segregation seemed a palpable embodiment of Antisemitism, but during our few months in Vienna we found many spoken evidences of it as well, in conversations with people good and bad, intelligent and stupid. The good and the intelligent were, if anything, the more trying, for they advanced humanity and reason in support of their prejudices. But the distaste of the well-bred whenever a Jew was mentioned was worst of all.

We were without knowledge of Jewry and felt at a loss when involved in Antisemite discussions. These puzzled us even more than the arguments advanced, which seemed to us childish; the discussion itself was the greater and the less understandable offence. At times we had to listen in patience, for some of the Antisemites were intelligent people. Yet at a moment's notice they would tell us seriously of hosts of Galician Jews who had come to Vienna without a penny and now owned fine properties and drove about in stylish cars: all by speculating on the exchange. These stories were as legendary as the tales of ritual murder in

Der Eiserne Besen. Many Viennese families had seen their money vanishing in the inflation; someone may have heard of a Jew from Galicia who had made money on the exchange; in a little he became an invading host of Jews. The misery in Vienna created its own nightmare. We did not know that the nightmare would end in the slaughter of a people.

The misery was more public than it had been in Dresden, for things had grown generally worse in Central Europe since we left that city. One bright winter day my wife and I were walking along the Ring when we saw a man half-sitting, half-lying on the wet pavement with his back against the wall of a great block of offices. He trembled continually and mumbled to himself. People kept passing; some of them threw him a worried glance, but no one stopped; they had no doubt got used to such sights. We waited beside the man and managed to learn from him that he was on his way home from a hospital where he had been treated for a wound in the head, an old war wound. He had walked for a long time till he could go no farther; he was still far from his home, and he had no money to pay his tram-fare. We stopped a taxi, helped him in, found out his address, and gave him some money. He made no response but kept muttering, 'My head! My head!' We saw how much Vienna had suffered when a people naturally kind could pass with indifference someone in such distress.

Yet in spite of their poverty the Viennese people kept up, as a sort of needy caricature of itself, their tradition of gaiety. There was a story going round at the time that while in Berlin people were saying, 'The position is serious but not critical,' the Viennese version was, 'The position is critical but not serious.' The people of Vienna were proud of this story against—or was it for?—themselves; it expressed their characteristic way of life, which had always been precarious in appearance and yet had worked for two hundred years; and it defined the Austrian brand of courage, which consists in recognizing that things are naturally incorrigible, yet are to be got round by tradition, tact, tolerance and a sense of honour. The old Austria was gone, dismembered by the Versailles Treaty; Vienna, the great capital, was now the chief town in a small country. The Viennese went on in their traditional way on their shrunken means, and still kept up a style, embodied in their faces, their elaborate and yet natural manners, and their public jokes, though now there was nothing except a memory on which to support it.

But the flower of Austrian life was already withered, and to know it as it had been we had to go to the work of Hugo von Hofmannsthal. We were under his enchantment at the time. I could easily have found ways of meeting him, for he was then living at Rodaun, a few miles from Vienna, but I refrained from a premonitory sense of the embarrassment which a writer must suffer on being confronted with an unknown admirer. I had heard stories of his fantastic sensitiveness, his charm, and his instantaneous dislikes which he could not control, though they were more painful to him than to those who occasioned them. I thought him then and still think him the greatest German poet of that age, the age of Stefan George and Rainer Maria Rilke. Unlike them he was devoted, with a life's devotion, to the part of Europe that bred him. He was committed to Austria, and when Austria was dismembered his heart broke; an experience Rilke was never to have, for he was unattached, and George knew only in the last year of his life. Before the disaster came Hofmannsthal had preserved in his poetry and prose the old Austrian life, as if it were an infinitely precious thing which might be lost, as it was now; his love still suffused it with a tender radiance. His description of the Austrian farm in *Andreas*, an unfinished novel, is unlike anything else in modern literature in its union of reality and enchantment and a sense that everything is rooted deeply and tranquilly in time. He knew that peasant life in a traditional land flowers into its own magic, as the life of industrial towns and great cities cannot; for it is tradition that nurtures enchantment, and when it collapses the natural shrinks into the bald shape of what is called 'real life': a theme for the ordinary novel. Hofmannsthal lived in a world where that transformation had not yet taken place; he saw tradition still shaping life, and for that reason his characters and scenes too are shaped, not copied, and exist beyond the reach of an art which concerns itself with those numb facts which, set down no matter how faithfully, tell us nothing more than that they are there. He had faith in what he knew and loved, and held that 'powerful imaginations are conservative.' His poems and plays preserve a lost world and give it back to us as part of experience.

His plays were still being produced in Vienna, but defeat and misery had bred curious perversities in the artistic life of the city. The tradition having collapsed, people turned to anything which would give them back the flavour of life, and they did not care if the taste was bitter. The plays of Wedekind, a writer admired by German intellectuals for some reason I have never been able to discover, were revived, and we attended a midnight performance of one of them, a play with a whole cart-load of perversions. And one afternoon we went to see Ernst Toller's *Der Deutsche Hinkemann*. At that time Toller was a communist incoherent with indignation at the wrongs of the poor, and he chose as the symbol of post-war Germany a soldier who had been castrated in the war. As we approached the theatre we found a huge crowd gathered outside, and policemen guarding the doors. After we entered we were told by some one that in Berlin and Dresden, where the play had already been produced, Nationalists had shot at the actors and stopped the performance. The Nationalists objected, quite naturally, to their country being symbolized by such a figure; but the shooting showed how fantastically the taste for violence had spread. The theatre was filled. I can remember little of the play except that the stage was dimly lighted and that the actors scuttled back into the shadow as soon as they had said their lines. About half-way through, as expected, a shot rang out from the gallery, and the stage was suddenly empty. Men jumped to their feet shouting, 'Weiber und Kinder still! Weiber und Kinder still!' though, as my wife remarked, the women and children were in fact quite still; it was the men who were making all the noise. Someone was led from the gallery, the audience quietened down, the dreary play went on. I have never been in any other theatre where the audience was so intent: everyone was waiting for the shot.

Both these plays were German, not Austrian, and it is curious how often the questionable is invoked by German writers when they set out with a moral purpose. The resolve to expose evil in its most squalid forms may be enough to account for this; but almost invariably something sordidly inquisitive comes into the treatment as well, adding to the moral confusion. The result is that the spectator is not cleansed, but involved in the impurities he is witnessing, and the moral intention is perverted into its opposite. The audience at Wedekind's play was a very curious one. Perhaps Hofmannsthal was thinking of such dangers when he violently repudiated plays which had designs on the spectator.

In the spring I was suddenly informed that *The Freeman* was to be discontinued. Neill was in Austria on his mountain, and to tide us over until we found some other way of making a living Willa wrote to him, asking if she could help again in his school; he sent her a warm invitation to come. The snow was melting and ragged patches of brown earth were spreading in the fields as we sat in the train to Rosenau, a little town at the foot of the mountain. When we got to the top after two hours' climb over slippery tracks, everything there was still deep in snow. In a week spring announced itself through the cuckoos calling across the snow; the southern slopes melted; and in a single day, or so it seemed, the fields were thick with primulas and gentians. A few weeks later a telegram came from an American publisher asking us to translate three of Gerhardt Hauptmann's poetic dramas. We wired back accepting the offer. It was the beginning of a period when we turned ourselves into a sort of translation factory.

Neill's school was housed in a wing of what had once been a monastery, and next door was a Baroque church stranded like a great ship on the top of the inland mountain. A cluster of houses nestled at its foot, displaying in their windows sacred badges, images and rosaries for sale to the pilgrims who came from all over the Danubian plain, sometimes as far as from Slovakia, in the idle time between the hay and the corn harvest. They came in straggling processions, men, women and children together; the men in front playing an assortment of instruments, pipes, brasses, fiddles; the women with large round bundles of bedding on their backs. They climbed the mountain, slept at the inn or in the fields, and early in the morning ascended in procession, singing, the great flight of steps that led to the church. It was both a pilgrimage and an annual holiday in which they could renew their acquaintance with the towns and villages along their road, and meet friends they had not seen since last year. To the children these wanderings and the wonderful last day must have been enchanting.

The great church had been erected on the mountain to celebrate a miracle. Centuries before, it was said, the Turks were advancing on Vienna when a spring broke from the mountainside a little below where the church now stood, bogging their horses so that they had to turn back.

The Sonntagberg stood on the edge of a line of foothills leading up to a higher range. From the top floor of the monastery we looked out on the plain of the Danube stretching away for sixty or seventy miles. There we would watch, for half an hour before they reached us, the majestic approach of the thunder storms, which were frequent in the late spring. Perhaps because of the configuration of the mountain range, the storm clouds always wheeled at a certain point; then they drove straight at us; the air became charged; and the building rocked as the wind struck. The lightning playing in the sky over that wide stretch of flat country held us at the window as if we were watching a gigantic Olympian game.

In the school we met again old friends from the Hellerau days, and visitors for Neill were always arriving from places near and far, Vienna, Sweden, England, America. We had our own room where we struggled with Hauptmann's verse and converted it into passable English measures. The life was lively and yet remote; there was company when we wanted it, and in the pine-woods one was free to gaze for hours at the little farms shining on the slopes, and scattered for mile after mile over the green landscape.

I had had a collection of poems accepted by Virginia Woolf for the Hogarth Press, and walking in the woods I felt the stirrings of a longer one, a chorus in which the dead were to look back at the life they had left and contemplate it from their new station. The idea greatly moved me, but my imaginative excitement never managed to communicate itself, or at best now and then, to the poem; the old disability which I had struggled with in Hellerau, a simple lack of skill, still held me up. In any case the theme was far too great for my powers—yet who can decide when or to whom a theme will come, or if it will come too soon or too late? There are a few lines in the poem which express my state at that time better than anything I could say now, and I shall quote them. One of my newly dead, looking back on his life, speaks of

> The stationary country where
> Achilles drives and Hector runs,

an image which had often haunted me, and after several more lines he ends with

> that ghostly eternity
> Cut by the bridge where journeys Christ
> On endless arcs pacing the sea.

These lines surprise me afresh when I read them, and bring back the days when I walked in the pine-woods on the Sonntagberg, and the difference between what I thought myself then and what I think myself now.

One of the disconcerting accidents of a writer's life is that if he reads again what he wrote, say thirty years before, as I have just been doing, he may appear quite strange to himself. These three lines seem so strange to me that I almost feel it was someone else who wrote them; yet that someone was myself. I fancy we all have sometimes this sense of strangeness, or of estrangement, when we look back, perhaps at some moment in our childhood, or at a body waiting for a girl he loved or thought he loved—both gone and almost forgotten, never in any case to be recovered—or at a young man loitering in a summer dream beside a river which flows now into a different sea. Time wakens a longing more poignant than all the longings caused by the division of lovers in space, for there is no road back into its country. Our bodies were not made for that journey; only the imagination can venture upon it; and the setting out, the road, and the arrival: all is imagination. We long most for the places in time where we were happy, and I was happy during these spring and summer months on the Sonntagberg, composing an abortive poem.

Yet our memories of a place, no matter how fond we were of it, are little more than a confusion of lights on a ground of maternal darkness. I remember the Sonntagberg by a sudden rush of spring flowers, a silver thread of water on a mountainside in sunset light, and only then to be seen, a patch of turf so quiet and clean that the light seemed to be more still there, a peasant woman shearing a sheep which she held affectionately on her knee, kissing its nose now and then to comfort it, and two snakes fighting so furiously in the middle of a mountain stream that they were swept, still fighting, over a cataract. But our memories are real in a different way from the real things they try to resuscitate. I was being driven through Austria by a friend twenty-three years after all this; I saw a collection of white buildings on a hill which I was told was the Sonntagberg; but I did not recognize either the hill or the buildings.

Yet when I dream of them, everything has a supernatural radiance. I remember two of those dreams. In one I found myself in a high field dotted with little conical heaps of dead leaves; as I drew near the leaves turned to stooks of corn; but when I went closer I saw that they were the dead, lying two by two, a numberless host who were harvested there. In the other dream my wife and I were walking hand in hand through a street in a ruined town. The sun had risen and its rays streamed down the street, irradiating the house walls on either side and making a tunnel of light. The cobbles shone, and tender green grass began to sprout between them; as we went on the grass steadily grew longer, the house walls crumbled, sending out green branches from the stone, and in a little square where we found ourselves next trees began to rise and blossom, filling the air with perfume, while farther away we heard the plashing of fountains and the singing of birds. The whole dream was filled with freshness and delight, and somewhere in it, strangely disguised, was the Sonntagberg. I have not had such dreams for a long time.

In July Neill decided to move his school to England, and we returned there too. We had been away for four years.

CHAPTER TEN

England and France

A friend had rented for us a small house in the village of
Penn in Bucks. It had once been the local blacksmith's
house; the smithy beside it had been used by a previous
tenant as a garage; we turned it into an extra workroom. The
house stood at the end of a bye-road on the outskirts of the
village; next door was a Baptist Chapel attended on Sundays
by seven or eight people whose voices we would hear raised
in forlorn song. Opposite was The Sportsman and His Dog,
a pleasant inn patronized by the farm-labourers who shared
the road with us and by people out for a Sunday jaunt.
Four years' absence had been enough to surprise us, for
the first time, at the number of religious denominations
in England and their social distribution: the gentry and
the farm-labourers, Church of England, the shopkeepers,
Methodists or Baptists; and in the middle of the village
green, facing the main road, a large notice with the words
'God First,' announcing another sect. This pattern seemed
to have been settled by an amicable arrangement between
the denominations, so that each was pleased with its own
position, which was ordained, or so it seemed, both by
history and the will of Providence. The conflict was long
over, and all the sides had won.

We had a novel of Gerhardt Hauptmann to translate,
and Leonard Woolf, at that time the literary editor of
The Nation and Athenæum, gave me books to review every
now and then. The summer began early and ended late,
a succession of days monotonously, deliciously warm and
bright. Sometimes Stephen Hudson (Sydney Schiff), the
novelist, came over in his car and took us to his house in
Chesham for afternoon tea or dinner. He and his wife Violet
were extravagantly kind and considerate, and enjoyed, as
if it were a rare treat, the company who came to see

them; an unusual thing in a married pair who shared so completely the life they had made between them. They had known Marcel Proust and often spoke of him with tender regard, his habits, his ill-health, and his devoted maid. Their delicate enjoyment of company seemed to me a spiritual gift, though Sydney was reluctant to use such terms. In his long autobiographical novel, *A True Story*, he pushed his honesty towards himself so far, I have always thought, that he was less than just to himself: an excess of sincerity rare among writers. Those who knew him and his wife, and the exquisite quality of their separate and so closely united lives, will never forget them.

We spent our summer at Penn translating, and too much of our lives was wasted in the following years in turning German into English. It began as a resource and hardened into a necessity. In the autumn we went to Montrose to stay for a while with my wife's mother, and there, still translating, we both fell ill, my wife seriously. The doctor was often in attendance, and one snowy evening during this time stands out from the monotony of dejection. The snow had come on in the afternoon, and the streets were unfamiliarly white under the lamps. I had gone to summon the doctor. I turned into the stone-flagged yard before his house, and after ringing the bell glanced at a little tree a few steps away. A lamp above the door shone straight on it, illumining it like a Christmas tree, and on one of the twigs a robin was sitting looking at me, quite without fear, with its round eyes, its bright breast liquidly glowing in the light. As I stared at it out of my worry, which was a world of its own, the small glittering object had an unearthly radiance, and seemed to be pouring its light into the darkness without and the darkness within myself. It astonished and reassured me.

A few years later, when we were living in Crowborough, and my wife and my young son and our maid were all ill together, and the house seemed to be steeped in illness, something of the same kind gave me an irrational reassurance. Our house was on the outskirts of the pleasant straggling town, and I was on my way to the local chemist's shop, about a mile away. Beside the road there was a house before which an old black dog, his great blunt muzzle grey with age, was always lying. I had got into the habit of speaking to him whenever I passed, but he had always stared back at me expressionlessly, like some stolid peasant Ivan or Misha in a Russian novel, and seemed to reserve his judgment on me: not even a wag of the tail. I was so depressed this day that I passed him without my usual greeting, and I had gone on a little distance when I found his warm blunt muzzle pushed into my hand. I looked at him; he looked at me; then he turned and walked back to his place with the air of one who had accomplished a necessary task. I fancy that he made this advance, so extraordinary in him, because by now he expected me to greet him, and wished to remind me, a little reprovingly, of my omission. But one can never tell from what quarter help may come, and as I went on I felt that the old dog knew I was worried and wished to comfort me. My feeling may have been quite false—I have no means of knowing—but the help was genuine.

My wife recovered after a while; and I was summoned to London to discuss with a publisher a German novel about which he could not make up his mind: later on it became a best-seller. In the spring we went to the south of France, so that my wife might recover; we had heard of the little fishing town of St Tropez, where the living was cheap. We took the German novel with us and translated it there.

We rented a furnished house a quarter of a mile out of the town. It was a pleasant place, with a quarry in its grounds, a number of almond trees and stone pines, and a little jungle of maquis. A pair of grass snakes lived there, sunning themselves in the recesses of the shrubs and leaving their cast-off skins on our door-step. St Tropez was filled with writers and painters, and a retinue of followers from England, America, France, Germany, Poland, Czechoslovakia; a foreign population with ways of their own, unlike those which they followed in their own countries, and quite unlike those of the St Tropez people.

It was now the middle of the 'twenties, and the cult of untrammelled freedom had become an established fashion among some of the intellectuals and artists. With the removal of restraint nothing, not even enjoyment, seemed to matter to them any longer, and life, under its assumed care-lessness, was joyless and without flavour. The convention of romantic love, the ideal of five centuries, had been discarded in Paris and Berlin and London, and to those who had got rid of it was no longer thinkable, or at best remained a blank area in their minds. These decent 'free' people therefore carried about with them a vague sense of loss, perhaps due to the permanent disappointment of discovering that, even though they followed their impulses, on principle or because they wished to, the result was quite different from what they had hoped. Ideal love had been nibbled at ever since Schopenhauer, who saw it as an illusion created by the Will to Live; marriage, its sacramental embodiment, had been questioned by Ibsen in the name of freedom; Shaw had invented the Life Force, an optimistic version of the Will to Live, and had shown it casting men and women together for its own purposes, which were intelligent according to him, but quite indifferent to mankind's longing to give its desires a high meaning. By now Ibsen and Shaw, having done their work, were almost forgotten, so that little was left but the freedom to yield to the mildest inclination in a 'civilized' way, knowing (and that was the root of the joylessness) that it did not matter in any case. There was something ambiguous in that life, for its freedom was not real freedom, but merely the rejection of choice. Innocence and experience had intermingled in a way so simple and baffling that each spoke with the other's voice, and there was no grace in innocence and no virtue in experience. Some years before, Aldous Huxley had described in *Antic Hay* the life of intellectuals in London who followed their inclinations. He made them vile; but the summer population of St Tropez were merely lost in a featureless world which gave them too easy an access to the satisfaction of their fleeting wishes; and these, being without meaning, remained beyond realization. They lived in an open landscape, without roads, or a stopping-place, or any point of the compass. Their brief love affairs resembled those of children who had acquired the knowledge and the desires of mature men and women, and in their conduct, perhaps even in their thoughts, remained children. They were lost and on the road to greater loss, and ready to accept any creed which would pull their lives together and give them the enormous relief of finding, even under compulsion, a direction for their existence, whether it had a spiritual meaning or not.

At the approach of winter we went to Menton, where we lived, still translating, in a little house on the side of a hill above the town. I began to write my story about Salzburg, and my wife sat down to a novel she had been turning over in her mind for a long time. Menton with its old-fashioned English colony, its Victorian grace, its superannuated old ladies dressed like Queen Alexandra, its modest incomes and regular habits, its aura of Cheltenham and Torquay, its English lending library still nursing the works of Marie Corelli, was a great relief after St Tropez. The delicious hills and valleys above the town had been chastened by the countless resigned, elderly English feet which had wandered among them; the very ants and caterpillars making their way across the little paths seemed to be conscious that a grave, watchful regard was upon them, and that they were expected to behave with decorum. We made friends with a delightful American couple, Arthur Mason and his wife Mary. Born in Ireland, Arthur had run away to sea at sixteen; after that he had led an adventurous life, had joined the gold-rush in the 'nineties, and known many conditions of life before settling down to write his stories of the sea, filled with humour and charm. He still owned a little gold-mine in some remote corner, and told us that if he were to work it, it might actually bring him in four pounds a week. Soon after we came, a Hungarian baroness set her cap at Arthur. She could not speak English and he could not speak German, and when she came over to the table where the four of us dined every evening, my wife had to translate for each of them in turn. The baroness would sit down beside Arthur, turn to my wife, and say: 'Tell him that he puts me into a fever; he glows like a volcano.' Arthur would listen glumly, and say after a pause: 'Tell her that the volcano is extinct.' The courtship of the baroness became more and more difficult, and at last she gracefully retired. Arthur and Mary returned to the States. I have not heard from them now for many years.

We stayed in Menton over two winters, and returned to England in the spring of 1927, when my wife was expecting a baby. We rented a furnished house in the village of Dormansland, near the Lingfield race-course. There was a path through the woods which led down to the course near the starting-point. It was a long, dry hot summer, and we often took the path to the race-course, for horses enchanted us and we could not think of any sound more exciting than the thunder of their hoofs as they swept down on us and flew past, a sound which made the ground hollow, like a great drum. We could watch them by ourselves, away from the bustle and noise of the stand, and without caring whether they lost or won; wishing them all, if that were possible, to pass the winning post together in one glorious line. They seemed to exist in a fabulous world of their own, oblivious of the watchers in the stand or even the jockeys on their backs; as if the race existed only for them.

Biographies were popular at the time, and I was commissioned by a publisher to write a life of John Knox. He was not a man I admired, but I had felt for a long time that he had had an influence on Scottish life which was still active. As I read about him in the British Museum I came to dislike him more and more, and understood why every Scottish writer since the beginning of the eighteenth century had detested him: Hume, Boswell, Burns, Scott, Hogg, Stevenson; everyone except Carlyle, who like Knox admired power. My book was not a good one; it was too full of dislike for Knox and certain things in Scottish life. Though dead for three centuries and a half, he was still too close for me to see him clearly, for I had met him, or someone very like him, over and over, it seemed to me, in the course of my life. The most surprising response to the book came from a Scottish minister. He told me he had never realized how badly the great reformer had behaved; it was clear to him that Knox was no gentleman.

Our son was born towards the end of October, and we went on living in the furnished house in Dormansland until the end of the next summer. By then we had managed to rent a house in Crowborough and bring our furniture into it. We were still making a tolerable income from translating. My wife had finished her novel, *Imagined Corners*, and I was working on a story of the Reformation, *The Three Brothers*. Our young son simplified life for us, and filled it with a daily sufficiency, beyond which we did not have any wish to look. Yet the poetry I wrote at that time was tinged with apprehension. The fears of writers living nearer the centre of things must have communicated themselves to us. 1930 had passed, and the poetry of Wystan Auden and Stephen Spender and Cecil Day Lewis had caught the general feeling that something must be done if we were not to be entangled in a war. It was the time of the slump, of unemployed processions and silent factories. We had lived remote from them in foreign countries; we were still isolated from them in Crowborough. Now and then, it is true, I would see groups of young men idly wandering down the road past our gate to the local Labour Exchange, but they seemed not quite real in a countryside where men and women were to be seen working every day in the fields. We scarcely realized the state of things which dictated these casual journeys to the Labour Exchange; the suffering of the cities was a distant dream, and the newspaper reports, because of the eternal ineffectualness of journalese, did not bring it nearer or make it more real.

Yet the apprehension had somehow reached us, and perhaps because of it, perhaps because of a feeling that we were living too far from the life of the time, we decided to move to London. By good luck we managed to rent a charming, dilapidated house in Hampstead. Curiously enough, my apprehension about the state of the world, which had darkened the poetry I had written in Crowborough, became far less troublesome now that I was in London, where everyone I met had been talking about it for a long time, until it had become an ordinary theme for conversation. Hampstead was filled with writing people and haunted by young poets despairing over the poor and the world, but despairing together, in a sad but comforting communion. Perhaps despair can be really felt only in solitude. It cannot reach its measure if it encounters other despairs. When it does, it can talk itself into a state of comparative rationality.

The poetry of Auden and Spender and Day Lewis, as I say, was being much spoken about. Dylan Thomas and George Barker were writing their first obscure verse; David Gascoyne, still in his teens, was interested in surrealism. Geoffrey Grigson was conducting his lively journal, *New Verse*. A new generation had appeared from a country which I had never guessed at; they had been nurtured on strange food and prepared, it seemed, by a secret discipline; now they appeared to belong in a specific way to the present, as if it were theirs exclusively, or as if they had been forged by it alone. My wife and I came to know most of them and had no difficulty in entering into the world their minds moved in; but to us there seemed to be a hiatus between it and the poetry they wrote, so that they seemed to be more real than their poetry. This was explicable enough; they were young, and their work was still to find its true shape.

To my surprise Holms, who was now living in London, was much impressed by the political poetry, and saw in it a new possibility. He had lived so long in his timeless world, where even words had lost their solidity, that the limitation the new poets imposed upon their work, the direct purpose they aimed at, may have given him the sense of present reality which he needed, and the hope of stepping out of his vast insubstantial dream on to firm ground. I did not quite believe in Auden's limestone country and deserted factories, and I misdoubted the adequacy of his purpose: he and his contemporaries have now left all that behind. The political interpretation of life which seemed so new at the time and so applicable, was only one of several that might have been made, and even combined with psychology, as it was later, it did not give any deep insight into 'the life of things,' but stopped at the reality of categories. With Lenin and Mussolini and Hitler the outlines of power had grown sharper than they had been for a century. To take sides, therefore, seemed to be the only choice for intelligent people, and where there are only two sides the choice becomes too easy.

There was at the time among young writers a great interest in Marx, whom they had suddenly discovered. I felt no temptation to become a Communist, for I had been a Socialist in my twenties, when we thought more of humanity and brotherhood than of class-war and revolution. I had studied the Communist theory at that time and been repelled by it. History as the unending anger of class against class seemed an empty idea which, like a curious mechanism, explained nothing but itself. A gospel which exhorted me to fan class anger until the pure flame of revolution should break out was a mere grammar of force which turned men and women of the dispossessed class into anonymous units, with no hope but the one hope, no desire but the one desire. I had been made a Socialist by the degradation of the poor and the hope for an eventual reign of freedom, justice and brotherhood. Instead of these things Communism offered me the victory of a class, and substituted the proletariat for a moral idea. It was as if a conjuring trick had been played with a hope as old as Isaiah, and what the heart had conceived as love and peace had been transmuted into anger and conflict. In these early days we could still pity the stock-broker distorted by money as well as the casual worker deformed by poverty. What claimed our love and compassion was misshapen humanity in all its forms, and we looked forward to the great release. Instead, Communism presented itself as a strange, solidly made object, very like a huge clock, with metal bowels, no feelings, and no explanation for itself but its own impenetrable mechanism; it was neither glad nor sad, and reverenced only its own guaranteed working.

I was struck by the difference between the feeling of the political poets and the feeling among Socialists twenty years before. The new poetry was influenced by Marx (as we were not): it knew a great deal about the present (which we did not); and it put its faith in revolution, and revolution as soon as possible. It seemed to exist so entirely in the present that it had inadvertently removed the future. Our dreams had been tinged by the radiance of peace. The new poets came of age in a time of danger and power. If they acted, and their poems were acts, they had no choice but to act in terms of power. The immediate future was all danger, the present all urgency; for the future had to be decided for good or ill in a matter of years or even of months.

To us, twenty years before, the present was not urgent nor the future dangerous; in our sleep-walking we saw an almost infinite peaceful expanse where by little change after little change the ideal society would at last come about, surprised to find itself there. We were so little in the present and so unconcerned about the immediate future because our eyes were on the end, which we never imagined we would see. Clearly the world in which we lived then was not the real world. The first war awoke some of us from our dream, but it did not quite awaken me, my hopes were too stubborn; and it is possible to live in the present world nursing hopes that belong to the past. But there are also immemorial hopes. The new poetry had left the immemorial hopes behind it; in no imaginable future would the lion and the lamb lie down together; they belonged to a mythology which Marx had exploded; and all that was left for the lamb now was to arm itself with the latest equipment and liquidate the lion. Better still if it could transform itself into a different kind of lion, more intelligent and more ruthless. Power as they saw it exercised in the world confronted the political poets with this choice; if a single other thought had intervened choice might have become free again. They acted honourably, desperately and mistakenly. And Marx provided them with an old-fashioned weapon.

In Hampstead, then, my old objections to Communism rose up again, as well as a new one which seemed to me at first far-fetched, but I think is humanly valid. I can only express it by saying that in the Communist scheme there is no place for forgiveness, except at the end of time; no chink through which mercy to a bad or lapsed Communist can steal, or admiration for a brave or good opponent. The religious man is bound to forgive; the ordinary man forgives easily. Without forgiveness our life would be unimaginable, and

> Humanity must perforce prey on itself,
> Like monsters of the deep.

It seemed to me that there was no place in the 'System' for great and magnanimous actions, any more than for the natural affections. To forgive an enemy was a sin against the system; to forgive an erring brother was reprehensible weakness. I tried to think of ordinary people, husbands and wives, fathers and mothers and children, lovers and friends, and to imagine them all as unforgiving and unforgiven, on principle and not merely by inclination; and I realized that it was impossible to wish this and to understand mankind. To think in such ways either kills or falsifies the imagination. It is easy for the false imagination to hate a whole class; it is hard for the true imagination to hate a single human being. I thought of the device the Scottish Covenanters displayed on their banners in their battles against Montrose: 'Christ and No Quarter.' How could one expect hatred and violence to achieve the ideal community, or the dictatorship of the proletariat to bring in universal freedom?

At that time conversion to Communism seemed to be easy, especially to the young. It was, I fancy, because people were hypnotized by the false alternatives. A girl we had known in Austria—she was now a refugee—dropped in on us now and then, and scolded us for hanging back from the great decision. A pleasant kindly girl, she had become embittered by persecution in her own country and the theoretical hatred which she had learned since. She had a strong sense of duty; now she had made her choice; and she was so sure she had done right that she could not understand why we did not follow her example. Looking round our pleasant little sitting-room, she accused us of hard-heartedness for living in such ease and idleness—actually we were working from morning to night—while the masses existed in misery. She had enjoyed a fairly comfortable life in Austria and Germany; she was poor now, scraping a livelihood as a refugee, and was greatly changed. She felt sure that only idleness or selfish interest prevented us from joining the Party. She was too much in earnest to be a good propagandist.

But I must not give the impression that we met many Communists at that time, and it is strange to me that, in spite of the general dread, and our drudgery turning German into English, and our periodical money worries, we were happy. I fancy that even under dictatorships, where apprehension is a daily part of life, people have a spring of happiness, not from any privately nursed ideal, but simply from the society of friends, an inexhaustible, hidden source. We have come to think so much of politics as colouring or overshadowing all our thoughts and feelings that it is easy for us to forget the truth, which is that the impulses of the heart come of themselves, and that our most precious experience takes place, happily for us, in a universal unchanging underground. There seems to have been no objective reason for our happiness in Hampstead, and when I try to resuscitate it now it seems to have been made up of a confusion of things, many of them quite trifling. First of all, we had many more friends than in the years when we had lived abroad or in the English countryside. Geoffrey Grigson and Donald and Catherine Carswell were three minutes away. George Malcolm Thomson, an old friend of ours, was a little distance up the hill. George Barker and Dylan Thomas dropped in at all hours. Hugh Kingsmill, who lived in Hastings now, came to see us when he was in London. And there were many more, whom it would be tedious to mention. Holms often came, bringing with him Peggy Guggenheim, who told us curious stories of the American colony in Paris after the first war. Looking back on our long abstention from society, we felt there was no pleasure greater than that of good company.

The house itself was a source of happiness. It was an old dilapidated Strawberry Hill Gothic house, which vibrated gently whenever the underground train passed beneath it. A plumber and repairer had attended to it for an absent-minded trust for forty years. Plumbing had developed during that time, but he had not. The roof of our bedroom leaked, and for the first few weeks we had to sleep with a large umbrella over our heads, in case of rain. We got him to put in a new bath, but he absent-mindedly left the waste-pipe hanging in the air, and the first time the bath was filled water poured down into the dining-room below, bringing a large chunk of plaster with it. The lavatory pan swayed precariously when you sat on it. The garden at the back was filled with small bones and oyster-shells. An elderly lady who had had the house before us had spent her days in bed, living on mutton chops and oysters, and throwing the bones and the shells through the open window. As I look back at our troubles with the house, they seem part of the pleasure it gave us, though they must have been exasperating at the time. The fact was that we were in love with its sweet, battered, Mozartian grace, and for that were prepared to forgive it anything.

We endured our maids too for the sake of the house: the quiet (Welsh) one who left to get married, taking a selection of our sheets and pillow-slips with her; the (Scottish and Northern English) ones who introduced suspicious characters into the house under our noses, and left secretly one night after having drunk all our wine and whisky; the sad little Cockney (from Camden Town) whom my wife engaged out of pity, but who felt lost away from her pub and her friends. At last our luck turned. On one day we got hold of Hilde, a refugee German, and Eja, a Finnish student who had come to England for a year to improve her English. The house grew stable under their reign, and Hilde, a remarkable woman whose story should be told sometime, became a close friend. She went with us a few years later, when we moved to St Andrews. Then, in 1938, she decided to return to Germany and get married; she thought she would be able to hold her tongue now. She did not marry after all, for she could not trace the birth certificates of her grandparents—a condition of marriage under the Nazi regulations. Impatient with the official nonsense, she took a post in a hotel. In the summer of 1939 she wrote to my wife asking if she could come and spend a holiday with us in September. Willa replied asking her to come; but before that could happen the war broke out. We thought we should never see her again, but we under-estimated her resource. In the third year of the war I had a letter from an English prisoner in Germany informing me that 'Hilda' had married an Italian. Eighteen months later a post-card arrived from a Scottish soldier beginning: 'Dear Edwin, As brother Scot to brother Scot, you will be glad to hear that Hilda has had a baby and that mother and child are both doing well.' When we left for Czechoslovakia, we gave up all hope of hearing from her. We were mistaken. Shortly after we left she had written to our address in St Andrews, and the letter had been returned to her. Then she wrote to a St Andrews girl who had sometimes helped her with her housework. The girl met our son in the street—he was studying in St Andrews at the time—and asked him for his parents' address. Presently we had a letter from Hilde in Prague. She was living in the little village of Cremia on Lake Como with her husband and son. When a few years later I was posted by the British Council to Rome, my wife wrote to her and asked if she would like to come to keep our flat for us. She arrived with her little boy and soon got a post as waiter for her husband. She had been bombed out of three separate houses in Germany and lost everything she had. In the last year of the war she had suffered great hardships, trundling a perambulator over the country roads to get food from remote farm-houses, and living as she could. She looked very thin and much older, but in a few months she began to recover.

All this was still in the future. In Hampstead Hilde established order in our house, and fed us twice as well as the other maids had done, at half the cost. When she first came she was still shaken by the things she had seen done in Germany. She had been crossing a square in Munich early one morning on her way to the hotel where she worked, when she saw a young Jew lying on the ground dead and covered with blood. Some young soldiers were standing by grinning, and she turned upon them, calling them 'Halunken mit aufgepflanzten Bayonetten.' They told her to be careful, else something might happen to her too. A few days later a hint was dropped to her that she had better leave the country. She got across to Switzerland and from there to England, where she took a post as a kitchen-maid in a large house. From it she came to us.

Hilde was an Aryan, born in Alsace, where she had spent the first few years of her life hiding in cellars in a village which was bombarded in turn by the Germans and the British. Her mother had a hotel in Germany, and Hilde spent most of her life there until the Nazis came into power; she became a hotel manager, and had a whole row of medals and diplomas. Her ambition is still to run a hotel of her own, and if anyone who reads this has good sense, imagination, an interest in hotels, and money to spare, he can do nothing better than hand some hotel over to her; in Italy if possible. It would repay him and give a remarkable woman the chance of her life. My wife and she still write to each other.

Hilde was part of our happiness in Hampstead. But Hampstead itself, its old streets and old houses, the Heath five minutes' walk away, the little shops like shops in a village, the sense of seclusion and leisure on the verge of a great city, the need to walk only a few steps if one wanted to see a friend: all these were parts of the happiness. Even our dog Matthew, a golden cocker spaniel, was woven into it, with his noble melting Colonel Newcome eyes, his unbridled appetites, his raffish air when he wanted to joke with us, and his habit of flopping down on the floor in sudden boredom and turning his mind at once to more serious and practical things. But how evoke the ghost of a happiness, or how account for happiness when Auden's 'sixteen skies of Europe' were so sombre, and we knew it so well.

We were still translating from the German, mainly from Hermann Broch and Franz Kafka. At one stage Kafka's stories continued themselves in our dreams, unfolding into slow serpentine nightmares, immovably reasonable. They troubled us, but not as real dreams would have done, for they did not seem to come from our own minds but from a workshop at the periphery of consciousness busily turning out, for its own private satisfaction, a succession of weird inventions. They had laws of their own, and this made them slightly unconvincing, not to be taken seriously.

But I was troubled by one dream I had in Hampstead. A friend of mine had written an enthusiastic review of a volume of my poems; a week or two later, having thought them over more carefully, he reviewed them again, coldly; then, after an interval, he reviewed them yet again, and had hardly a word to say for them. A vague apprehension that he might go on reviewing them for ever, in a steady scale of depreciation, sometimes came into my mind, and one night I dreamt of him. He had turned into a frisky young colt, steaming with fire and mischief, kicking up his heels and galloping up and down the street before our door. At last he trotted in through the gate and rang the door-bell. I had been watching him from the window, and when I opened the door I was surprised to find that he had changed to his human shape again. Without saying a word he snatched a dagger from his pocket and struck at my breast. But the dagger did not go in; it was one of those trick daggers where the blade slides back through the sheath when the point touches anything. We looked at each other in surprise, not knowing what to say. Then he hurried away, throwing a cheerful 'Good-morning' over his shoulder. A comic image of a fanciful fear.

Our happiness was abruptly terminated one hot summer day, when a young girl came to our door, gasping out, 'Oh, Mrs Muir, your little boy has been run over.' We ran down the street towards the Heath and found a small crowd waiting beside the main road. Our son was lying on the grass, one of his feet sagging to the side, as if it had no connection with his leg. An immense oil-tank was drawn up near by. Gavin was very pale and quite silent. An ambulance was coming down the hill. He was carried into it, we went in with him; the hospital was a little distance up the road. His leg had been broken in two places, and he was suffering from concussion. He was five at the time.

We were told how the accident had happened. Gavin had been out on the Heath with our Irish maid and was coming home. He was running ahead; the maid was following with the dog Matthew on a lead. The oil-tank was coming down the hill, and Gavin, being a daring little boy, thought he could beat it. He might have succeeded, but at the last minute he hesitated. The lorry driver braked desperately, but could not quite avoid him. The nurse stood chained to the dog.

Gavin was in the hospital for two weeks; then we brought him home with his leg in plaster, and he lay for a few weeks longer on the sofa in the sitting-room and in good weather on a swing-settee which we had set up in the garden. But when he was able to walk again he twitched and trembled whenever a car passed, and we saw that we should have to leave Hampstead for a quieter place. A friend got a furnished house for us in St Andrews. But first we went to Orkney, so that our son should have a complete rest. We lodged in a farmhouse off the main road. It was run by a young farmer whose family had tilled it for centuries. He and his pretty young wife and his mother lived there in a serenity which reminded me of the Italian family who had given us coffee and let us dry our clothes at their fire many years before. But how different the house was, how clean and airy and bright. From the windows we looked down on the isle of Damsay, with its one farm and the ruins of a chapel said to have been built by Adamnan, the disciple and biographer of St Columba. A path across a field led down to the beach, and we spent most of our time there. I had not been back to Orkney for many years; few of the people I had known were there still; but the beauty of the light showered from the wide sky and reflected from the spreading waters, and diffused, a double radiance, over the bright fields, was the same beauty I had known as a child; and the loneliness of every shape rising from the treeless land, the farmhouses and the moving outlines of men and women against the sky, had, as then, the simplicity of an early world. The peace helped to still Gavin's fears. After a month we moved south to St Andrews.

CHAPTER ELEVEN

Scotland

My wife had been a student at St Andrews, and because of
her pleasant memories of it and the quietness of the little
town, we had chosen it as a place to live in. It had been a
lively place when she was there; and the town-life she knew
had been made by the students. We were now in our middle
age, and when we wanted company we had to resort to our
sad compeers. The minds of people seem to grow older more
quickly in small towns than in great ones; they get fixed in
their place; and the fixity and the steady advance of time
between them beget a sanctioned timidity, where no one
any longer expects much. We could find no one to talk to.

All this time the world was growing darker. The Spanish
war had broken out; and presently a committee formed itself
in the town for the support of Basque refugee children,
some of whom were already quartered in the houses of
kind-hearted women. The emergency brought a number
of people together, Liberals, Socialists and churchgoers,
and ourselves among them, and created a centre in the
self-contained, averted little town. Without knowing very
much about the situation, we were on the side of the
Republicans; George Orwell had not made his first-hand
report on it yet. We were, of course, right to be against
Franco, but wrong to take the other side so self-righteously.
Everyone who serves a political movement must be appalled
later by the confident blindness of his choice.

The internal political pressure was also increasing. The
campaign for a popular front to include Liberals, Socialists and Communists was warming up, and after a few
discussions with odd acquaintances we became perfectly
convinced that it was the policy to be supported. Soon afterwards the town was split in two over the policy of Neville
Chamberlain. People who had been fast friends passed each

other in the street without speaking. The Spanish War dragged on, the second world war was approaching. And in a region of their own a group of Buchmanites flourished, leaving tracts at house-doors.

It was a depressing time, and there was no one with whom we could discuss the dangers we felt coming but our two friends, Drury and Oscar Oeser. Oscar was a lecturer in psychology at the University. They were intelligent, honest and pessimistic. With them we decided to start a small informal club to discuss the questions of the day. The members met on Sunday evenings at one another's houses; the Oesers and ourselves, a congregational minister, two teachers from St Leonard's Girl's School, two trade unionists, a local dustman, and some others. Like all who discuss political things, we assumed that we knew more about them than we actually did, and consequently came to no decision or to inadequate ones. The friendship which sprang up among us was the chief good produced by our meetings.

Though I took part in political discussions, I was really concerned during these years with something quite different. I had been happy in London; I was more unhappy in St Andrews than I had been since the time of my obscure fears and the course of psychoanalysis that dispelled them. I had come to a point from which, looking back, I was profoundly dissatisfied with myself. The turning of German books, good and bad, into English, had become meaningless as a way of life, and more and more difficult to support because of its meaninglessness. I began to keep a diary, as a sort of judgement on myself, and I find in it entries such as this:

> After a certain age all of us, good and bad, are guilt-stricken because of powers within us which have never been realized; because, in other words, we are not what we should be.

That observation was directed against myself, and the question continued to obsess me during these years:

> I am astonished by the contrast between the powers I am aware of in me and the triteness of my life. As I grow

older I feel more and more the need to make that barren astonishment effectual, to wrest some palpable prize from it; for I cannot see that the astonishment itself is of any use to me. I have a body, affections, desires, needs, like all men. I lead in essentials much the same life. My time is spent in the routine of sleeping, eating, working, and sleeping again. I say the same things as everyone else, am daily troubled by the same cares, perform the same actions, the actions which keep us alive. There is nothing extraordinary in all this. But when I turn to the thoughts and images in my mind—I admit I do this only at exceptional moments—what a difference. What an unbelievable difference.

My dissatisfaction with myself made me turn against other people as well:

The other night at a party in Edinburgh. Scientists mainly: good people; clever: honest: disinterested. But without a soul among them. Take H., for instance. He is a pleasant fellow; has an acute mind; is an amusing talker; surprisingly 'human'; a good husband; an indulgent father; with a love for poetry; engaging; but without a soul. Mitrinović, my old Serbian acquaintance, used to say of Bertrand Russell: 'When he die, the angels, they find nothing to eat on his bones.' H. gives me nothing to eat. Yet I am fond of him, and sorry for him as if he were a changeling.

I was sometimes haunted by animal traits in human beings, as I had been many years before, sitting in a Glasgow tramcar looking at a man like a pig:

The cold considering eye which one human being sometimes turns on another without being aware of it. J. R., for instance. I caught him last night looking at me in that way, as if he were asking: Well, what the devil are you? The same look that one animal gives another at their first encounter. I know I must look at people like this sometimes, and probably quite often. Yet how hateful it is, and how hateful it makes human nature.

Shortly after this there is another entry, written at a very low ebb:

> We all come out of a hole and go back into a hole. Leave hiding and go back into hiding. The distance between is disguise.

During these years I wrote very little poetry, and I think it must have been out of my obsession with animal traits flitting across human features that a poem called *The Face* emerged like a frightening monster:

> I should have worn a terror-mask, should be
> A sight to frighten hope and faith away,
> Half charnel field, half battle and rutting ground.
> Instead I am a smiling summer sea
> That sleeps while underneath from bound to bound
> The sun- and star-shaped killers gorge and play.

After that there came a turn for the better:

> I can see men and women as really human only when I see them as immortal souls. Otherwise they are unnatural, self-evidently not what they are by their nature; they do not exist in their *own* world.

This dialogue with myself went on. Meanwhile the world was darkening, and our work was growing precarious. Then my wife fell ill and had to go into a nursing home. After she began to recover, I was returning from the nursing home one day—it was the last day of February 1939—when I saw some schoolboys playing at marbles on the pavement; the old game had 'come round' again at its own time, known only to children, and it seemed a simple little rehearsal for a resurrection, promising a timeless renewal of life. I wrote in my diary next day:

> Last night, going to bed alone, I suddenly found myself (I was taking off my waistcoat) reciting the Lord's Prayer in a loud, emphatic voice—a thing I had not done for many years—with deep urgency and profound disturbed emotion. While I went on I grew more composed; as if it had been empty and craving and were being replenished,

my soul grew still; every word had a strange fullness of meaning which astonished and delighted me. It was late; I had sat up reading; I was sleepy; but as I stood in the middle of the floor half-undressed, saying the prayer over and over, meaning after meaning sprang from it, overcoming me again with joyful surprise; and I realized that this simple petition was always universal and always inexhaustible, and day by day sanctified human life.

I had believed for many years in God and the immortality of the soul; I had clung to the belief even when, in horrifying glimpses, I saw animals peeping through human eyes. My belief receded then, it is true, to an unimaginable distance, but it still stood there, not in any territory of mine, it seemed, but in a place of its own. Now I realized that, quite without knowing it, I was a Christian, no matter how bad a one; and I remembered a few days later that Janet Adam Smith had told me, half-teasingly, while I was staying in Hampstead, that my poetry was Christian poetry: the idea then had been quite strange to me. I had a vague sense during these days that Christ was the turning-point of time and the meaning of life to everyone, no matter what his conscious beliefs; to my agnostic friends as well as Christians. I read the New Testament many times during the following months, particularly the Gospels. I did not turn to any church, and my talks with ministers and divines cast me back upon the Gospels again, which was probably the best thing that could have happened. I had no conception of the splendours of Christendom; I remained quite unaware of them until some years later I was sent by the British Council to Italy.

The war came at last, and our income from German translations stopped. I was writing a novel review for *The Listener* every fortnight; I had begun when Janet Adam Smith was literary editor, and when Joe Ackerley followed her he kindly asked me to continue. I was doing a weekly review for *The Scotsman* and occasional work for the Scottish B.B.C.; but all this did not bring in enough to keep the house going. My wife and I applied for teaching posts; she had a degree in classics and experience as a teacher, and

received offers from schools in distant parts of Scotland, but
to accept any of them would have meant breaking up the
family. No answer came to my applications, for I had no
degree and had never taught. At last my wife was offered
a badly paid post in the little local prep school which Gavin
was attending, and I got a job in the Food Office in Dundee.
Before that I had joined the Home Guard and was drilled
in the evenings by a retired sergeant, on the grounds of
the University, along with professors, divines, teachers
and shop-assistants. At night I took my turn guarding the
telephone exchange, armed with a silver-mounted shot-gun
which had been presented by a local landowner, but with no
ammunition. To pace alone around the telephone exchange
from two to four in the morning emptied the mind of
the cares of the day and removed the war itself to an
inconceivable distance. In the room where we slept between
our turns of duty, there was peace and a complete sense of
identity among us, except for occasional flurries of gossip
in which the secret cupboards of the town were opened
with almost affectionate candour. My return in the morning
through the empty streets prolonged the tranquil pleasure of
these night vigils, until, with breakfast and the newspaper,
the war and my personal worries rushed back again.

The town was a unity as it had never been before.
Shopkeepers and workmen who had had army experience
were set above professors and lawyers, and the change was
accepted as natural though surprising. We were without
arms, but we observed good discipline, and though we
had nothing to defend ourselves with, looked forward in
excellent heart to the possibility of an invasion.

This was in the early days, and arms were presently supplied to the Home Guard. But before that I had to leave it.
One evening I overstrained myself carrying sand-bags; what
they were intended for I have quite forgotten. By this time I
was working in the Food Office and taking evening classes
on English Literature to make a little more money. I began
to have pains in my chest. A local doctor came to examine
me and told me that if I did not rest completely for six weeks
he could not guarantee that I would live for another year. I
lay in a room on the top floor of the house, trying to forget

that money was needed and I was not earning any. My wife was away all day with Gavin at the prep school. My meals were sent in from a boarding-house next door. It astonishes me that I summoned a few moments of peace there, in spite of my worries and the knowledge that my wife was not well.

When I got up—it was spring again—my wife had to take to bed; she did not get any better, and was driven off to a nursing home to undergo a difficult operation. She awoke from it in such weakness that the doctors feared for her life; for some days she had to be kept alive with sips of champagne. One day when I went to see her I realized that my being there no longer had any meaning for her; she had gone too far away and she did not have the strength to reach out her hand to me. That was our worst day. Then very slowly she began to recover. We were in another spring, and again as I walked back from the nursing home one day the children were playing at marbles on the pavement, rehearsing their perennial ceremony. It was a long time before my wife recovered, and when she came home at last she had shrunk as if by some chemical process, and life, of which she had been so full, had sunk to its inmost source. Years passed before she returned to the semblance of what she had once been.

In the autumn of 1941 I had a letter from Harvey-Wood, the Scottish Representative of the British Council, asking me if I would give a talk on contemporary English literature to a group of Polish officers stationed in Edinburgh. My talk was liked and the Poles asked if they could have me again. This was my first connection with the British Council; it lasted for eight years, and was a very happy one.

In the beginning of 1942 Harvey-Wood wrote offering me a post in the Council. He had started certain international houses in Edinburgh: a Polish House, a Czechoslovak House, a French House, where soldiers and refugees from these countries could meet one another and the people of Edinburgh. He wanted someone to provide evening programmes for the houses—an American one was added after America came into the war—and engage lecturers and arrange concerts. I agreed willingly, and on the morning of March the second, 1942, in a snowstorm, I began my duties in the Edinburgh office. My wife and son were to stay in St Andrews until I could find a flat.

I still remember my first day in the Edinburgh office. As I had to know all the people I would be dealing with, Harvey-Wood had arranged for a number of them to come, and the day passed in a continuous sequence of introductions and discussions. During the past years my wife and I had seen only a few people; now in a day I met more of them than I had done in a twelvemonth; and when I returned to my lodgings in the evening I went up to my room and did not stir from it again for fear of meeting someone else. But I soon got used to talking to many people; my new work was interesting; and I felt at last that I was doing something useful, like everybody else. Under the inspiration of Harvey-Wood, the work of the Council in Edinburgh was universally admired at that time, and it had attached to it the intelligence of the city, old and young, so that Edinburgh enjoyed an excess of life and enterprise. This made my own work easy. I drafted programmes for the foreign houses, arranged concerts, and wrote scripts, and was out for three or four evenings a week to see that everything was going as it should. Lecturers were willing to talk to our audiences in the friendly houses; Sir Herbert Grierson, though old now and lame, gave a great deal of his time to them; and when we wrote to London, T. S. Eliot and Stephen Spender and John Betjeman and Hugh Kingsmill and many others willingly came.

I was too busy to have time for the agonized introspections of St Andrews, and I felt again, as I had done in Hampstead, that it was good to be among people and to make friends. I got a flat at last, and Willa and Gavin came down from St Andrews.

All sorts of things were discussed in the friendly atmosphere of the houses: the war, the future of Europe, on which our hopes were beginning to fix themselves, the habits and traditions of different lands. The terrible memories which the refugees brought with them became more distant and bearable as they fell into the mould of a story, often repeated. I spent a great deal of time on tramcars, travelling to and from the office and back and forward among the houses. Sitting on the top, looking at the windows flying past, feeling as if I were in no fixed place, as if I were nowhere, I found odd lines coming into my mind again, after such a long absence; and though my time was busily occupied, I wrote more poetry in Edinburgh than in all the years in St Andrews.

In my last two years in the Edinburgh office, it was clear to everybody that the war was coming to an end. Peace arrived at last; I felt that my work in Edinburgh was done; and as I had known Czechoslovakia before, I applied to the Council to send me there. They offered me the post of Director of the British Institute in Prague.

CHAPTER TWELVE

Prague Again

At the end of August I set out for Prague. My wife had to stay behind for a while to dispose of our furniture and settle our other affairs. My son was studying at St Andrews University.

I was asked to take out a private car belonging to the British Council Representative. The official Council car was being brought out by the librarian, Cyril Saunders. Before leaving England he and I met a young man who was going to a post in the Information Service of the Embassy, and we decided to drive down together with him through Belgium and Germany to Czechoslovakia.

When we reached Germany there seemed to be nothing unmarked by the war: the towns in ruins, the roads and fields scarred and deserted. It was like a country where the population had become homeless, and when we met occasional family groups on the roads they seemed to be on a pilgrimage from nowhere to nowhere. In the towns and far out in the countryside we met them pushing their belongings on hand-carts, with a look of dull surprise on their faces. Few trains were running; the great machine was broken; and the men, but for the women and children following them, might have been survivors of one of the mediaeval crusades wandering back across Europe to seek their homes. Now by all appearances there were no homes for them to seek.

As we passed through Aachen there were crowds at what had once been the street-corners; haunting, perhaps, the places which they had once frequented when the town was standing. They looked like industrial workers, grimy and apathetic, gathered before the gates of factories which had shut for good. Few cars were on the roads, yet they paid little attention to our cortege of three as it passed.

In a few hours we reached Cologne and drove through the fine straight avenue leading into it from the north. All the houses were standing, and for a moment the sense of a settled peaceful life came back. It was an illusion. The spacious houses were roofless, the windows empty gaps. Presently the sour stench of the corpses buried under the ruins rose about us. The stench, the unreal houses, the crumbling pavements, prepared us for a dead city; yet people were out as usual for their Sunday evening walk in their Sunday best, the children decked in chance remnants of finery. It was a lovely late summer evening, and the peaceful crowds in that vast graveyard were like the forerunners of a multitude risen in a private resurrection day to an unimaginable new life. It was moving to see a simple courteous inclination of the heart so calmly surviving, upheld by nothing but its own virtue after the destruction of all that had nourished it.

Our journey to Prague took us longer than we had expected. Ten miles or so past Godesberg the car I was driving began to rattle alarmingly and then stopped. The young Embassy man drove back to Godesberg to get help from the British Army. Saunders and I waited in the broken-down car. There was a little farm a mile away, and on a height opposite us a fair, bearded man was sitting in the evening light with a collie at his feet. He looked as if he were keeping watch. Presently a woman came along the road leading a little girl by the hand. I got out and wished her good evening. She stopped for a while, as people do in country places, and talked with peasant resignation of the hardships of the war, which had passed over this quiet spot. The child had been sent to her from Munich, where its parents had been killed in an air raid. When I told her that I had just come from England she looked at me in wonder. As we went on talking I felt that England was a place beyond her imagining, a distant fabulous country, more strange to her than wicked. She had been to a prayer-meeting and was returning to the little farm. I learned later that in this quiet neighbourhood a band of Displaced Persons, as they were called, were living in the woods; they had raided several farms and committed some murders. Perhaps that was why the man with the dog was keeping watch on the hill.

Late at night, in pouring rain, an army lorry arrived to tow us back to Godesberg. The commanding officer, a young major in the Guards, gay and kind, had a meal waiting for us when we arrived, and lots of wine. When he heard we were going to Prague he pretended he could not believe his ears and strongly advised us against it. 'You'll never get through,' he assured us, half in earnest. And during our stay he would say now and then: 'When I visit the salt mines in Russia in twenty years' time, I'll look down and say, "What, is that you there still, Muir and Saunders? Well, you should have taken my advice."' He installed us in one of the luxury summer villas that bordered the river and never tired of entertaining us and shaking his head over us.

We were told that it would take a few days to repair the car, and during that time we walked about the streets of the little town, which still seemed to express a wish to please. But the shop windows showed nothing but packets of dried vegetables, neat and sordid. The people were subdued or unfriendly, and a middle-aged lady whom we were always meeting put her nose in the air and glared at us whenever she passed. The Guardsmen told us that they had no connection with the townspeople. These tall men, striding about with the traditional pride of their regiment, must have made the Godesbergers unfairly conscious that they were in a conquered country.

I spoke to a German policeman one day. He was all on our side, and began by assuring me that he had never belonged to the Nazi Party. We talked for a while about the war, but then the blood rushed to his face and he started blaming Britain because she did not stop Hitler before he became too powerful. I said that the Germans themselves should have seen to that, but he cried, 'We couldn't! We couldn't!' He would not admit that Germany, the true Germany, was to blame for anything.

We were told at last that it would take several weeks to put the car right; spare parts would have to be brought out from England; so we decided to proceed in the two remaining cars. At Frankfort we ate in the mess of the American Army and slept in a hotel which had been split in two, so that the passage outside our bedrooms had only one wall and hung precariously over nothing. Crowds of young boys wandered the streets, confidently begging from the soldiers; they looked lost and gay. We stopped at Nuremberg and clambered ever the ruins of the old town. I remembered a few days I had spent there with my wife during our stay in Hellerau. The town had enchanted us; so much affection had gone into the building of it; every house was a simple embodiment of the impulse which makes people create a little world around them to which they can attach their affections. Now nothing was left but jagged blocks of masonry. As I clambered over the debris I tried to find Dürer's house and the little fountain in the square, but nothing seemed to be left except some fragments of the city wall.

In Nuremberg we were not far from Czechoslovakia. We entered it next morning and drove on in some trepidation towards the point where we should reach Russian territory. At a little house by the wayside we were stopped by a soldier with fixed bayonet. He was short and compact, with a pale face tinged with yellow, his eyes quite expressionless and giving out the interior light of glowing, highly polished stones. We showed him our papers; he turned them over in his hands and tried to read them from every side, as if at last he would find the right one, then gave it up and carried them into the little house. An officer appeared; he discussed the papers for some time with the soldier, came over and spoke to us in some language we could not understand, shrugged his shoulders, returned to consult with the soldier again, and with a puzzled look retired into the house. In a field beside the road a Russian soldier was standing in the middle of a field of winter wheat, keeping watch over some horses which were grazing on it and trampling the tender shoots. Some time passed; the sentry was again at his station; the road was empty; there was no sign of the officer. We wondered if he had forgotten us or was still trying to decide whether he would let us though or send us back. Then he reappeared, looked at us again and after a short inspection turned back into the house. The soldier stood in the middle of the field; the horses went on grazing. Then the officer came to the door and had another look, seemed put out because we were still there, but turned back and appeared at last with our papers in his hand. Walking across he pushed them at the young Embassy man, gave us all a sharp and knowing look, and waved imperiously to indicate that we should drive on.

In the late afternoon we reached Prague and drove through dense crowds to the Embassy, where we had to report. We learned that General Montgomery had paid a visit to the city that day. Saunders and I went off to a hotel where rooms had been booked for us.

Prague was still recognizable as the city I had known twenty-four years before, and I spent an hour or two proving that I could find my way about, and recognizing houses and streets which I had forgotten. In some indefinable way they looked different from my memory of them, and by a detail here and there insisted on their individuality, which had been worn smooth in the process by which the mind helps to make everything entirely conformable to it. The new impression was more vivid and less agreeable than I had expected; it was as if whole series of familiar objects were presenting themselves a second time and asking to be disgested again. During my first few weeks in Prague I felt I was in a strange place, and was teased by the fancy of another city, the same and yet not the same, whose streets I or someone very like me had walked many years before.

It had been arranged that we should have our meals in a restaurant in the Small Town, which served as the Embassy Mess. In the hotel and the restaurants no meat could be had, but only dried vegetables served with a thick and ambiguous sauce, and *knedlik*, a kind of heavy dumpling of which the Czechs are fond. The shop windows showed the same repulsive dry packets which we had seen in Godesberg; that trade mark of the short Nazi empire must have been scattered over the greater part of Western Europe at that time. The crowds in the streets looked undernourished and apprehensive; here and there I saw a man jerking his head over his shoulder, as if the memory of being watched and followed still lingered in his nerves. The Czechs as I had known them were a noisy, somewhat unruly people; but now they hardly spoke. Russian soldiers were everywhere, short powerful hairy men, who seemed to be lost in the alien city and only half-aware of the power they possessed and the fear they inspired. I was told that the Russians who first entered Prague were fine, handsome men, with excellent discipline and considerate manners; but they had been withdrawn and replaced by troops from beyond the Urals.

It took me some time to find my bearings in the impoverished uneasy city. When I had left England the Russians were much admired, and everyone remembered Stalingrad and felt that Russia would remain friends with us. I discovered that the Russians were unpopular in Prague. The day after I arrived Czechs came to me with stories about them, and several times as Saunders and I walked through the streets, people, hearing us talking in English, ran after us, sometimes with tears in their eyes, to tell us how glad they were that we had come; as if 'we' were the precursors of a relieving army for which they had been waiting.

Britain at that time was greatly admired. At the risk of their lives people had listened to the B.B.C., and followed the lessons in English broadcast by it. Scores of young Czechs had learned to speak English from these lessons, partly in protest against the German Occupation. When the authorities made it a crime punishable by imprisonment or death for anyone to possess a radio set which could receive foreign broadcasts, they invented a little gadget called a Churchillka to overcome the difficulty. Almost every house had its Churchillka, which was so ingeniously hidden in all sorts of places that it was always getting lost.

During our first stay in Prague my wife and I had been enquiring visitors; we looked on at a life strange to us, but were not involved. I had come now with express instructions to get in touch with people and organize an Institute in which they would learn something of English literature and the institutions and ways of Britain. A skeleton British Council staff was all that existed in Prague when I arrived, and it was housed in a small flat in a side street. One room was reserved for the Council Representative and a tiny closet for his secretary; the rest of us had to do our work at a large table in the remaining room. An unoccupied palace had been promised to us in which the Institute could hold its classes. But the tug between East and West in the Czechoslovakian government had already begun; excuse followed excuse, and the prospect of occupying the palace seemed remote. Meanwhile the staff increased as more people were sent out from England; our table became overcrowded; there was no place to keep our papers, and we had to clear them away every day when our luncheon was brought by car from the Embassy Mess.

In spite of this we had somehow to start our work. It was arranged that I should take a class in English Literature at the Charles University, and other classes were started by the members of my staff. The University had just re-opened after being closed for the latter years of the Occupation. All the young people who had been prevented from studying thronged to it; and the professors and lecturers could not deal with the inrush. The university library was in confusion; books had been stolen or destroyed; the English Literature section was pitiably bare, and English books were still not to be had in Prague because of some currency regulation. In my lectures I had to use any English books I could get hold of and have passages in verse and prose typed out by my students and distributed among them. For the first six months I improvised English literature from memory to a class which could only take my word for the things I said. When the palace at last passed into our hands and the British Council had furnished it with a respectable library, things became easier.

I think I should say something at this point about the work of the British Council, for it has been much and unfairly criticised. It has been blamed, for instance, for sometimes housing its Institutes in such places as the palace I mentioned a little while ago. The truth is that after the war there were scores of unoccupied palaces in Czechoslovakia, while the schools and universities were overcrowded, and the business premises were urgently needed for other purposes. Our own particular palace was chosen because it was a small one and would house conveniently the offices of the Council and the class-rooms of the Institute; in the end it turned out to be cramped. The Council has been blamed too for sending theatrical companies abroad. It sent the Sadler's Wells Ballet to Prague in the summer of 1946, and that company did more than our classes could ever have done to show the vitality and inventiveness of the English to a foreign people. The Germans had painted England as a land of medieval castles and privileged universities, idle lords and ladies who spent all their time at race-courses, and a populace dull and supercilious. The picture still lingered in the minds of Czechs we met: people of the Right who sentimentally adored it, and people of the Left who detested it. These ideas, unreal but influential, had to be corrected, and the British Council did a great deal to substitute a genuine picture for a false one, and it did this, working on ridiculously small means. Its work was necessarily miscellaneous, and the Council was bound sometimes to make mistakes. But the mistakes have been picked out for ridicule by people who know nothing of the work.

The British Council is a non-political body. Even if we had been inclined, we could not have taken sides in the political debates of the Czechs or have pushed any political propaganda of our own. But people from all parties naturally came to us: the Catholic People's Party, the Czech Socialists (roughly corresponding to our Labour Party), the Social Democrats, and the Communists. It took us some time to understand these political divisions and the tensions between them.

There were many things which puzzled me at first. When I arrived almost every shop-window displayed portraits of Masaryk, Beneš and Stalin; Stalin always in the middle, and generally raised slightly above his companions. I assumed that he had been set there by popular worship. Then in October, on the anniversary of the foundation of the republic, something happened. The portraits of Stalin disappeared. Their removal could be construed as a matter of propriety, for after all the anniversary was a purely national one. But they did not appear again. The Russian army was still in Prague. A few weeks later it took its leave, cheered by huge crowds who tossed flowers and bottles of wine to the soldiers as they sat on their army lorries, apparently as glad to leave as the Czechs were to see them going.

Underfed and depressed, the Czechs now had the capital to themselves. The first breath of gaiety came at Christmas. In spite of the shortage of electricity the city council decided to set up Christmas trees in the squares and streets and illumine them with brightly coloured bulbs. There was a Christmas tree opposite the hotel where my wife and I were staying, and we listened to the first sound we had heard of singing in the streets, a strangely forlorn and yet reassuring sound. And one early spring day as we were walking beside the river we saw a young couple wheeling a perambulator who stopped now and then to look at their baby and smile at each other. The sight struck us as quite extraordinary.

There was still a large Russian colony in the city, and I was curious to meet them. I found it almost impossible. We were sometimes invited to receptions where we were told we should meet Russians, but they never turned up. The Czechs too found it difficult to get hold of them. Once I did meet a small Russian group. Some representative function or other was being held in a large hall, I have forgotten why. Britain, France, the United States and Russia had been invited, and I was asked to attend. The tables for the different countries were set on a raised platform at one end of the hall, with the national flags displayed on the wall behind them. I was introduced to the Russian delegation; they bowed stiffly and turned away. But later in the evening, when drink had loosened his tongue, a young Russian came over and spoke to me. We talked about Tolstoy and Dostoevsky, and were getting on excellently—he had just promised to come and see me—when I looked up and saw the other Russians staring across at us from their table; in a little while a dignified elderly Russian made a sign to my young acquaintance and he rose and went away. I never saw him again. I realized how strange the ways of the Russians were, and how hard it was to communicate with them.

All this time my wife and I had been living in the Šroubek Hotel, which was uncomfortable, cold, noisy and expensive. At last we managed to get a flat in a pleasant open part of the city. The Russian Embassy was at the end of the street, and beyond that stretched a large public park. On either side of us and in most of the street officials of the Russian Embassy were living; and on special days Russian soldiers were to be seen standing on guard among the flower-beds in some front garden. The walls of our sitting-room were pitted with bullet marks; the flat had been occupied first by German officials and then by Russian officers, and we could tell where a portrait of Hitler had hung; it had been so often shot at that its outline was clearly picked out. The flat was so quiet and our Russian neighbours so inconspicuous that in time we quite forgot they were there.

In the first few months we heard little of the internal politics of Czechoslovakia. Everyone spoke of the Occupation. The question of collaboration often came up. The men and women who had carried out underground work in the heart of Prague or in the mountains of Slovakia were admired by everyone. But business-men who continued their work because business had to go on, and officials who remained at their posts knowing that if they did not they would be replaced by worse men, were sometimes unjustly blamed. A man of high character, the curator of a historical museum, had stuck to his post during the Occupation simply because he regarded himself as the guardian of irreplaceable national treasures. He was blamed by some and highly praised by others. It was indeed hard to distinguish genuine virtue, such as that of the curator, from virtue of an easier kind. There was on the whole a disposition to admit the difficulty of the choice which many people had had to make, and to judge each case fairly.

A few months after we went to Prague my wife and I were having tea one day in the house of Vera, a young Czech writer. The late Hermon Ould, then general secretary of the International P.E.N. Club, was there; the talk naturally turned to the Germans, and Hermon Ould, who wished the peoples of the world to live in perpetual friendship together, hoped that the Czechs would now be reconciled with their enemies. During the war Vera's husband had been the head of an underground group which collected secret information and sent it to Britain. The work was dangerous; the members of the group were picked up and executed one by one, and Vera was arrested a few weeks before the war ended, along with her husband. At the headquarters of the Gestapo he was interrogated and afterwards tortured, but he could not be got to name any of his friends. Finally, after extreme torture, the Gestapo confronted him with his wife and told him that if he did not speak she would be tortured as well. But by then he had been so maltreated that he could not recognize her, and a young Gestapo man strangled him.

Hermon Ould did not know of these things when he spoke of reconciliation with the Germans. We did, and for a moment we sat in deep embarrassment at the pretty tea-table. Then Vera started up, rushed from the room, and came back with a curious box in her hands. It was a shallow, oblong, silver-edged black cardboard box such as shops use to display shirts in their windows. She snatched off the lid. Inside, under a film of cellophane, was a white shirt neatly folded, but blotched with blood-stains and little scraps of torn skin. It had been sent to her by post, evidently as a matter of routine, after her husband's death and her release from prison. She held it out to Hermon Ould and cried: 'They sent me my husband's shirt in this box, and you ask me to call them my friends!'

The past was indeed very close to the Czechs during these months. But I did not realize until later how far back it reached. One day Vera showed us a photograph of some local Gestapo men which had come into her hands. The photograph had been taken when they were in the country outside Prague for a day's holiday. The young men were ranged in two rows in their neat uniforms, and they stared out at us with professionally menacing but unhappy eyes from that recent past now dead. They all seemed to be in their late twenties, and it suddenly came into my mind that they had been bred by the first world war. They had been children in 1919 when Germany was so wretched, and young girls and boys sold cocaine in the streets of Berlin and gave their bodies to anyone for a free meal.

After the relief of Prague these young men were hunted through the countryside, Vera told us, like wild game, and all of them taken and killed. She pointed at one young man and said without expression: 'That is the one who strangled my husband.' But it might have been any of the others. They stared out from the photographs with the confidence of the worthless who find power left in their hands like a tip hastily dropped by a frightened world. Though they had done so many things to satisfy their revenge on mankind there was no satisfaction in their faces, and no hope.

Perhaps it was fanciful to see these young men as I saw them then. Evil works itself out from generation to generation, but to observe it happening, to be confronted with one particular illustration of the universal law, is like a violation of the ordinary faith which makes us believe that all men can be saved. I could not believe that the Gestapo men in the photograph were enjoying the summer light and the country air, and thought that the light itself must have come to them twisted and splintered as they lived out their daily waking nightmare. The torment of their childhood had made them tormentors; they had done infamous things; and now they were wiped out. I heard other stories as bad as this, but I have no wish to relate them.

My lectures in the Institute and the Charles University brought me in contact with a great number of young Czechs. Most of them were poor and working at various jobs as well as attending the university: at part-time teaching, journalism, translating, office-work. They had been idle by compulsion during the Occupation and now they never seemed to rest from morning to night. They appeared to believe that the good life consisted solely in hard work; perhaps they had been encouraged in this by old Masaryk, a remarkable but pragmatically moral man. I suggested that, if they worked all the time, they would have no time left for thinking; but they did not take my words seriously. They read and read, wrote and wrote, worked and worked, in a continuous fury which would have exhausted an ordinary student. Perhaps they were half-aware already of history behind them driving them on, and history in front warning them that they might have very little time to do what they wanted to do. The republic had set out twenty-seven years before in faith and confidence; now it had to make a new start, and the second beginning is always harder than the first; it cannot summon spontaneous enthusiasm, and it needs determination more than faith. To these young Czechs the thing that appeared most needful was hard work and more hard work.

They were excellent students, responsive and eager, and their incessant industry generated a sort of intoxication which failed them only at the rare times when they could find nothing more to do. In the second winter they began to give parties and organize dances, and they flung themselves into these as if they were working at some task. They were like pleasure-seekers who cannot endure a hiatus or silence in time, but must find something to fill it, no matter what. They filled it with literature, history, science and philosophy.

In the spring and early summer Prague was enchanting, in spite of its dark memories. The park at the end of our street, the Stromovka or place of trees, was really a stretch of open wooded country, and before the republic decided to change its name had been known as the Kralovska Obora, or royal hunting-forest. It stretched down to the Vltava river through a labyrinth of paths, and one could find complete solitude there. Across the river was the old town of Troya with its eighteenth-century manor house and its secluded park. I had known these parts during my first stay in Prague; they were still delightful, but my memory of them was more delightful still; perhaps their freshness had been tarnished by the many feet which had trudged over them since; in any case they had assumed a radically democratic appearance. A zoo had been installed behind the manor house, and the exquisite little park had the look of things which it is not the particular business of anyone to care for.

And spring could not dispel the insistent memory of the Occupation. The first time we went for a walk through the Stromovka we came upon a little shrine where two paths met. Behind a pane of glass it showed the photograph of a young man, scarcely out of his teens, who had been shot there by the Germans. We came upon these little memorials in all sorts of places; set in the windows of houses, at street corners, and sometimes against hoardings covered with advertisements, a humble and forlorn memento to find in such a heartless situation. The names and ages of the victims were inscribed on cards beneath their photographs, along with an account of the ways in which they had met death. Most of them encountered it alone, unprepared, through a mistake or a rash word, without witnesses.

In 1947 there were recurring flurries of apprehension. That summer we went to Mariánské Lažné, once known as Marienbad, for a holiday. There we were warned that the Communists were preparing to make trouble. The popularity they had enjoyed in the last months of 1945 had long since faded; the elections were to come off in the May of 1948; everyone expected a sharp decline in the Communist vote, and some feared that the Party would frustrate it by taking direct action. A conference of the Social Democrats was to be held in a few months, and a great deal depended upon it. A section of them, led by Fierlinger, wished to join with the Communists; if that happened the united vote would be formidable. The conference, when it came, was stormy, but by a large majority the Social Democrats decided to preserve their independence; some of the delegates shed tears of relief at the thought that now everything was saved.

Then, in the early days of 1948, as everyone knows, the parliamentary crisis suddenly flared up. The Minister of the Interior was accused of packing the police with Communists and dismissing the police who remained faithful to the régime. He made no reply and went on. At last the ministers resolved to take a step which by the rules of the constitution would make it necessary for the President to appoint a new government. They handed in their resignations and waited for him to take the necessary step.

All this happened very quickly. The public was expecting the nomination of the new government. But the Communists left in office insisted that they should be empowered to form a government along with the trade unions, then assembled in Prague for their annual conference. Beneš refused to accept the resignation of his ministers, and said that he would not countenance any change until after the elections. The trade unions called a token strike.

The night before this the students of the English faculty gave a party to which my wife and I were invited. A choir sang Scottish songs; the traditional Czech dances were danced. But everyone was depressed and troubled and I found a young Czech girl crying in a corner and saying over and over, 'What is to become of us?' During the war she and her mother had escaped from a train which was taking them to Ausschwitz and the gas chambers, and had made their way to Prague through bye-roads to arrive a day or two after the Germans had been driven out. I tried to comfort her by saying that nothing would happen.

The police, most of them young lads, were everywhere and in high spirits. Two days after our party they raided the offices of the Czech Socialist Party and announced that they had found among the papers evidence of a plot against the State. No one was to leave the country without permission. The day after, the offices of the Social Democratic Party were raided, and the university students sent a message asking the President to appeal to the people to die rather than abandon their liberties. The Ministers of Posts and Transport were forcibly removed from their offices; it was rumoured that certain 'high officials' had been arrested. Most of the newspapers failed to appear. The President still had not announced his decision.

Then on the Thursday, the newspapers appeared after all, under Communist editorship, and all saying the same thing. At last, in the late afternoon, Gottwald announced over the radio that the President had accepted the Communist government.

That evening I listened to the radio. A great outdoor demonstration was being held in the main square; and Gottwald was the chief speaker. Graham Greene had written a few days before from Vienna to say that he intended to stop in Prague on his way to England. He was in our flat that evening; a Communist member of the Czech P.E.N. Club appeared along with him; the Party was already keeping an eye on distinguished foreign visitors. We listened to the rehearsed, timed, threefold shouts that greeted Gottwald, and I could not help saying to the young Czech, 'Why, it's "Sieg Heil! Sieg Heil! Sieg Heil!" all over again.' He threw a startled glance at Greene, wondering perhaps how he took it, and protested. 'Not at all! Not at all!' These shouts, which sounded like the brute response of a huge mass machine and had no resemblance to the spontaneous cheers of a crowd, brought back mean and bullying memories. We seemed to be back in 1939 again, with Europe fearing and preparing for war.

Next day people recognized that all was over. Stories came through of happenings which had not been reported in the newspapers. We heard of the attempt of the students to reach the President. The police had blocked the main street to the Castle, and the students took another route. When they reached the Castle they found it shut and soldiers on guard. An officer raised his sword as a warning to them to keep back. Then they began to sing the national anthem, and the soldiers, in obedience to traditional discipline, stood to attention. The students rushed forward. A shot was fired from behind by one of Gottwald's militia; a student fell. But accounts were confused; some denied that the student had been killed.

The stories kept coming in: a high Russian official had arrived in Prague just before the trouble began: Beneš had been prevented from speaking to the people over the radio. When people do not believe what is said by the newspapers, they create their news for themselves.

As soon as the new Government was in power it announced that the President would speak, but his voice was never heard again.

In these first days the people were stunned. The revolution was like a trick which had been played upon them behind their backs.

It is simple now, after the event, to explain how a Communist revolution could be successful in a democratic country where the great majority of the people were against it. But it is easy enough to account for. In the government the Communists had from the start controlled the police and the radio, and they had a collaborator at the head of the army. This enabled them to build up the police into a Communist corps, to divert at a moment's notice the radio and the press to their purposes, and at the last moment to mobilize the army. The *coup* had been long planned, a replica of similar revolutions in other countries, a piece of safe and well-tried plagiarism. Once the machinery was set going, an atmosphere of urgency and danger had naturally to be manufactured; the story was put about that the Sudeten Germans, in American uniforms, were massed at the borders of the country, ready to march in. And the Czechs were even more afraid of the Germans than of the Communists.

I had been in Prague for two and a half years, had made friends there, had seen the city forgetting the fears bred by the Occupation, and growing prosperous. The people in the trams talked to one another freely, as in the days before the Occupation, without needing to be reminded of old Masaryk's saying that he would know Czechoslovakia was a democracy when anyone could stand up and say in public, 'God damn the government.' In Prague houses no one started with apprehension when the door-bell or the telephone rang. Now all was changed. The old stale fears were back. No one opened his mouth in the trams. No one said 'God damn the government,' knowing he would be arrested if he did. No one dared to tell what he really thought, except in his own house or to a friend he could trust. No one telephoned if he could help it, though in a very short time people knew by the slight diminution in the volume of sound when the line was being tapped. And men at last became suspicious even of their friends.

Then there were all the direct and indirect forms of intimidation: the newspapers which in a few days became minatory; the radio broadcasts blaring from loud-speakers strung along the streets, following you after you passed them and waiting for you as you approached them; the application form of the Communist Party lying on your desk when you arrived in the morning, telling you that it must have your urgent attention. All this bred a sense of pressure and apprehension. And if a man signed the form, knowing that his signature would secure his post, his ration book and the livelihood of his family, he felt degraded. A young Czech woman came to us in tears and told us that her husband, who worked in a government office, had just signed the form. She cried: 'We're dishonest! We're dishonest! We shall never be able to hold up our heads again.'

The position of writers was little better. A few days after the Communists came to power the writers held a congress to decide on their attitude to the new order. One who was there told us that the discussion was quite open and friendly; the Right and the Left were very accommodating; the Centre remained intransigent. The conference passed two resolutions: one affirming its loyalty to the new government, the other asserting the freedom of the writer. In the newspapers next day the first resolution appeared; the second was not mentioned. The organisers of the conference were called before the Central Committee of the Party and reprimanded. And when a few weeks later a group of young Communist writers went to the Committee for permission to start a literary review, they were told: 'Certainly. Go ahead. Here are the names of the editorial board.' They protested that this was not the review they wanted and were informed that they could have it or none at all.

We were living in the midst of these changes, without any clear notion of what was happening, but aware of a constant invisible pressure, which seemed more dangerous than the isolated acts of intimidation or terror which came to our ears. The pressure produced, as by an exactly calculated process, a deepening of the apprehension which already anticipated the future; people were not so much afraid of what was happening as of what would happen yet. At first the apprehension seemed the worst effect of the new State; then the moral anguish of those who had to choose Communism against their conscience to keep their families alive seemed worse still: until at last one saw that the impersonality of the system which imposed these miseries was the worst of all. Its acts had a look of cynicism; one imagined the Communists sardonically smiling at the discomfiture of their enemies, yet I feel sure that they did not; in their own eyes they were simply carrying out by rational means a necessary change. Their morality told them that the sufferings of individuals did not matter in comparison with their great impersonal aim.

I came across an instance of this. A Czech lady whose husband had been killed in the Resistance was offered a choice. Her father and mother, both of them invalids, lived on a pension she had been granted after her husband's death, and on a small salary she earned in a government office. She was asked to join the Party or lose her pension and her work. Her parents, who like herself were Catholics, would not speak to her again if she became a Communist; if she did not, they would starve. The problem was completely impersonal, and completely insoluble: the only choice left for her was a false one: to declare herself a Communist and remain a Catholic. I do not know how she dealt with it, for I left Prague shortly afterwards. What the Communists asked of her must, I think, have appeared quite reasonable in their eyes, since their theory did not take the soul into account. Persuading her in friendly voices to do what she could not do, they may have thought that they were behaving with indulgence. Freedom to them was a strange aberration, almost a nothing; for real freedom was necessity; and so what they offered the lady was necessity. They did not hate or dislike her, I feel sure. They did not realize that she had become their victim; they merely did not understand. As a Catholic she fell into a category, it is true; but she was also, in their eyes, a possible convert. What they did not realize was that she was a human being. Their categories, the working class, the capitalists, the bourgeoisie, the communists, the anti-communists, were far more real to them than she was. Their moral judgments were judgments of their categories. The worker, the obscure hero of their myth, was a good worker if he conformed exactly to the idea of his class, and bad if he deviated from it by some useless or lively human quality. They could understand a good worker, but a good human being was an abstraction which fell outside their sphere of thought and therefore a source of confusion. So they could not believe that my Czech friend really found it hard to give up her religion, or cut herself off from her parents. History, the masses, revolution, the dictatorship of the proletariat, and the final utopia when, at the great halting place of history, the state would wither away and all would be changed; what could a private person's beliefs and affections matter compared with these great things?

The problem of the Czech lady troubled me at this time. Impersonality is an admirable quality in a historian, so long as he has human understanding as well. But to observe the long struggle of humanity as one observes a scientific demonstration heats the brains of men and petrifies their hearts; and to deal impersonally with the living human beings around us or beneath us, knowing that we have the power to do so, is merely a particular form of inhumanity. It was put into effect as soon as the *coup* was accomplished. People were forced to declare themselves Communists, for it was expedient that the revolution should be able to show that it had the support of the 'masses.' As soon as the revolution was safely entrenched, the paper Communists were purged. The deliberate humiliation of these helpless people for a temporary end was an infamous act. But those who decreed it, I feel sure, did so with a good conscience, and looked upon it merely as the necessary next step.

What they did was eminently reasonable in their own eyes; but in practice it seemed a sort of madness, all the more dangerous because it was methodically thought out. The feeling among our Czech friends was that they had been overtaken by a great calamity, and when they looked into the future their apprehensions were lost in their certainty of the lasting desolation which awaited them. As outsiders, we could say nothing to mitigate that prospect. The change was felt as a calamity, rather than a human error, because it did not 'recognize' the human being or take into account his ordinary qualities: kindness, intelligence, frankness, suspicion, cheerfulness, gloom. So it seemed both irresistible and unnatural, for it is unnatural for human beings to act impersonally towards one another.

Some time before the *coup* I had come to know two nieces of Franz Kafka, daughters of his favourite sister Ottilia and her Gentile husband. They showed me some photographs of their mother. She was a gay, kind and charming woman, whose house in Prague had been open to everyone. Once she had taken a young girl off the streets, had looked after her, and at last had married her off, happily, to a respectable young man who knew her story. This girl had kept house for Franz Kafka for a while when he took the whim to live in the Street of the Alchemists, a little street of dolls' houses—they were hardly bigger—built against the Castle wall. Perhaps his obsession with low roofs and confined quarters in his stories attracted him to these pretty, poky dwellings. He did not stay there long. He was a tall man, and these houses were built, one would have said, for a race of dwarfs or of children who never grew up; perhaps the alchemists who once lived there were associated in the minds of the princes who supported them with those earth spirits who reside in the hollows of grassy mounds.

When the Germans invaded Czechoslovakia Ottilia insisted that she should be divorced from her husband, and cut herself off, for their sake, from her family. She got a post in a nursery school for Jewish children. When she had been there for some time, orders came from the authorities to get the children ready for travel; she was to take them to a centre in Sweden. Instead, they were sent to Ausschwitz, where they all died in the gas chambers. But Ottilia's sacrifice had saved her daughters.

The impersonality of the Nazis was more cruel than that of the Communists, but also more comprehensible, for it was animated by human hatred. Yet it was the impersonality of its working that made it infamous. Systematic thought had to be exercised before one could regard the family relations of the Jews as indistinguishable from those of domestic animals, and the killing of a Jew scarcely different, except in its profitlessness, from the killing of an ox. A human problem did arise where a Gentile had married a Jew, and a clean animal had coupled with an unclean one. Then the Gentile had a choice as reasonable and impossible as the choice demanded by the Communists from the Czech lady. The husband could put away his wife and leave the children to what judgment was reserved for them. Ottilia's divorce saved her children. The stories about the Nazis when I first came to Prague, and those I heard now about the Communists, called up a vast image of impersonal power, the fearful shape of our modern inhumanity.

At Easter, two months after the *coup*, my wife and I and

two members of the Institute staff went down to Piešťany, a little town in Slovakia, for a holiday and the sulphur baths. As we passed through the pastoral Slovak countryside—it was Easter Friday—the people were everywhere streaming to the churches. The town itself looked dead. At the hostel where we stayed we heard of countrywomen being haled to prison for selling eggs without a permit: probably they were still unaware of the new regulations. A Czech we met told us he had decided to stay in the country in the hope that things would get easier when corruption set in: a mistaken hope, for corruption works in incalculable ways. He was an honest man, but prided himself on being realistic, and like many Czechs he was troubled by the question: at what point did realism pass over into cowardice, and had he and his country crossed that line? It was a painful imaginary torment; for when the government controlled the police, the news, and the armed forces, what could the population do?

On Sunday we walked out to a church on the outskirts of the town. Inside the door an image of Christ was lying on a bier, his body covered with flowers of the spring, a thin veil through which one seemed to feel the trembling of the Easter resurrection. Inside, peasant women were kneeling before images of their Lord; one of them, just in front of me, with a worn, kind, handsome face, knelt motionless, and my eyes came back again and again to the worn and patched soles of her boots, a battered image of her own constancy and humble faith. I did not feel that this ancient humanity could ever be destroyed by the new order.

We returned to Prague a few days later, and I resumed my lectures at the university. But all was changed; my class, once eager to discuss everything, was silent. Two Communists were in attendance, taking down what I said. I could speak to my class, but I no longer had any contact with it. Yet in spite of this I felt in a privileged position, compared with the Czech professors and lecturers who were in the employment of the State. I did not try, therefore, to modify the tone of my lectures to suit the new demands. I was ploughing through the Victorian Age at the time, and when I came to John Stuart Mill, I gave my students a summary of his ideas on liberty. The two Communists grew agitated; the students seemed to be fearfully enjoying a forbidden pleasure: I felt them coming to life again. But it was a temporary revival; the class quickly dwindled.

I could still mention liberty; but the Czech professors were in a more difficult position. They too had their Communist observers, and a single imprudent sentence might bring their dismissal and the withdrawal of their livelihood, and I do not know what else. Yet there were some who calmly ignored the diurnal intimidation, and went on lecturing as if there were no Communist government in Czechoslovakia. Their steady courage, summoned day after day, their composure in face of unvarying danger, filled their friends and their students with admiration and dismay. I do not know what has become of them since, for I have never dared to write to them, knowing that a letter from the West might make things worse than they are.

At last I felt I was not doing any good in Prague. When my students came to see me at the Institute or at our house, I could offer them what comfort I could think of, but I could not give them encouragement without the risk of getting them into trouble. It was a hopeless position, and when the Chairman of the Council came out to Prague, I told him that I wished to be transferred to some other post. He promised that he would see what could be done.

The summer term came to an end, and my wife invited my remaining students to a party at our home one blazing hot afternoon. There we said good-bye. I have heard from a few of them since, from Greece, from Italy, from the United States, but not, understandably enough, from their own country. We began to make preparations for our return. Officials came to check our belongings, from the pillow-sheets to the coffee-spoons, so as to assure themselves that we were not taking any Czech property out of the country. On the last day of July we found ourselves on the train to the border. It stopped there for two hours, in a hot dusty station. People here and there were ejected, and luggage flung out of windows. At last the train went on, and we were running through the American zone of Germany.

CHAPTER THIRTEEN

Rome

A friend had booked rooms for us in a boarding-house in Cambridge. As soon as I arrived I had a breakdown, and fell plumb into a dead pocket of life which I had never guessed at before. It was hard to live there, simply because it was unimaginably uninteresting. I awoke each morning feeling that I had lost or mislaid something which I was accustomed to but could not name; I slowly realized that it was the little spring of hope, or of interest, with which the day once began. It had stopped playing, and it did not return for several weeks. This left a blankness which was very disagreeable; and wrapped in it I had neither the power nor the wish to regret the loss of what had been a part of myself; yet I was not resigned either, but merely apathetic. Memories of Prague now and then shivered the surface of my mind, but never sank deep into it. I wandered about the colleges, seeing but not feeling their beauty; I navigated a punt on the river, played clock-golf and table-tennis on the lawn behind the house, and read detective stories. I was a poor companion to my wife in these weeks. At last things began to become real, pleasurable and painful again.

After leaving Cambridge we stayed with friends in London for a while, then in a boarding-house in Hampstead, where our old happy memories of the place gathered round us. Meanwhile the British Council was trying to find me a suitable post. Several appeared, and then faded again. At last, in December, I was asked to go to Rome as director of the British Institute there.

My wife had been ill during most of this time, and I had not been able to settle down. The kindness of London, born during the blitz, was a comfort to us after the chilly suspicion that had closed over Prague; and it helped to relieve a succession of dead months.

Early in January my wife and I set out for Rome. My affections are still too deeply attached to the Italy I discovered then—for the few months I had spent in it twenty-three years before had told me little or nothing—that if I were to write at length about it now, gratitude would make me say too much, or dread of appearing extravagant tempt me to say too little. Perhaps the fact that Rome made my wife well again and let me forget Prague was enough to account for part of the gratitude. Perhaps the free environing warmth of Italian life after the chills of Prague intoxicated us both a little at first. But it was the gradual revelation of Italy during the next year and a half which came to mean so much to us. We did not idealize our Italian friends; we had instead the pleasure of being able to take them as they were. I fancy the good and the bad are distributed among Italians in much the same proportion as among other races. The poor, certainly, were dreadfully poor, and the rich senselessly rich. But it was a new experience to know people who spoke from the heart, simply and naturally, without awkwardness, and put all of themselves, heart and soul, into what they said. I had known fresh and natural speech among Orkney farmers living close to the cattle and the soil, but not till now among men and women moulded by city life, and sometimes of subtle mind. From such people what one expects is sophistication, but here there was something quite different, for which sophistication seemed a vulgar substitute. The people we knew had the air of stepping out completely into life, and their speech, even at its idlest, had something of the accent of Dante, who spoke more directly from the heart than any other poet but one. I was reminded of the figures in the paintings of Piero della Francesca and Michelangelo, not so much by the faces of our friends, as by their expression and carriage, which seemed an image of full humanity. The humanity was perfectly natural, but I knew that naturalness does not come easily to the awkward human race, and that this was an achievement of life.

One comes to know a people not by statistical accounts or mass observation, but by making a few friends. I was fortunate in my first friends: the staff of the Rome Institute. My predecessor as director was Roger Hinks, and he had been so loved by his staff that I felt, the first morning I called at the Institute, that I was breaking into an Eden which could never be quite the same again, now that he was about to leave it. He inducted me into my work and gave me a great deal of useful advice before he left. But the staff naturally felt uneasy at the change, and Laura Minervini, the secretary and moving soul of the Institute, took me aside one day and told me how happily they had all worked together till now, and how much she wished they might do so still, now that I had come. She tried to give me an idea of the Italian character, saying that Italians would do anything for love of their friends and their work, but they could not be driven. I was greatly touched and told her that she need have no fear. The Institute remained a sort of talkative Eden and was the most friendly, kind, busy place imaginable. In it and from it I made most of my friends.

Meanwhile we had got a furnished flat in the old town, on the top of a tall block looking out on one side to the Tiber and the distant Alban hills, and on the other, across a multitude of red-tiled roofs, to the Quirinale. The flat was small but had a wide terrace running along three sides, and there we spent most of our time. On spring evenings we sat on the terrace for hours watching the swifts cutting scimitar-like curves in the sky. There were tens of thousands, and their shrill screaming, a fierce exciting sound, filled the evening. They boiled in the air high up over the roofs between us and the Quirinale, and swooped down, sometimes almost brushing our heads in their flight, turning and tacking at full speed, plunging into the canyon-like street below, setting in motion the curtains of open windows with the wind of their flight, and working at full stretch until the light failed. Then in a few minutes they had disappeared into their nests beneath the roof-tiles. A whole township of them lived in a curious, squat, little tiled tower across the street. One day we looked for them and they were gone.

We had never been in Rome before; at first we were a little overawed by its splendour and its age; what we did not know was that we should come to love it and think of it as the most friendly place. We saw the usual sights, sometimes enchanted, sometimes disappointed; but it was Rome itself that took us, the riches stored in it, the ages assembled in a tumultuous order, the vistas at street corners where one looked across from one century to another, the innumerable churches, palaces, squares, fountains, monuments, ruins; and the Romans themselves going about their business as if this were the natural and right setting for the life of mankind.

The history of Rome is drenched in blood and blackened with crime; yet all that seemed to be left now was the peace of memory. As we wandered about the Forum we could not summon up the blood-stained ghosts; they had quite gone, bleached by centuries into a luminous transparency, or evaporated into the bright still air. Their works were there, but these cast only the ordinary shadow which everything set up by mankind gathers at its foot. The grass in the courtyard of the Temple of the Vestals seemed to be drenched in peace down to the very root, and it was easy to imagine gods and men still in friendly talk together there.

But it was the evidences of another Incarnation that met one everywhere and gradually exerted its influence. During the time when as a boy I attended the United Presbyterian Church in Orkney, I was aware of religion chiefly as the sacred Word, and the church itself, severe and decent, with its touching bareness and austerity, seemed to cut off religion from the rest of life and from all the week-day world, as if it were a quite specific thing shut within itself, almost jealously, by its white-washed walls, furnished with its bare brown varnished benches unlike any others in the whole world, and filled with the odour of ancient Bibles. It did not tell me by any outward sign that the Word had been made flesh. Instead there was the minister; yet if he came to visit us in our house, he was still recognizable to me, while I stared at him with all the experience of childhood, as a human being like other human beings. Mr Pirie, the minister of Rousay, whose church we attended while we lived in Wyre, was a man of sweet and gracious character, loved by all his congregation. After we moved to Garth we went to the church of Mr Webster, who thundered like a Hebrew prophet and might have sat for Michelangelo: a tall, nobly handsome, white-bearded man, greatly admired, but not, like Mr Pirie, universally loved. In figures such as these the Word became something more than a word in my childish mind; but nothing told me that Christ was born in the flesh and had lived on the earth.

In Rome that image was to be seen everywhere, not only in churches, but on the walls of houses, at cross-roads in the suburbs, in wayside shrines in the parks, and in private rooms. I remember stopping for a long time one day to look at a little plaque on the wall of a house in the Via degli Artisti, representing the Annunciation. An angel and a young girl, their bodies inclined towards each other, their knees bent as if they were overcome by love, 'tutto tremante,' gazed upon each other like Dante's pair; and that representation of a human love so intense that it could not reach farther seemed the perfect earthly symbol of the love that passes understanding. A religion that dared to show forth such a mystery for everyone to see would have shocked the congregations of the north, would have seemed a sort of blasphemy, perhaps even an indecency. But here it was publicly shown, as Christ showed himself on the earth.

That these images should appear everywhere, reminding everyone of the Incarnation, seemed to me natural and right, just as it was right that my Italian friends should step out frankly into life. This open declaration was to me the very mark of Christianity, distinguishing it from the older religions. For although the pagan gods had visited the earth and conversed with men, they did not assume the burden of our flesh, live our life and die our death, but after their interventions withdrew into their impenetrable privacy. There is a church in Assisi built above an older one, reputed once to have been dedicated to the ancient gods. In the lower church all is darkness and mystery; in the upper one, all clear colour and light; and ascending to it is like passing into another age. But to deal with these impressions, so vivid at the time, and yet so hard to define, is beyond my power, and I shall say no more about them.

When my work in Rome allowed me, I was sent on lecture tours to various towns in Italy; my wife shared in them when she could. In this way we became acquainted with a string of cities from Venice in the north to Syracuse in the south, astonished again and again by the prodigious energy which had created in a few centuries such a wealth of beautiful forms in painting and stone. The daughter cities of Tuscany and Umbria, Florence and Siena, and Perugia and Assisi, looked young after the maternal agelessness of Rome, and still kept, as they had done for centuries, their springlike innocence and grace. They looked like new incarnations sprung from the inexhaustible source of metaphysical felicity, and though they had witnessed violence and crime, they rose above it into their own world and their own light. Christendom was still young there.

We had looked forward to a long stay in Italy, and had planned to see many things. But after a year and a half our stay was cut short; the grant on which the Council did its work was drastically reduced, and its branches in Rome, Naples, Venice and Palermo were closed. We said good-bye to our Italian friends and to Italy.

I had no experience of teaching, and little of lecturing, before I joined the British Council. My experience in Edinburgh and Prague and Rome had given me a love for the work, and when in the spring of 1950 I received an invitation to take up the post of Warden of Newbattle Abbey College I gladly accepted it. The sole institution of its kind in Scotland, it had been commandeered by the Army during the war, and was now to be re-opened. As soon as I returned from Rome I began work there. In October the students appeared: clerks, fitters, turners, tube-makers, railwaymen, typists, journalists, teachers, civil servants. They came to follow up for a year, in a residential college, studies which they had begun in evening classes or in their spare time. They were eager, and more intelligent than I had ever dreamed they could be, and to watch over them and see their minds unfolding was an experience which I am glad not to have missed. The Abbey building had been generously given by the late Lord Lothian, as it was when he lived in it, to be used as a centre of liberal education, non-vocational and non-political. The students mostly came for a year; some afterwards returned to their previous work;

some went on to universities. In the second year one of them, a miner, won a scholarship to Cambridge with a dissertation on Kant; in the third, another, a tube-maker, won a similar scholarship with an essay on *Paradise Lost*. I feel that, scattered in all sorts of odd jobs, in all parts of the country, there are countless men and women with an intellectual passion or an undeveloped gift, and that in most cases these remain lost or half-shaped, to their own misfortune and the general loss.

I have written this continuation of my autobiography at Newbattle, in scraps of spare time and during vacations. What is left to say when one has come to the end of writing about one's life? Some kind of development, I suppose, should be expected to emerge, but I am very doubtful of such things, for I cannot bring life into a neat pattern. If there is a development in my life—and that seems an idle supposition—then it has been brought about more by things outside than by any conscious intention of my own. I was lucky to spend my first fourteen years in Orkney; I was unlucky to live afterwards in Glasgow as a Displaced Person, until at last I acquired a liking for that plain, warm-hearted city. Because a perambulating revivalist preacher came to Kirkwall when I was a boy, I underwent an equivocal religious conversion there; because I read Blatchford in Glasgow, I repeated the experience in another form, and found myself a Socialist. In my late twenties I came, by chance, under the influence of Nietzsche. In my early thirties I had the good fortune to meet my wife, and have had since the greater good fortune of sharing my life with her. In my middle thirties I became aware of immortality, and realized that it gave me a truer knowledge of myself and my neighbours. Years later in St Andrews I discovered that I had been a Christian without knowing it. I saw in Czechoslovakia a whole people lost by one of the cruel turns of history, and exiled from themselves in the heart of their own country. I discovered in Italy that Christ had walked on the earth, and also that things truly made preserve themselves through time in the first freshness of their nature. Now and then during these years I fell into the dumps for short or prolonged periods, was subject to fears which I did not understand, and passed through stretches of blankness and deprivation. From these I learned things which I could not otherwise have learned, so that I cannot regard them as mere loss. Yet I believe that I would have been better without them.

When we talk of our development I fancy we mean little more than that we have changed with the changing world; and if we are writers or intellectuals, that our ideas have changed with the changing fashions of thought, and therefore not always for the better. I think that if any of us examines his life, he will find that most good has come to him from a few loyalties, and a few discoveries made many generations before he was born, which must always be made anew. These too may sometimes appear to come by chance, but in the infinite web of things and events chance must be something different from what we think it to be. To comprehend that is not given to us, and to think of it is to recognize a mystery, and to acknowledge the necessity of faith. As I look back on the part of the mystery which is my own life, my own fable, what I am most aware of is that we receive more than we can ever give; we receive it from the past, on which we draw with every breath, but also—and this is a point of faith—from the Source of the mystery itself, by the means which religious people call Grace.

From *Yesterday's Mirror*:
Afterthoughts to an Autobiography

Note: This essay was published in *Scots Magazine* New Series,*Vol xxxiii No 6* (Sept 1940), pp. 404–10. The first three pages only are given. Much of the rest was revised, and included in *An Autobiography* at the end of the 'Dresden and Hellerau' chapter.

I wrote my autobiography some time ago. While I was working at it I tried to make clear the pattern of my life as a human being existing in space and moving through time, environed by mystery. After I had finished I went over the manuscript many times, seeking to make the pattern clearer, and felt like a man with an inefficient torch stumbling through a labyrinth, having forgotten where he entered and not knowing where he would come out. At last the proofs arrived; I made the last correction; there was no further turning back. And suddenly I felt that now that my autobiography was finished, I could really write my autobiography. I had cleared up a few things in my mind. But then I reflected that to clear up a few things merely makes one aware of other things to be cleared up; if these were cleared up in turn, there would be still others; the process would be endless. To write a book describing one human being is strictly an impossibility; for what we require for real self-knowledge is the power to stop the sun and make it revolve in the opposite direction, taking us back stage by stage through manhood to youth and through youth to childhood, missing nothing, until it conducts us to the mystery from which we started. But at most we can take only a few chance leaps backward while Time hurries us on; and these fortuitous leaps we afterwards call our life.

A book by André Gide was once described as a novel

about a novelist writing a novel. The most satisfactory kind of autobiography would be about an autobiographer writing an autobiography: for he learns more about life by writing his life than he will ever manage to convey. Writing an autobiography at least forces us to think about life, however reluctantly; yet once we begin we cannot stop at the point where we intended to stop, for we realise that there is no stopping point, a daunting yet animating discovery. The same is true of the tapping of memory. While I was writing my life many memories which I had completely forgotten came up, and they have been coming up ever since, quite disregarding the fact that the book was finished and that as a writer I had no further use for them. For most of our lives we ignore ourselves, or at least the self which it would be best for us to remember: and the reason for this is simply our selfishness, which seizes only the importance of the present moment, since it is most vital to us, and jealously excludes those past moments where we could recognise if we liked, by an effort of imagination and understanding, the self which has always been there through all the hours' changes. There is a law by which the momentary self continuously ousts the permanent self. Consequently to know what we are we must cease for a time to be what we are. Otherwise we live in a perpetual bright oblivion of ourselves, insulated in the moving moment and given a meaning only by the moment.

This came home to me very sharply after I had finished my autobiography. It is not an original idea; religion has reminded us of it a countless number of times. Yet what matters in an idea is not its originality, but its clarity. And I saw more clearly than I had ever done before that our knowledge of life comes from yesterday, a yesterday which can never change again and is therefore beyond confusion; and that there is the glass into which we must look if we want to see what life is. Our feeling of life comes from the present, our knowledge of life from the past. Our feeling of life is real only if we project ourselves into life and feel all round us the struggle, suffering and enjoyment of the world; our knowledge of life significant only if we read into the pattern of our own past the universal pattern of human existence.

There, in the present, which to us is all space, and in the past, which to us is all time, lies our earthly meaning.

Art is the sum of the moments in which men have glanced into that yesterday which can never change; and when we read, or look at a picture, or listen to music, we are released from the moment to contemplate that mirror in which all the forms of life lie outspread. There is accordingly something divine in art, since it moulds a living world out of our dead yesterdays, reliving life, and since in dealing with what can never change again it lets itself be purified by the Unchangeable. The subject of art is always the same, life that has been lived and can never alter; but the pictures of life made by the artist are numberless, for he looks at that unchanging world with a changing eye, which can never be simply comprehending and without shadow of doubt, since he is in the fairway of time and cannot be sure either of himself or of what he sees.

I can think of three ways in which men may look into that mirror which shows life as it is lived, and each would give back a different picture. There is the glance of experience which discerns a world where wrong triumphs and right suffers, where greed succeeds and generosity fails and selfish illusion reigns. This is the world of the realist, who has forgotten his childhood or has dismissed it as unimportant, as if he had been born fully equipped to deal with life at the age of thirty. Then there is the glance of the man who in maturity has kept a memory of his childhood. Perhaps simply by virtue of that memory he sees in the mirror an indefeasible rightness beneath the wrongness of things; a struggle between good and evil, and not merely the victory of evil; and to him the rightness of human life has a deeper reality, a more fundamental appositeness, than the evil, as being more truly native to man. This, to our credit, is our normal view of life. The third glance into the mirror is given only to the greatest poets and mystics at their greatest moments, and is beyond rational description. The world the mystical poet sees is a world in which both good and evil have their place legitimately: in which the king on his throne and the rebel raising his standard in the market place, the tyrant and the slave, the assassin and the victim, each plays a part in a supertemporal drama which at every moment, in its totality, issues in glory and meaning and fulfilment. This vision is too dangerous for us as human beings struggling in the arena: it would be safe only if we felt no touch of evil; and it is given to men only when they are at the very heart of good, and, in a sense very different from Nietzsche's, beyond good and evil. St Augustine saw it and so did Blake; it is the supreme vision of human life, because it reconciles all opposites; but it transcends our moral struggle, for in life we are ourselves the opposites and must act as best we can.

Extracts from Diaries

Note: When *The Story and the Fable* was turned into *An Autobiography* the first five chapters were not much altered; the sixth chapter, originally called 'Prague and Dresden', was considerably cut and some of the material was transferred to the new chapter 'Dresden and Hellerau'. The seventh chapter 'Extracts from a Diary 1937–39' was omitted, though some of the entries were used for the new section on St Andrews. These extracts were mostly taken, revised, from a notebook, now in the National Library of Scotland; and some from another source now lost. The extracts given here are printed in the revised form from *The Story and the Fable* with the addition of dates, except that the dream about T.S. Eliot is taken from the notebook.

23 April 1938
Bad night last night. Dreamt of T.S. Eliot who was taking Willa and myself to his country house: very kind and even mildly jolly, as he has become in the last few years, pleasant and yet with a trick of willed bonhommie which gives the pleasantness a slight appearance of falseness, though it is perfectly real: perhaps all the more real for being willed? Yet I was uneasy. The road to his home led through a wood: it was quite dark, yet we walked among the trees, without stumbling or knocking into anything. At one point—we were near the house now—we passed a family sitting in a drawing-room (I think it was) which was nevertheless in the open air: two walls were ordinary walls with pictures hanging on them, while where the other two walls should have been there was nothing but wood, with the trees set in open order. Sofas and easy-chairs were standing about in the room, which was lit softly with a shaded standard lamp; and in the chairs and sofas were sitting a few obviously

well-to-do people, one of whom, a young man, stared over with interest as we passed, while Eliot, who seemed to be on familiar terms with them all, waved his hand and said good-evening. The young man was clearly taking in E.'s latest visitors, and it occurred to me with surprise that perhaps W. and I were figures after all, who merited such scrutiny.

Soon we reached Eliot's house and were conducted by him into an old English sitting room with a fire burning in a wide open hearth: the walls looked somewhat dilapidated and had large patches of damp. As we stood in the middle of the floor, I realised that there was another wide open hearth on the other side of the room and Eliot mentioned that he had this put in lately. Suddenly there was a whirring noise just above the lighted hearth and a little grey animal slipped rustling through a hole in the roof there, which was covered with tall rough grasses. When the little beast dropped on the floor I saw that it was a very long, thin grey cat with a great thick tail somewhat like a squirrel's. I bent down to pat it and show that I knew how to deal with cats: and it responded just as a normal nice cat would, in spite of its queer appearance. We stood like this for a time, and then Eliot, still standing up, began to change his clothes, beginning with his trousers. This did not surprise me at all, but I suddenly realised I should have taken my evening suit; and I saw E.'s behaviour as an indirect rebuke to my remissness. I felt more and more uneasy: acutely not at home, taken at a disadvantage, not really wanted: I think the disadvantage of the Scot confronted with the Englishman and of the proletarian (or one-time proletarian) confronted with a man of middle- or upper class upbringing. Also something about E. himself, much as I like him, and nice as he has always been to me. And perhaps something suspicious and touchy and morbid in myself. I woke feeling my short-comings, how little I had made of my life, and the guilt that comes from the feeling that I am not what I should have been, and have not realised the powers within me that I should have realised. Do all people or most people who have reached my age have that feeling?

Lying awake it occurred to me that Eliot's concern with

social conventions which some people think snobbish—and there may be some snobbishness in it—is really a result of the extraordinary solidity with which he sees everything, his insistence on looking at things as they are, without reacting against them or blindly accepting them. He looks on these conventions as real: a novel standpoint, but a true one, nevertheless.

15 June 1938

Yesterday I was down in Edinburgh, and in the evening went to a restaurant for supper. The restaurant was up a stair, and I took a seat by a big window where I had a fine view of the street and the people passing by. I drank some claret with my supper and sat at the window, my mind growing more and more luminous. It was a beautiful evening; the street below lay in clear shadow; in a green square to the west the leaves of the trees were like gold feathers. Down below people kept getting out of tramcars singly or in groups or in couples; I watched them strolling or hurrying away, and every one seemed to have some secret business, which idly pleased me. Then, as if a formidable engine had started or a great wheel had begun to revolve, a number of things happened simultaneously; everything was changed; and a half-nightmare, half-pleasant oppression seized hold of me, as if I too, the observer, were caught in that wheel. The solid street lay below me, flanked with ponderous buildings; immediately opposite a tall, narrow lane led to another street a little distance away, whose traffic I could see passing in the gap. A girl got off a tramcar and set off down this lane. At the same time two young men came out of a pub opposite, and a big woman with a blind, hanging face and blind, hanging breasts came striding along the pavement at right angles to the girl and the two young men. From the waist down she had the legs of a tall man; she was going at a great speed, blundering along; her long skirt flapped round her lower body like a great gown billowing on a clothes-line. Her feet were enormous, and flapped as they swung along. And then, at the farther end of the short lane, a long, thin, furry dog slid past. At that distance I could distinguish neither head nor tail nor legs; it was simply a uniform round length of hair floating past six inches from the ground. And all these things were related to each other like the parts of an intricate and monstrous machine. I sat in astonishment and horror, feeling, as one feels only a few times in one's existence, the enormity of human life. I felt that there was literally nothing that could not be thought about human beings.

This mood lasted only a short time, and led to a more frequent one in which I fancy that if you could see everybody as an immortal spirit it would change the very basis of imagination, and through that life itself. I have occasionally tried to do this for a few minutes at a stretch, but I know that it is impossible as a consistent vision. I tried to see as an immortal spirit the girl who had gone along the lane on her pleasant errand. She was pretty and cheerful and at home in her body, and all these things made it hard for me to see her as an immortal spirit. If she had been ugly, or ill, or old, or merely sad, it would have been easier. But her qualities seemed to have a relation only to this world, as perfect health and perfect cheerfulness have. Then I tried to think of other people; children and old people I found easy; and, seeking a really difficult subject, I thought of a certain rich man who has acquired a fortune and some dubious public respect by all sorts of flinty-hearted rascality. I was surprised to find that I could easily see him as an immortal spirit; but as an evil one. And when I reached this point my dream of the glorification of life was abruptly checked; for I had thought that my vision would bring reconciliation, and instead I saw that it would only deepen in our consciousness the pattern of good and evil, and extend it into eternity.

21 June 1938

I was down in Edinburgh again yesterday. I went to the same restaurant and sat again at my window, but nothing happened. The sun shone as before; the people got off trams and hurried or strolled away; but they had no business of their own; they were ordinary and lost. I saw care or foolish freedom from care in their faces; eternal anxiety, eternal defensiveness: the look of people who work in offices or serve at counters, and who accept as a self-evident thing that they should work in offices and serve at counters. Looking at them, I felt neither grief nor satisfaction—merely that official indifference in which we pass ninety-nine hundredths of our lives. I sat and looked at them almost contentedly through the scales that covered my eyes, like a mildly damned spirit, a spirit pickled delicately in a discreet solution of damnation, while something far within me, as faint and forlorn as a hunter's horn in an immense forest, cried that I wanted to see.

13 August 1938

Spent an evening in Edinburgh talking with A. and L. about immortality. When I returned to the hotel I sat down on my bed and stared at myself in a long mirror on the wall. My face, especially the bony ridge of forehead, *came out*, and I saw the skin and flesh shrivelling from it, and the bone underneath: a terrifying, absolute vision, like Time being stripped off. And simultaneously a feeling of journeying on beyond Time with that forehead as a prow, and an assurance that the naked bone, there, would flower into new flesh and sprout new hair, fragrant and beautiful beyond conception. At the same time a feeling that I was doing a dangerous balancing feat on the edge of a precipice, that I had gone too far, and that it is not wise to play with death for the sake of immortality.

23 August 1938

Yesterday morning, as Gavin was so eager for it, I got up at half-past four to see the sunrise. The streets lay in the brown half-light of a spacious cavern; there was a crescent moon, yellow, with scarf-like clouds around her. When we came to the sea the East lay like a translucent shell lighted from behind. We went along the East Sands, the light steadily growing: the land no longer rich and dark, but picked out in bare, primitive colours: the red roofs of the farm looked new, as if red had just been invented. In a little while I grew aware of light as a thing in itself, not as a mere medium for showing objects:

the world was flooded with light flowing in a level river from the horizon. The East had been ramparted with black, mountainous clouds standing along the sea; now their sides were lighted up, and above them some thin scarves of clouds flushed rose, with umber bars here and there; the soft conflagration spread and began to die away. Then, under the black range of clouds, the sea turned crimson: the colour deep, alive, and moving. Part of the cloud rampart seemed to have caught fire from the other side, and the fire began to eat its way through: there was a core of molten yellow—the sun. And then in a few minutes, deliberately, in great circumstance, in great majesty, the sun rose: deep, golden, molten, living fire. In a little it had paled and no longer looked molten, but a neat, dry disc. Then we turned home. The deliberation of the whole magnificent process was overwhelming. I was struck particularly by the feeling that as the sun rose it was creating all the objects its light fell upon: everything *appeared* as if at a word of command, a spell spoken, and as if for the first time.

Summer 1939

I thought of John Holms to-day and his sad and easy death. And of the cremation in that brick chapel, with its clergyman who *looked* like a clergyman. He said some words to which I did not listen, then pressed a button. Two little folding doors clicked open; the coffin, piled with masses of flowers like a little perambulating garden, sidled towards the opening and the flames, genteelly *withdrew*, the flowers anticly nodding and shimmying, as if terrified by a premonition of the annihilating heat, like a bevy of giggling girls being slowly slid into a furnace; they seemed to be giving out inaudible little cries and shrieks. A woman sitting in one of the pews and staring in agony at the sliding coffin fell forward from the waist on to the back of the pew before her with her arms out-stretched: a sheer plunge like a wave breaking. The ceremony was like a dreadful violation of death, too horrible for tears. But afterwards, walking about outside along a brick wall crowded with niches and urns, I cried at the thought that he had died so easily, for that was the saddest thing of all: as if Death had told him to come, and like a good child he had obeyed, unresistingly letting Death take him by the hand.

Note: The following piece is undated and placed at the end of 'Extracts from a Diary 1937–9' in *The Story and the Fable*.

In *Le Temps Retrouvé* Proust describes how he set out to resuscitate in himself 'the Eternal Man.' The Eternal Man is what has possessed me during most of the time that I have been writing my autobiography, and has possessed me too in most of my poetry. To resuscitate the Eternal Man was an heroic attempt, and Proust was a great writer. Yet I cannot help feeling that that resuscitation was only a beginning. There remains the problem of communion between the Eternal Man in Proust and the Eternal Man in other people, and also their communion with the Eternal Itself. I should have a philosophy to cover these things, but I have not: I think that in the end I rely purely on faith, perhaps too purely. I console myself with the thought that all philosophies pass, and that any philosophy I might formulate would pass very quickly; also, that when St Paul spoke of the three things that were needful he did not call them philosophy, hope, and charity.

I am not a good theologian, and the existence of evil remains a mystery to me; I prefer that mystery to any explanation of it that I know. The writer who satisfies me most on the problem of evil is Jacob Boehme:

> Reason says that because man was found disobedient God cast His fierce anger upon him . . . Thou must not think such thoughts. For God is Love and goodness, and there is not one angry thought in Him. It was man, who should never have punished himself.

I like this sentence from William Law too:

> From eternity to eternity no spark of wrath ever was or ever will be in the holy triune God.

It seems to me that to read these words is to be convinced of their truth.

There is surely no writing about the soul more wonderful than some of the *Upanishads*:

> The Self knows all, is not born, does not die, is not the effect of any cause; is eternal, self-existent, imperishable; how can the killing of the body kill Him?
>
> He who knows the soundless, odourless, tasteless, intangible, formless, deathless, supernatural, undecaying, beginningless, endless, unchangeable Reality springs out of the mouth of Death.
>
> He who desires one thing after another, brooding over them, is born where his desires can be satisfied; but the Self attained, one desire satisfied, all are satisfied.
>
> The Self is not known through discourse, splitting of hairs, learning however great. He comes to the man He loves; takes that man's body as His own . . .
>
> He who has found Him seeks no more; the riddle is solved; desire gone, he is at peace. Having approached from everywhere that which is everywhere, whole, he passes into the Whole.

I was born before the Industrial Revolution, and am now about two hundred years old. But I have skipped a hundred and fifty of them. I was really born in 1737, and till I was fourteen no time-accidents happened to me. Then in 1751 I set out from Orkney for Glasgow. When I arrived I found that it was not 1751, but 1901, and that a hundred and fifty years had been burned up in my two days' journey. But I myself was still in 1751, and remained there for a long time. All my life since I have been trying to overhaul that invisible leeway. No wonder I am obsessed with Time.

Every summer, during my two weeks' holiday, I travelled back that hundred and fifty years again. What a relief it was to get back to the pre-industrial world, and how much better everything was arranged there! And even in Glasgow I could make little excursions into it on Saturday afternoon and Sunday by taking a walk in the country. On these walks I often met other Glasgow people doing the same thing. They thought they were 'nature-lovers,' but what really drew them into the country was a personal or racial memory of a protective order which had existed before the modern chaos came upon us. Most of these country-lovers did not have such a tough stomach as I had, for they had been brought up in the town. So they turned up their noses at the byre and the midden, which are at the core of that fostering order. Also they could look with pleasure at a potato field lavishly flowering, and not with my sense of gay-hued disaster. And I don't think they could have got the feeling of fatness and wealth which a row of stacks in a farmyard will always give me, making it the most satisfying and beautiful sight in the civilized world.

I was brought up in the midst of a life which was still co-operative, which had still the medieval communal feeling. We had heard and read of something called 'competition,' but it never came into our experience. Our life was an order. Since the Industrial Revolution there has not really been an order except in a few remote places; for competition is the principle of anarchy. The hiker flying from that anarchy to 'nature' is really, without knowing it, looking for an order. But he will have to look elsewhere for it now.

This is the point I have reached, after starting two hundred years ago; and with that I bring myself up to date. I do not think there is anything admirable in being up to date, apart from the fact that it is necessary. And to be born outside your age and have to catch up with it and fit into it is a strain. Yet I would not for any price have missed my knowledge of that first pre-industrial order; for it taught me something which is inherent in every good order.

Note: The following extract is taken from 'From a Diary', published in *New Alliance* IV (Sept.-Oct. 1943), pp.6–7.

I dreamed last night what must have been a symbolic pictorial representation of human life, with heaven above and hell beneath, angels ascending and descending, concentric beams of glory falling from the height, the animals in their places, and man in the centre. The picture did not present itself instantaneously, but grew detail by detail; the last detail, completing it, being a quaint little animal or sprite insinuated at the bottom of the right hand corner in the manner of an artist's signature (it looked very like one, except for the fact that it kept wriggling apologetically). This is all that remains clearly of the picture now. I think of it sometimes as a little fluffy dog sitting on its hind legs and fawning on an invisible master, and then as a neat, small, friendly, domesticated demon playing on a flute an air first learnt in hell but adapted a long time ago (perhaps in Eden) to the human ear and the human soul; the oldest music in the world. This little dog or demon or signature tune is all that remains. Yet I feel that if I found a propitious moment I could construct from that little hieroglyph the whole design, the glory and abasement, the summits and deeps, the light and darkness, the powers and dominations, and man himself in the centre.

Thinking over this dream again, I do not feel so sure that I could reconstruct the picture; but that does not matter much, for what it has left behind is a sense of order, and that was the principle of the picture; the order was everywhere in it. Every complete vision of life—and by complete I do not mean including everything merely, but including everything in its place—is a vision of life glorified. Where everything is included without order, we get a vision of life nullified. A vision of a few things arranged neatly in order, with all the rest left out, is a false vision. All three are worth having, since they are visions. But most of our lives we live without any vision at all, in our street, with our acquaintances, our habits, our worries, our comforts.

Last thoughts on the dream. It seems to me now that it was a dream of man finally redeemed, at the end of time, with the glory achieved, the peril past; and now I think of the little dog or demon as merely a vestigial survival of a vanished hell, all that was left of the busy firemen and furnace fiends, a little mannikin sitting on the grass-grown caved-in sides of hell and piping his solitary air, which is a necessary part of the symphony, since in the moment of ultimate harmony this note too was needed along with the rest; this weird, ageless, haunting, infernal melody, now, in its context, no longer infernal.

Note: The following extracts are taken from a notebook, now in the National Library of Scotland, used by Muir during the last year of his life.

6 November 1957

Dreams in the last few weeks. Dream of the watchers in a dark place (coming on the words somewhere, 'The Well of Life', I have associated them with that, though the words came later, in some poem or other in a book). Except for the watchers, all was deep darkness, and I could see only their faces, which were lighted by a brilliant beam of light: a horizontal beam which lighted the heads only, all else, above them and below in complete darkness. It seemed to be an underworld, and how the beam of light came, and from what source I did not know. The faces strongly radiant, serene, almost indifferent, hard to describe: 'indifferent' a too cruel word for them, for there was a sort of hidden tenderness. No, I cannot catch the expression, very beautiful. Radiance above all, unearthly.

Sometime later, another dream. Of a woman, or muse, or sibyl, speaking, it seemed, of human life, but in a dark and very spacious place. The story she told was great and elevated, uttered with solemnity. I thought of her as very tall, her voice of more than human volume, yet easy and full. On wakening I could not remember what she said, but thought it told of our life from birth to death, a great story, with nothing small or mean. I have associated it since with the Well of Life dream, and fancied to myself that this was how she would have begun her story, and that the rest of it would have been told in the same spirit, exalted and mysterious, to the end. Perhaps this is contrivance, but it might help. I've reflected since that, seen in this way, humour and irony are mere devices to hide the real nature of our life, which is infinitely serious and real, and a great event.

Other dreams, not of this kind. One about F.G. Scott, my old friend, who has lately relapsed into senile decay, though a wonderful creature. I dreamed I met him, and that he was handsome and young, younger than when I first met him, a handsome and radiant young man in his twenties. At the same time I thought that my hair had grown quite white and very neatly barbered (it seemed to suit me).

15 May 1958

Suddenly thought of my father and mother to-day. Saw their goodness, their gentleness, their submission to their simple lot; thought that, if they had been known, they would have been called saints. How can I forget them for stretches of time, as if they had never been, and remember them only now and then. It is fifty years since my father died, and a few years after my mother died too. How she must have suffered, living in that place, so strange to her. I realise this now, but I scarcely realised it then, I was too busy with my own discomforts in Glasgow. How cheerful she was, and how she sacrificed herself for us all. Human ingratitude is bottomless.

My father survived his coming to Glasgow only for a year. My mother had to suffer seeing Willie and Johnny dying, and it was Johnny's long and dreadfully cruel illness that brought on her own death. She was suffering herself from an inward pain, a tumour, but paid no attention to it, did not even tell of it, never complained but went on nursing her son. I remember one evening when Johnny threw his arms around her neck as she was bending over his bed—he had been complaining, driven mad with pain—and kissed her and asked her forgiveness. What things happen in life! Past imagination or invention or fantasy. And when Johnny was dead, and my mother went to see a doctor and was taken to hospital she died there in a few days. I remember still a day in Victoria Road, weeks after this, when I was walking back from my work in the evening catching sight of her on the pavement, and realising as I came nearer that it was not her, but a little woman somewhat like her, and becoming aware of the terrible difference between life and death: the finality of death. It is as if we cannot cherish those we love until we have lost them. We do not have enough humanity to be human. And how she would jóke, so gently and light-heartedly, and make up little rhymes to surprise and please us. And cook for us and look after us, she such a frail little woman. And I can forget her for weeks, for months, for years, as if she had never been. How hard the human heart is. I shall try to keep her in remembrance and make some recompense, after so long, and in remembering her simple and delicate humanity try to become more human myself. Perhaps I shall meet her again and have the infinite joy of her forgiveness. I do not know how to conceive immortality, though I still believe in it. If I meet her in another world, I know—and that is the infinite comfort—that I shall see her as she is, at last, the imperfections of mortality past, and that she will see me, and forgive me, for what I am. 'And throughout all Eternity, I forgive you, you forgive me.' What we desire above everything and what we can never find in this life. But remember, remember: we begin to die when we stop remembering.

Index

Auchen, 247
Aberdeen, 111
Aberdeen University, 4
Abraham, 201
Achilles, 33, 34, 201
Ackerley, Joe, 242
Adam, 174
Adamnan, 237
Æ, 166, 168
Alban Hills, 272
Alexander, 80
Alexandra, Queen, 225
Alfieri, 181
Alsace, 234
America, U.S. of, 218, 223, 244, 255, 269
Anderson, Willa, 147, 148, 149, 150, 152, 156, 176, 182, 183, 184, 186, 217, 245
Angus, Miss, 32
Annan, Miss, 62
Arnold, Matthew, 68, 144
Assisi, 274, 275
Athens, 170
Athos, Mount, 170
Auden, Wystan, 227, 228, 235
Aurelius, Marcus, 88
Ausschwitz, 261, 267
Austria, 181, 200, 231
Ayrshire, 90, 91

Ballantyne, R. M., 63
Barker, George, 228, 232
Barns, 2
Baudelaire, Charles, 139
Bavarian Alps, 212
Bax, Belfort, 104
Baxter, Rev. Doctor, 18, 48
Beardsley, Aubrey, 186

Beethoven, 145, 194
Belgium, 247
Benes Edward, 254, 262
Bergson, Henri, 115
Berlin, 176, 214, 216, 257
Betjeman, John, 245
Bizet, 145
Black Christ, 208
Blatchford, Robert, 102, 103, 276
Bohemia, 177
Boswell, James, 226
Bridge of Allan, 161
British Council, 234, 242, 244, 245, 246, 252-4, 270, 275
British Museum, 226
Brooks, Van Wyck, 178
Brown, George, 53
Browning, Robert, 88
Bruce, Robert the, 69
Bu, 4, 8, 26, 31, 35, 36, 48, 50, 54, 55, 57, 70, 82
Buchan, 4
Burns, Robert, 69

Caithness, 1
Caivit, 4
Calvin, John, 99
Cambridge, 270, 276
Camden Town, 233
Canada, 134, 135
Capek, Karel, 181, 183
Carlyle, Thomas, 6-9, 88, 140, 226
Carpenter, Edward, 103, 107
Carrara Mountains, 205, 207
Carswell, Donald and Catherine, 232
Cathcart, 83
Caucasus, 170

Chamberlain, Neville, 238
Charing Cross, 103
Charles University, 253, 258
Chesham, 221
Chesterton, G. K., 142
China, 170
Clyde, 85, 126, 140, 144
Coleridge, Samuel Taylor, 68
Cologne, 248
Como, 234
Copinsay, 1
Corelli, Marie, 225
Cormack, Edwin and Elizabeth
    (grandparents), 1
Cormack the Sailor, 1
Crabbe, George, 68
Craftie, 75, 76
Cremin, 234
Crosshill, 81, 87
Crowborough, 149, 150, 222,
    226, 227
Czechoslovakia, 223, 233, 246,
    247, 250, 253, 256, 263, 267,
    269, 276

Dalcroze, Jacques, 194
Damsay, 237
Dante, 143, 201, 271, 274
Danube, 213, 218
David, King, 48
Deerness, 1, 8, 52, 58, 59, 73
Deslys, Gaby, 196
Donne, John, 173
Dooley, Mr, 96
Dormansland, 226
D o s t o e v s k i , F y o d o r
    Mikhailovich, 116, 255
Douglas, Major, 140
Dresden, 187, 192, 193, 194,
    196, 200, 214, 216
Dryden, John, 68
Dunbar, William, 146
Dundee, 243
Dürer, Albrecht, 250

Eday, 59
Edinburgh, 9, 32, 48, 51, 57, 71,
    81-4, 111, 134, 240, 245, 275

Edinburgh Castle, 134
Egilsay, 6, 7, 59
Eja, 233
Elbe, 193
Eliot, T. S., 201, 245
Elijah, 48
Elizabeth, Queen, 170
Ellis, Havelock, 107, 115
Emerson, Ralph Waldo, 90
Epicetus, 88

Fairport, 121, 122, 124, 125,
    128, 133, 135, 143
Faldside, 128, 133, 134, 136
Farrar, Dean, 67
Ferrar, John, 171
Ferrar, Nicholas, 171
Fierlinger, M. Z., 260
Finland, 170
Florence, 205, 209, 275
Folly, 1, 2, 4, 74
Fontainebleau, 165, 167
Forster, E. M., 115
Forte Dei Marmi, 204, 205, 206
France, 107, 170, 223, 255
Francesca, Piero Della, 271
Franco, General, 238
Frankfort, 249
Freud, Sigmund, 150, 197

Galicia, 214
Galsworthy, John, 115
Gardield, President, 18
Garth, 57, 58, 59, 61, 69, 71, 72,
    73, 82, 202, 273
Gascoyne, David, 228
George, Stefan, 97, 98, 198, 215
George V, King, 90
Germany, 100, 170, 176, 196,
    223, 231, 233-4, 247, 249,
    269
Glasgow, 42, 43, 54, 66, 71, 72,
    76, 79-81, 82-4, 87, 90, 92,
    96, 99, 101, 102, 103, 105,
    111, 117, 118, 120, 122, 123,
    124-6, 133-4, 138, 140, 141,
    142, 147, 148, 161, 163-4,
    184, 187, 190, 195, 240, 276

Glasgow University, 145
Godesberg, 248, 249, 251
Goethe, 175
Goldoni, 181
Goldsmith, Oliver, 19, 68
Goliath of Gath, 36
Gorbals, 86
Gosse, Sir Edmund, 89
Gottwald, Klement, 261, 262
Graham, Cunninghame, 74
Greece, 269
Greene, Graham, 261
Grierson, Sir Herbert, 245
Grigson, Geoffrey, 228, 232
Grimsquoy, 59
Grimster, 59
Guggenheim, Peggy, 232
Gundolf, Friedrich, 198
Gurdjieff, 165, 167, 168

Haa, 4, 12, 14, 20, 52
Habreck, 4
Haco, 1
Halévy, D., 120
Hamburg, 176
Hampstead, 227, 230, 232, 234, 235, 236, 242, 270
Hans, 210, 211
Hardy, Thomas, 90, 114
Hastings, 232
Hauptmann, Gerhardt, 217, 218, 221
Hector, 33, 34, 201, 219
Hegel, G. W. F., 109
Heine, Heinrich, 108, 109, 110, 112, 117, 119, 138, 139, 140, 151
Hellerau, 192, 193, 194, 195, 197, 199, 200, 203, 219, 250
Helye (Helzigartha), 4, 26, 32, 54, 57, 77, 138
Hercules, 37
Hilde, 233, 234, 235
Hinks, Roger, 271
Hitler, 189, 190, 191, 193, 198, 200, 228, 249, 250
Hofmannstahl, Hugo von, 210, 215, 217

Hogarth Press, 218
Hogg, James, 226
Hölderlin, Friedrich, 200
Holms, John, xix, 161, 163, 166, 171, 173, 174, 175, 185, 187, 192, 193, 201, 203, 204, 206, 207, 209
Hruga, Kolbein (Cubby Roo), 4
Hudson, Stephen, 221
Hughie o' Habreck, 29
Hugo, Victor, 69
Hume, David, 69, 114, 226
Hundred Acre Dyke, 83
Huxley, Aldous, 224
Hyndman, Henry Mayers, 141

Ibsen, Henrik, 107, 114, 224
Inganess Bay, 58, 59, 63
Italy, 203, 242, 269, 271, 274, 275

Jack, Flora, xix
James V, 19, 20
James the Rose, Sir, 20
James, W., 162
Jehovah, 160
Joubert, Joseph, 174
Joyce, James, 115
Jung, Charles Gustave, 150

Kadman, Adam, 168
Kafka, Franz, 50, 186, 266, 267
Kafka, Ottilia, 266, 267
Kant, Immanuel, 276
Kapuzinerberg, 211, 212
Karlsrhue, 171
Kelvinside, 90
Kensington Gardens, 148
Kingsmill, Hugh, xix, 150, 161, 166, 171, 175, 232, 245
Kinsky Park, 185
Kirkwall, 24, 51, 54, 57, 59, 61, 63, 66, 69, 71, 72, 73, 74, 75, 76, 77, 79, 90, 104, 105, 111, 145, 202, 276
Kirkwall Burgh School, 60, 202
Knox, John, 226

Kralovska, Obora, 259

La Forgue, Madame, 104
Lammas Market, 51
Landor, Walter Savage, 146
Lavrin, Janko, 170
Lawrence, D. H., 115
Lear, King, 43, 44
Leith, 58, 65, 75, 81, 182, 202
Lenin, 228
Lessing, Gotthold Ephraim, 89
Levy, Dr Oscar, 118
Lewis, Cecil Day, 227, 228
Linklater, Eric, 4
Little Gidding, 171
London, 47, 147, 148, 152, 164, 167, 170, 223, 227, 239, 270
Lothian, Lord, 275
Lucca, 205, 208
Lucken, Ivo von, 199, 208
Lucknow, 5

Macaulay, Thomas, 68
MacDonald, Ramsay, 103, 210
McEwan, Mr, 60
McNeill, John, 76
MacPherson, Mr, 76, 77
Maezto, Ramiro de, 141
Maggie, Aunt, 6, 15, 48, 50, 56, 57, 75, 111, 202
Magnus, St, 16
Magnus, St, Cathedral, 59, 61
Mainz, 171
Mala Chuchle, 184
Mala, Pani, 177, 184
Mala Strana, 179
Mariánske, Lazné, 260
Marie, 177
Marienbad, 260
Marlow, Christopher, 68
Marx, Karl, 114, 136, 141, 190, 228, 229, 230
Masaryk, Thomas, 258, 263
Masaryk, President, 180, 181
Mason, Arthur and Mary, 225
Matthew, 235, 236
Maximilian, Emperor, 117
Menton, 225

Meredith, George, 90, 114
Michelangelo, 271, 273
Mill, John Stewart, 268
Millport, 85
Milton, John, 68, 90
Minervini, Laura, 272
Mirabellen Gardens, 212
Mitchell Library, 84
Mitrinovic, Dmitri, 168, 169, 170, 240
Molière, 141, 181
Mönchsberg, 212
Montaigne, 114
Montgomery, General, 251
Montrose, 147, 176, 222
Morris, William, 68, 89, 91
Moses, 201
Mozart, 145
Muir, Clara, 57, 72, 75, 76, 82, 86, 94
Muir, Elizabeth, 71, 72
Muir, Gavin, 236, 237, 243, 244, 245
Muir, James (Father), 111
Muir, Jimmie, 71, 81, 82, 84, 85, 86, 90, 93, 95
Muir, Johnnie, 20, 68, 71, 72, 81, 84, 85, 86, 92, 93, 94, 95, 99, 101
Muir, Willie, 64, 65, 71, 72, 84, 85, 86, 88, 93, 101, 111
Mull Head, 58
Munich, 183, 234
Murry, John Middleton, 150
Mussolini, 228
Mütze, Frau, 192

Naples, 275
Neill, A. S., 194, 200, 212, 217, 218, 220
Neustätter, Frau Doktor, 194, 198
Newbattle Abbey College, 275, 276
Nietzsche, F. W., 43, 110, 113, 118, 119, 120, 133, 141, 144, 145, 160, 161, 163, 276
Norway, 53

Novak, Pam, 183
Novakova, Pani, 183
Nuremberg, 250

Oeser, Drury and Oscar, 239
Ontario, Lake, 134
Onziebist, 4
Orage, A. R., 115, 118, 139, 140, 141, 150, 164, 165, 167, 168, 169, 170, 175, 195
Orkney, 1, 2, 4, 6, 18, 30, 47, 48, 49, 52, 53, 54, 66, 68, 70, 71, 73, 76, 81, 84, 90, 92, 107, 111, 118, 189, 190, 191, 201, 203, 205, 236, 271, 273
Orwell, George, 238
Oslo, 170
Ould, Herman, 256, 257

Palacky, Frantisek, 180
Palermo, 275
Palestine, 208
Pascal, Blaise, 89, 114
Paton, John, 142
Penn, 221, 222
Persia, 170
Perugia, 275
Piestany, 268
Pirie, Mr, 9, 49, 274
Pisa, 205
Plato, 114, 118, 174
Plutarch, 166
Poland, 223
Portugal, 36
Pound, Ezra, 116, 168, 201
Prague, 9, 152, 167, 170, 176, 177, 179, 180, 181, 184, 185, 186, 234, 246, 247, 248, 249, 251, 252, 253, 254, 256, 257, 259, 260, 261
Proust, Marcel, 188, 222

Queen's Park, 81, 87, 93
Queen's Park Football Club, 87
Quirinale, 272
Quoydandy, 59

Rabelais, François, 163

Racine, Baptise, 181
Rendall, Robert, 53
Reid, Dr George, 62
Renfrew, 86
Rilke, Rainer Maria, 215
Ritch, John, 20, 52, 111
Rodaun, 215
Rome, 234, 270-1, 273, 274-5
Rome Institute, 271
Rosen, Kunz von der, 127
Rosenau, 217
Rossetti, Dante Gabriel, 91
Rousay, 5, 7, 9, 30, 49, 51, 55, 59, 273
Rugby, 171
Ruhr, 200
Ruskin, John, 68, 88
Russell, Bertrand, 240
Russia, 170, 249, 252, 255
Russness, 4

Sadler's Wells Ballet, 254
St Andrews, 32, 233, 236, 237, 238, 239, 245, 276
St Andrew's Halls, 145
St Andrews University, 247
St Columba, 237
St Tropez, 223, 224
St Vitus, 179
Salt Market, 98
Salzburg, 209, 210, 225
Sanday, 1, 64, 202
Sandhurst, 171
Saunders, Cyril, 247-8, 251, 252
Saurat, Denis, 145, 147
Schiff, Sydney, 221
Schiff, Violet, 221
Schopenhauer, Arthur, 224
Schubert, 145
Scott, Francis George, 145, 209
Scott Library, 89
Scott, Sir Walter, 226
Selver, Paul, 182
Shakespeare, 68, 90, 114, 163, 181
Shapinsay, 6, 58
Shaw, G. B., 107, 114, 116, 168, 210, 224

Sheringham, 147
Shetland Islands, 70
Siena, 275
Sieyès, Abbé, 140
Simpson, John, 73
Sinclair, Freddie, 23, 32, 33
Skaill, 1, 107
Slovakia, 217, 256, 268
Slovenia, 170
Smiles, Samuel, 88, 186
Smith, Janet Adam, 242
Sonntagbert, 218, 219, 220
Sophie, Aunt, 107, 110
Sophocles, 181
Sorel, Georges, 115
Spain, 36
Spence, Fred, 74
Spender, Stephen, 228, 245
Spengler, Oswald, 190
Spenser, Edmund, 68, 146
Spurgeon, Rev. Charles Haddon, 18
Stroubek Hotel, 255
Stalin, 189, 190, 191
Stalingrad, 252
Stendahl, 141
Sterne, Lawrence, 69
Stevenson, R. L., 226
Strindberg, 181
Stromness, 81
Stromovka, 259
Sutherland, 2, 6, 7, 12, 13, 15, 20, 21, 27, 28, 30, 33, 50, 52, 57, 65, 73, 75
Sweden, 218
Swift, Jonathan, 43, 68
Swinburne, Algernon, 68, 69, 91
Syracuse, 275

Talmage, Rev. Doctor, 18
Tankerness, 58
Temple of the Vestals, 273
Tennyson, Alfred Lord, 68
Teresa, 204
Testaquoy, 4
Thaelmann, Ernst, 200
Thomas, Dylan, 228, 232
Thomson, George, 116, 117
Thomson, George Malcolm, 232

Toller, Ernst, 216
Tolstoy, Leo, 255
Toronto, 135
Torquay, 225
Torrey, Dr, 80
Traherne, Thomas, 173, 197
Tristram, 201
Troy, 33, 201
Troya, 259
Tuscany, 275

Ulysses, 201
Umbria, 275
Urals, 252

Vaughan, Henry, 173, 197
Velky Chuchle, 184
Venice, 275
Victoria Infirmary, 89, 93, 95
Vienna, 170, 180, 186, 212, 213, 214, 215, 216, 218, 261
Vinci, Leonardo da, 206
Vinohrady Theatre, 181, 182
Vltava, 177, 184, 259
Vogelweide, Walther von der, 210

Wallace, 69
Wallenstein, Albrecht, 177, 180
Watts-Dunton, Theodore, 89
Webster, Mr, 273
Wedekind, Frank, 216, 217
Weininger, Otto, 186
Wells, H. G., 116, 168
Whitman, Walt, 107
Wideford Burn, 59, 63, 75
Willie, Uncle, 107, 110
Wilson, President, 181
Wood, H. Harvey, 244, 245
Woolf, Leonard, 221
Woolf, Virgina, 218
Wordworth, William, 68, 89, 144, 172, 173, 201,
Wyre, 4, 5, 7, 13, 17, 19, 30, 33, 35, 48, 49, 51, 52, 54, 55, 56, 58, 59, 60, 63, 201, 202, 273

Yeats, W. B., 92, 167